BREAKFAST, LUNCH  DINER

Stories, characters and favorite dishes from fascinating restaurants in

ST. LOUIS

and beyond.

ROBERT RUBRIGHT

BREAKFAST, LUNCH & DINER

Stories, characters and favorite dishes from fascinating restaurants in St. Louis and beyond.
By Robert Rubright

Editor: Christine Frank, www.ChristineFrank.com
Cover and Interior design: Wendy Brookshire, wendybrookshire@mac.com

Robert Rubright
Breakfast, Lunch and Diner: Stories, characters and favorite dishes from fascinating restaurants in St. Louis and beyond.
ISBN 9780979594465

Publication year 2009

TABLE OF CONTENTS

Lunch Restaurants

Diners

ACKNOWLEDGMENTS

PLENTY OF BREAKFAST and lunch pals helped me tuck away meals along the way. Carl Campbell and Peter Enslin were my Tuesday lunch confederates at over 750 restaurants spanning fifteen years. Albert Barton, Robert Officer, David O. Fischer, Ramon Gass, and Dr. William Fogarty, Sr. joined our threesome at times and so did Jim Hershfelt and Roy Weisheit from the First Presbyterian Church of Kirkwood. Ron Coleman and Dr. Jeffrey Smith were breakfast regulars. A perennial luncheon gathering of Westminster College classmates included Dr. Joseph K. McKinney, Van-Lear Black III, Michael Tchoukaleff, Charles F. Betz, John E. Marshall, Paul Ross, Calvin R. Yeckel, Jr. and Morton Mallory.

I am indebted to Dr. Marlene Birkman who teaches a writing class at Webster University in St. Louis. For several years, I tested opening paragraphs and whole chapters of this book with her classes. Many of their thoughtful ideas are included in Breakfast, Lunch and Diner.

Over many a meal out, my sons Ted and Dan have been great encouragers. Their comments, notes, and critiquing have been both touching and invaluable.

My wife, Lynn, has been a loving and indispensable creative partner who helped me conceive, assemble, write, and produce this book. Christine Frank, whose editing and guidance was extremely valuable; Wendy Brookshire, our talented graphic designer; and Dan Thompson of Big River Distribution were key members of our publishing team.

INTRODUCTION

"OUR RESTAURANTS DEFINE US," Ruth Reichl, preeminent food chronicler and editor of *Gourmet* magazine, once observed in the *New York Times*. "Americans have never patronized restaurants just because they fed us well; we go for the people or the ambience or the way they make us feel. We choose restaurants as much for what they say about us as for what they feed us."

"A recent survey found that seventy percent of all diners had not selected their destination when they left their homes to dine out," wrote Richard Pillsbury in his stimulating book, *No Foreign Food*. "Is the diner primarily going to a restaurant to satisfy hunger—in essence to feed the body—or is the consumer dining away from home to enhance or create an experience—to feed the soul?"

In this book, which is a feed-the-soul, comfort tour of restaurants in the highly decentralized St. Louis region, we stop by eighty-four non-chain establishments not to review or critique them but to savor their character, charm, history, and local cast of characters, and to sample their food. This book will also help you choose a restaurant *before* you leave home!

Over many years, my friends Carl Campbell and Peter Enslin and I have taken lunch each Tuesday at 750 different restaurants in and around St. Louis. From this list I have culled some sixty lunch spots and added to them breakfast joints and diners that my sons, Ted and Dan, and wife, Lynn, have favored—some of them for decades.

With each chapter, our main emphasis is on the stories and lore that envelop a restaurant and shape its special persona. Some of these stories are about:

- Loyal or regular customers and how restaurants honor them through gifts, discounts, or special "walls of fame."
- Customer quirks and manners.
- Special and signature dishes such as "the Stretch" at Columbia's Broadway Diner or "The Wilbur" omelet at Goody Goody Diner in St. Louis and how they were named.
- Restaurant "culture" as reflected in seating arrangements, hospitalization or death of customers, order-taking, and exceptional policies for the most loyal regulars.
- Menus and how they reflect owners, customers, the neighborhood, or the times.
- How family photos, customer snapshots, tin ceilings, old-fashioned counters and stools, trees, murals, and paintings give area restaurants their distinct characters.
- Restaurant owners and managers who have memorable personalities.

Years ago I attended a lecture by historian David McCullough. "You can put a lens down here in St. Louis and see all of America," he said.

So here my lens beams toward a fascinating group of restaurants, most in St. Louis and nearby Illinois with some scattered in outstate Illinois and Missouri. Some restaurants, such as Hodak's and Pietro's in south St. Louis and Fischer's Restaurant and the Shrine restaurant in Belleville, Ilinois, are "destination" locations because of their vast draw. On the other hand, many restaurants in this book are, by various degrees, either overlooked, unheralded, under-appreciated, or simply forgotten. Whatever their status, all of them deserve a visit.

Robert Rubright

BREAKFAST RESTAURANTS

Bevo Mill

St. Louis

SOME LANDMARK BUFFS say that the two most memorable architectural structures in the St. Louis area are the Arch and Bevo Mill. Bevo Mill, capped by an 18-foot Flemish windmill with aluminum blades, is a most indelible building.

Bevo Mill opened in 1916, a $250,000 dream of August Busch, Sr., who headed the Anheuser-Busch brewery and coveted a restaurant setting to sell his new pre-Prohibition non-alcoholic near-beer, Bevo. Busch also sought a drinking and dining spot that lay halfway between the brewery and his home, Grant's Farm, where he and his friends could relax with sauerbraten and schnitzel and try some Bevo.

Bevo Mill consists of a main dining room, the octagonal Mill Room, and the downstairs Oak and Bavarian rooms, a space originally known as the Yacht Club. Breakfast is served in the main dining room, whose centerpiece is a mammoth Bavarian fireplace. "August Sr. and August Jr. brought stones for the fireplace directly from the grounds of Grant's Farm," says Dave Gilbert, Bevo Mill manager. What appear to be coat racks on the dining room's dark walls are antlers from small European deer shot in Germany decades ago by Busch. "We have covered the antlers with trekker hats so people won't hang

Once weekend customers are seated, they are treated to a plateful of maple walnut cookies as a token of Chris' appreciation. "When we first opened we gave out little cups of fruit," says Saracino. "After a while we switched to raisin scones then we switched to the maple walnut cookies. People like them so much, I'm afraid to change to something new. We serve the cookies until we run out, which is about 12:30 P.M. if we don't sell a lot of cookies in bulk. Some customers will order three or four dozens of cookies to take home. These people are lucky because I give them more than a baker's dozen, which is thirteen. I put sixteen to eighteen cookies into my dozen!"

Chris' Pancake and Dining
5980 Southwest Avenue, St. Louis

☎ (314) 645-2088

🕐 6 A.M. to 10 P.M. Monday through Thursday
6 A.M. to 11 P.M. Friday and Saturday
7 A.M. to 9 P.M. Sunday

♿ Wheelchair accessible

🚬 Some smoking permitted

Cowan's Restaurant
Washington, Missouri

OVER THE KITCHEN door a small sign states: My Kitchen and Me Welcome Thee. Not far away eight town fathers sit around the BS Table sipping coffee and discussing the universal topics: weather, sports, sex, and local matters. As regulars at Washington, Missouri's Cowan's Restaurant (locally famous for its homemade mile-high pies), the Coffee Boys convene at a long table reserved just for them.

The historic Missouri River city of Washington was until 1946 home to America's only zither factory. It remains the home of Missouri Meerschaum Company, whose forbears made corncob pipes for President Herbert Hoover, Tennessee Ernie Ford, Carl Sandburg, Norman Rockwell, artist Thomas Hart Benton, and General Douglas MacArthur. Local lore holds that MacArthur had a Washington-made corncob pipe clamped in his mouth in February 1945 when he waded ashore on the Bataan peninsula near Manila Bay, where he and his forces, vastly outnumberd by the Japanese, had fled in 1942. "I Shall Return," he had said, and he did, with his corncob pipe leading the way.

On most weekdays, two shifts of regulars sit down at the BS Table, personally named by restaurant owner Jerry

Gildehaus. Shift one arrives around 6:30 A.M.; shift two begins to appear between 7:30 and 8 A.M., though there is always some overlap. Generally, the first shift contains still-working Coffee Boys while the later shift has moguls, professionals, retirees, and semi-retirees. Next to the BS Table is the BS, Jr. Table, which attracts "anyone who can stand being near us, including some women," a Coffee Boy explains. Rarely is there conversation between the two tables.

A few years back, the first shift depended on the presence of former mayor Ernie Hillerman, a prominent nurseryman. "I'm here to give information," he would say. "I just brought the boys up to speed on the local airport situation," was a typical statement. "We like to give the mayor our feedback," a Coffee Boy recalled, "especially on his public speeches. If Ernie isn't here, we leave his seat open just in case he shows up." When Hillerman leaves the table, his parting words might be "Got to go and unlock City Hall." Another Coffee Boy—a dentist—would blithely state, "Well, I must go and inflict some pain," when he adjourned for the morning.

The second shift included—and still does—Gary R. Lucy, a local artist whose massive oils highlight the history of America's inland waterways, especially the nearby Missouri River. "I use some of the Coffee Boys as models for my paintings," he says, which easily explains his popularity at the BS Table. In one oil rendering, for instance, he had Coffee Boy Paul LaPlant posed next to the pilot house of the Bright Star and Bob Jones perched on the rail of the boat, a ferry that operated between 1865 and 1875. In "Eating Up the Light," which means marking the river channel for safe passage, Lucy has Al Westrich standing on the river boat that does the marking and Dave Craig as an oarsman. Another Coffee Boy who has appeared in

Lucy works is Steve Lochirco, president of Happy Apples, Inc., a local company that turns out more than ten million candy apples annually.

Buck Sincos, once the local postmaster and longtime unofficial mayor, was a founding Coffee Boy back in 1958. One day, recalls Lucy, Sincos stopped him on the street and said: "I live my whole life to have coffee with you boys in the morning and before I die I want you to paint my portrait." Sincos gave Lucy a $750 deposit. When Lucy finished, the oil was unveiled in Cowan's back room. Not long after that, Sincos suffered a stroke. Recuperating in a nursing home, he had the new oil hung over his bed. Later on, partially recovered, Sincos rejoined the Coffee Boys at Cowan's until one sad day when he had an apparent heart attack while seated at the BS Table. Stoically, he walked three blocks to his home, where he died later that day. At the Sincos wake, some of the surviving Coffee Boys were heard to say that Sincos had been "a Buck well spent."

One firm Coffee Boys rule is that no wives or any other women are allowed at the BS Table. "If you bring your wife in here for breakfast," Lucy once said, tongue somewhat in cheek, "we say 'Oh My God!' Coffee Boys don't bring their wives here. If a woman sits down at our table, say between shifts, men come in and purposely don't talk to them. Soon the women move to another table. When getting their coffee in the morning, men want only to talk to other guys."

As for breakfast, some of the Coffee Boys order a bagel and a cup of coffee. Others opt for a half order of biscuits and sausage milk gravy. (Biscuits and gravy is a Cowan's signature dish). "When you order only half the biscuits and gravy," explains Lochirco, "it makes it appear as if they're only half the calories, half the bad stuff." Coffee Boys like to substitute cornbread for their biscuits. "Cornbread with coffee is like drinking good Scotch instead of plain whiskey," Lochirco opines. On special days, Coffee Boys order the popular Cowan's Scramble, which the menu describes as "… homemade biscuit with 2 scrambled eggs, melted cheese, topped with our own sausage milk gravy. Your choice of ham or sausage." A few of the Coffee Boys order a slice of one of Jerry Gildehaus's mile-high pies, particularly the coconut cream, crowned with fluffy meringue, often so high that Gildehaus can barely remove it from the oven. Gildehaus's meringue secret? "Basically, I beat the hell out of it," he replied.

Lest one infer that Cowan's is merely a Coffee Boys bastion, Gildehaus quickly asserts that his restaurant attracts locals and outsiders of all stripes who find his pancakes, scrambles, combos, and egg dishes all equally attractive. As the Cowan's business card says, the restaurant is the town's oldest and "still the place to meet."

Cowan's Restaurant
114 Elm Street, Washington, Missouri

 (636) 239-3213

 Closed Tuesdays
6 A.M. to 8 P.M. Monday through Saturday
6 A.M. to 7 P.M. Sunday

 Wheelchair accessible

 No smoking

4

Duff's

St. Louis

IN THE WINTER of 1973-74, when President Richard M. Nixon was still in office, a local character on Euclid Avenue in St. Louis operated an off-kilter joint called "Jerry Breakfast."

Jerry opened his place at 1:30 A.M. Posted by the back door off an alley—the only entrance—and supposedly out of view of city health inspectors, Jerry greeted his patrons, mostly entertainers, pub crawlers, and off-duty waiters and waitresses. Sometimes people such as Herb and Adelaide Karp, owners of Balaban's, perhaps the city's best-known bistro back then, took turns as "guest servers" on Jerry's breakfast buffet line.

During daylight hours, Jerry Breakfast proclaimed himself the "mayor" of Euclid. From the side door of a tarnished aluminum Airstream trailer that he called "the Euclid Country Club" he sold oranges and other produce to street people. As membership cards, he handed out stones that he had salvaged from the Mississippi River levee in downtown St. Louis.

One reason that Jerry Breakfast started his after-midnight breakfast place was that a wee-hours breakfast service that had begun one year earlier at Duff's Restaurant, next door to Jerry, had run asunder. "We began serving breakfast around midnight but it was too rowdy a venture for us, so we stopped it," says Karen Duffy, longtime co-owner—with Tim Kirby—of Duff's.

Duff's, which opened in 1972, offered lunch and dinner in a dining room and bar area with furnishings that a local critic described as "early Goodwill mixed with gross misjudgment." "Every table has a story here," Karen says, "but I can't remember any." *The West Pine Weed*, a neighborhood newsletter, termed Duff's "a new coffee house," even though its main luncheon fare early on was a "surprise burger" for ninety-five cents. Some thirty-five years later, Duff's burger contents still remain a surprising secret.

In earlier years, the Duff's space housed the Women's Exchange Tearoom and later Aumon's Tearoom. Across the street from Duff's is the beautiful red brick Euclid Building where Tennessee Williams took writing lessons and the famed mid-twentieth century contralto Helen Traubel learned to sing. As Duff's business grew, antique shops, quaint bars, bookshops, and other businesses moved in. The renaissance prompted Karen Duffy to begin offering brunch on weekends, one of the first local places to do so. Duffy credits Adrienne Bergh, now a St. Louis police lieutenant, with the brunch idea. At the time of the idea Bergh was a waitress and sometime cook. She introduced omelets, egg specials such as huevos rancheros, and pancake specials such as banana pancakes topped with pecans. Then she added soups, muffins, and French toast, and the brunch idea was off and running.

Jim Voss, chef since 1973, and his brother, Matt, furthered the Duff's brunch idea. Their pancakes, particularly the ricotta strawberry, whole wheat, and the blueberry blue cornmeal, became best sellers. So did their Parmesan rosemary biscuits with chicken herb gravy and the cheddar cheese biscuit. Their turkey-apple sausage, to which pureed apples and breadcrumbs are added, continues to outsell traditional bacon. Their Creole Eggs Benedict has been in demand since brunch debuted.

Brunch profits have risen measurably since Duff's installed an outdoor patio with a wrought-iron railing and matching chairs and tables. "We didn't just slap tables and chairs out front; we decorated most tastefully," says Matt Voss. "If we hadn't put in an outdoor café, we would have lost business to competitors. Right now, our place is a landmark of brunch." In the patio, house sparrows and blackbirds can poop on customers and bees sometimes sting them. But, says longtime waitress Margaret Kelly, "customers will wait forty-five minutes to sit outside because they want to be seen there for some reason, but they will barely wait fifteen minutes for inside seating."

In 1986, Karen Duffy took a long-distance call. "Karen, can we have Jimmy?" asked the manager of the Grateful Dead. The manager had dined at Duff's and respected Jim Voss. Karen said yes and that was the beginning of a nine-year stint for Jimmy as part-time co-chef for one of the world's most famous entertainment groups. Using his Duff's kitchen skills and utensils, Voss joined the band on some of its month-long tours. The Grateful Dead, says Voss, were "down-to-earth American eaters. I started out to do fancy things with them, but learned that they really enjoyed turkey with stuffing, meat loaf, lasagna, spaghetti, and grilled fish."

Over the years, Duff's has hosted a Monday night poetry reading and jazz series, welcoming celebrity guests such as the Grateful Dead who came in twice in the 1990s to escape the hazards of the road and eat dinner. Duff's also welcomed the crew of *White Palace*, a movie starring Susan Sarandon. Duff's was portrayed in the film as a representative New York pub.

Vincent Bommarito, owner of Tony's, the city's premier fine dining restaurant, is a Duff's fan. "I sometimes say 'Vince, watch the door for me,'" says Duffy. "He loves to stand and schmooze."

In 1990 Duff's expanded into the space next door, once known as Europa 390 (1961-1987). Europa, my favorite St. Louis bar and lunch spot in those days, was known for its thick roast beef sandwiches. "The roast beef arrives from Chicago by train every day or so," bartender Tony Mormino would remind all of his fiercely loyal patrons. Duffy christened her new space "The Grand Canyon Room" in tribute to a large acrylic painting by the late artist Bill Kohn that depicts a setting in the Grand Canyon. It dominates the south wall.

Duff's has served nearly two generations of customers in its time. "We've always welcomed families but these days we find we have a large baby clientele," observes Duffy "We have eleven high chairs and often they are all in use at the same time. We've even put in a diaper changing room on our balcony. It's important to get those babies lined up as future customers. But we won't serve them Cheerios—they're too messy to clean up."

Duff's
392 N. Euclid Avenue, St. Louis

 (314) 361-0522

 11 A.M. to 10 P.M. Tuesday through Friday
10 A.M. to 11 P.M. Friday
9 A.M. to 10 P.M. Sunday

 Wheelchair accessible

 Smoking

5

Fran & Marilyn's

Jerseyville, Illinois

FRAN & MARILYN'S restaurant, "famous for homemade pies," sits squarely in the middle of downtown Jerseyville, Illinois, a town founded in the 1830s not by European immigrants, but folks from New Jersey

"From 1834 to the present time, the Old Jersey has emptied itself with a steady and increasing current, into the New Jersey of Illinois," declared the Reverend Marshall M. Cooper in the *History of Jerseyville, Illinois 1822 to 1901.* "…Waves of migration from New Jersey have continued to roll hitherward," the pastor went on. A generation later saw the formation of the Jerseyville Old Settlers Society, the Ladies' Tourist Club, and the Bachelor Maids' Club. If it had been in existence, those clubs would probably have met for pie and victuals at Fran & Marilyn's.

"Pie—the sweet staple of pioneers—is the quintessential American dessert," points out Pascale Le Draoulec in *American Pie.* The old settlers and the ladies' groups would be pleased to learn that Fran Fosha, the restaurant manager, makes about ten pies on weekdays and twenty-five on weekends and that chocolate cheese and apple pie upside down—both sugar free and regular—are the top sellers, and that you can buy whole pies or slices at the pie display case near the front door.

Pie devotees include the 185 members of Fran & Marilyn's Coffee Club whose members—mostly regulars—sit at three round tables in this cavernous building that once was home to the Jersey Theatre (1938 to 1963). The theatre packed them in for Dick Tracy and Lone Ranger serials and for live shows with stars from KMOX radio in St. Louis, such as "Little Patsy the Pest," "Hal, the Smiling Cowboy," "Roy Queen and his Gang," and "Susie the Gal From the Hills." Fran & Marilyn's packs them in, too.

Every morning the restaurant's round tables are filled with regulars. Sandy Freand, now a cook at Fran & Marilyn's, is a fixture at Table 1. Ten years ago, Sandy was drinking up to forty cups of coffee daily, starting out at 3:30 in the morning, a half-hour before Fran switches on the lights and officially opens for business, then returning at noon to basically drink lunch, at 2:30 to "jaw with everybody until 4:00," at 6:00 for supper, and at 7:30 for a few cups to wash down the day. (Sandy has cut her coffee intake to ten to fifteen cups today.) In the early morning then—as now—a parade of regulars dropped by Sandy's table. There was the milk-route driver for Prairie Farms Dairy who delivered buttermilk that went into the buttermilk pancakes in Jake's Special, one of the restaurant's top sellers. Another regular showed up at 5 A.M., then left to unlock the local Elks Club so the morning gin rummy game could start on time.

At 6 A.M., Ellis Holleman would appear. "Here comes Ellis. He's a corker," Sandy would say, sipping and grinning. "What's new?" Ellis asked, much as he does today. The regulars briefed him. "Since we don't have a daily paper here, if something happens in Jerseyville overnight, we find out at Fran & Marilyn's the next morning," Holleman explains.

Another round table group, the Paul Horn Coffee Club, sits at the front of the restaurant. Nonagenarian Horn, who died in 2006, was a banker and former owner of the Jersey Theatre. Coffee drinkers at this table, many of them retired professionals, order more coffee than food, discuss local affairs, toss in dollar bills for football and basketball pools, and plan social outings. "When one of us takes a trip somewhere," says a stalwart, "the rule is that you have to bring back a gift for everyone, including Fran and the waitresses. After a trip to the Bahamas, I brought everyone big straw hats. You're chintzy if you don't bring us something."

The "Farmer's Start Beakfast" with two eggs, bacon, sausage or ham, hash browns, and toast is part of the top-selling breakfast trio along with the "Lumber Jack," which adds pancakes to eggs and hash browns; Franny's Omelet; and the Jake's Special, the sausage and buttermilk pancake classic created by retired grain farmer Jake Gettings (still a daily presence). "We should have patented our Jake's Special because now McDonald's and Hardee's are selling it, too," Gettings laments.

Caring managers, such as Fran Fosha, know their regulars and something about their daily routine, general health, eating habits, and domestic life. Fosha keeps a stack of get-well, thinking-of-you, and condolence cards in order to be on top of illnesses, hospitalizations, nursing home-moves, and deaths.

When a member of the Coffee Club dies, that person's cup is presented to the surviving spouse or significant other. "I take pie or soup to our bereaved along with the coffee cup," says Fosha. "A waitress may come with me for the presentation. If I take the cup to the spouse in the funeral home during the wake, the first thing they usually say to me is 'There's going to be an empty spot at the table.'"

At least once during the early morning coffee hour, Fosha brings trays of chocolate chip or oatmeal cookies, banana bread, or even piecrust with sugar on it for the regulars to munch on. She keeps "a soldier's wall" that honors residents serving in Iraq or Afghanistan and displays American flags in the front window. Fosha has organized Disney Days and Fifties Days, where waitresses jitterbug through the restaurant taking breakfast orders. For four days each year, the restaurant shuts down. For two of those days, the staff thoroughly cleans Fran & Marilyn's; for the last two days, the group may take off to the Ozarks or somewhere else. "All the girls here are like my family," says Fosha. "Most call me Mom."

Fran & Marilyn's
1131 S. State Street, Jerseyville, Illinois

 (618) 498-4912

 4 A.M. to 8 P.M. Monday through Saturday
6 A.M. to 8 P.M. Sunday

 Wheelchair accessible

 No smoking

6

Gruchala's
Columbia, Illinois

IN MID-SUMMER THE best way to find Gruchala's restaurant is to drive to the corner of S. Main and E. Plum in historic Columbia, Illinois and look for the corn corner. That's right, the corn corner. When he bought the old Ollie's restaurant in 1988, Dennis Gruchala planted six corn plants at the intersection. Twenty years later, the corn keeps growing and is now taller than the street sign at Main and Plum—thanks to Gruchala's regular applications of Miracle-Gro.

Gruchala's exterior, cream with burgundy trim, is reminiscent of a quaint cottage in Nova Scotia or Ontario's Georgian Bay region. Flower boxes of cascading petunias, rows of orange and red zinnias, and huge pink and red hibiscus plants bring botanical garden beauty to the building in summer months.

Inside the handsome edifice, part-owner and waitress Jeanne Kish understands the relationship between a small-town restaurant and its breakfast regulars.

"We know our people by what they eat," Kish says. "We put in their order when they appear and we set up their drinks. We know what they want. When I approach them at their table, I say 'This is your big chance to change something, since I already put your order in.'"

On Gruchala's menu, the "Full Breakfast" offers a choice of bacon strips, sausage patties, or ham plus hash browns, two eggs, toast, or biscuits. The "Small Breakfast" reduces the meat, allows one egg, and keeps the potatoes and the toast and biscuits. Gruchala's is the only restaurant around that offers a "Cook's Choice omelet with everything" as well as chewing gum and candy bars.

"Women think that they are getting less calories if they order the Small Breakfast," observes Kish. "If you order the Full Breakfast, you are seen as a big eater. Men order the Full Breakfast because that makes them feel macho. Men tend to order the sausage and women the bacon. I don't know why."

Besides the Full Breakfast, Gruchala's touts the "McOllie" breakfast sandwich as a breakfast best seller. The McOllie—sausage, ham or bacon smothered with eggs and cheese and served on toast—is named for Ollie Hoock, who owned the business, then called Ollie's, from 1974 to 1988.

"Ninety-five percent of our morning customers are regulars," Kish tells me. "And we have our newbies, such as you. We try to be very nice to newbies. We're particularly nice to clergymen. We feed every minister in town for free; lately, though, we seem to be getting some ministers from out of town."

Waitresses at Gruchala work furiously, take most food orders without writing them up, and are equally considerate of regulars and newbies. "Excuse me," my waitress warned on my first visit, "I'm coming in with a messy cup." Arriving at my table, she yanked a napkin from the tightly packed tabletop holder and in one swift move slipped it under my coffee cup. It is rare for restaurants to have saucers these days.

"Our regulars say whatever they want to say because they know this is their place," says Kish. "Customers are always adjusting our wall thermostat, complaining that it's 'too cold' or 'too hot.' Customers will walk to our kitchen, peek in the door, and ask us to cook their sausage a little longer or heat up something. They bring their food plates with them.

"One of our customers, 'Sleepy,' whose real name is Jim, and who can fix anything, eats here free every day and everyone knows it. Yesterday he fixed the door on our walk-in cooler. The other day he replaced a blade on a ceiling fan. A while ago a customer sat back on a bar stool and popped a rivet. Sleepy took the bar stool home with him, did some welding on it and had it back the next day. If need be, Sleepy will ask you to get up from your bar stool so he can take it home to fix. We have had quite a few rivets pop."

In Ollie's era, as today, the restaurant sold Illinois lottery tickets. Ollie's policy was that if an employee made a mistake in selling the tickets, the employee must pay for them. "One day a waitress ran off one hundred extra lottery tickets," says Kish. "The waitress bought half the tickets and Ollie generously bought the other half. Luckily the waitress bought a winning ticket and won ten million dollars. People still come in here and ask if there are any mistakes lying around."

Customers eat in the ground-floor dining area north of the bar or walk up some stairs to the "back" dining room, the former living room and bedroom of a home that Gruchala's gutted in 1993 to create more eating space. "Mr. and Mrs. Bergmann lived there when they owned the place before Ollie Hoock," says Kish. "The family still comes in to eat."

The older Gruchala's building site has historic roots that date to 1820 when the town was first laid out. Juengling's stage-coach stop supposedly occupied the site in those days. Later the site housed the Franklin Inn, then Buck's Tavern. How the town got its name is blurry. "Since the early settlers of Columbia had fought in the Revolution, it is possible they heard the (popular) song 'Columbia, Columbia to Glory Arise,' sang it, and decided it was a patriotic and appropriate name for the town they founded, our own fair Columbia," a local historian surmises.

Gruchala's
210 S. Main, Columbia, Illinois

 (618) 281-9901

 6:30 A.M. to 8:30 P.M. Monday through Friday
6:30 A.M. to 7 P.M. Sunday

 Wheelchair accessible

 No smoking

The Happy Cow

Caseyville, Illinois

In 1993, Cheryl Lauer and her partner, Gene Johnson, moved their kitchen tools and dinnerware into the long abandoned, but once thriving, space that had been Simpson's Drive-In in Caseyville, Illinois. Simpson's had a credible hamburger reputation and a sign out front that read: "Our hamburgers come from cows that die happy." Maintaining a connection to the past, the partners named their fledging operation "The Happy Cow." Unfortunately, that Happy Cow suffered financially and had to shut down.

"Our customers really missed us," said Lauer, who regained financial strength, leased the building across the road, kept the name "Happy Cow," and painted a sign on the new building that proclaimed: "Our hamburgers are still made from cows that die happy." Hamburgers aren't on the breakfast menu, but cows are all around.

Physically, Happy Cow comes in three parts: the Booth Side, the Big Side with large tables by the front window, and the Back Side. Cow knickknacks dominate the restaurant—hundreds of bovine porcelain and plastic figurines, drawings, wood carvings, painted skillets, cartoons, stuffed cows, and assorted you-name-its. Cows are simply everywhere you look, some even hanging from the ceiling and most of them black-and-white Holsteins, although a Guernsey or two are posted near the kitchen where a sign announces: "Udder Chaos."

Sitting in a far booth, Lauer points to her 'art collection.' "The things I've had the longest are the two calves with pacifiers in their mouths. See them there on the top shelf by the window? I got them at the Hen House in Okawville, Illinois. The cow on a swing came from the Ozarks. My daughter and her friends got the flying cow at the Mall of America in Minneapolis. Some people ask if any of the cows are for sale but I say no because most of them were gifts to us from family or customers."

Cows that sit around all day are certain to gather dust, so Lauer and her waitresses perform a cleansing ritual every three months. "We get together on Monday, the day we are closed, take everything off the walls and shelves, wash the walls, the shelves, and the cows, and put everything back again. The stuffed ones get the dirtiest."

On one visit, I saw an older woman leaning across a table to cut up a sausage link on the plate of her older friend, a rather common sight along with couples that pray before tucking into their meals. "Seniors are ninety percent of our business," explains Lauer. "Many of them come from St. Stephen's Catholic Church or the Caseyville Methodist Church, who are our neighbors. We also get workers from other neighborhoods such as Cahokia Mounds and Fairmount Park race course."

(Caseyville does have a religious legacy of sorts. Georgia M. Engelke wrote in her 1983 book, *The Great American Bottom*, that Caseyville was founded by Zadoc Casey, a preacher who later became lieutenant governor of Illinois and a member of the U.S. House of Representatives. "Before going to bed he

(Casey) would offer prayer on his knees," Engelke wrote. "One night he became ill while praying and the next morning was found dead on his knees.")

"During breakfast," says Lauer, "we are best known for our 'COW'ntry Special," consisting of three meats, potatoes, two eggs, one biscuit, and some gravy. "Half the people at breakfast order it." The other half prefer either the four-ounce ribeye steak (since it comes from a cow) with two eggs, potatoes, toast or biscuit, cheese or western omelets, and old-fashioned biscuits and gravy.

The Happy Cow has a small kitchen and limited storage capacity. Lauer, the main food buyer, keeps an eye on dwindling supplies. "We have to hope that we have the right amount of everything on hand," she says. "We make a lot of trips to the Shop 'n Save in Collinsville to keep up. I go there every other day but some weeks I have to go every day."

The Happy Cow
601 N. Main Street, Caseyville, Illinois

 (618) 346-7421

 6 A.M. to 7:30 P.M. Tuesday through Friday
8 A.M. to 7:30 P.M. Saturday
8 A.M. to 2 P.M. Sunday

 Wheelchair accessible

 No smoking

Hy Ho Restaurant
Belleville, Illinois

AT THE HY HO, a 24-hour restaurant on the southern edge of Belleville, Illinois, most of the breakfast regulars are called "family," but others—a tiny fraction of them—may be called to task for culinary indiscretions.

Debbie Curtis, Hy Ho's owner, muses about the word "regular" and how one becomes a regular at the Hy Ho. "You become a regular when you *want* to become one. We have people who come in here three times a week but don't fit in because they don't open up and talk to anyone or show any friendliness. When you're a regular you become part of each other's lives. As an example, one family of regulars here has 'adopted' one of our longtime waitresses. On her breaks, the waitress comes to sit with the family. They buy each other presents and get together on birthdays and holidays. That's what I mean about regulars.

"At breakfast, the Hy Ho counter is like a neighborhood bar. But customers have to come in a lot to get to know each other," says Curtis. "Regular counter guys bond. Maybe three or four of them talk every morning, all sitting on their stools and leaning forward or backward to see one another. Then one day, one of them will say, 'Let's start sitting in a booth so we can talk better.' As they bond more, they'll leave the booth and switch to a table in our main dining room."

On the other hand, the Hy Ho frowns on extraordinary customer missteps, even among its regulars. One longtime customer was banned for life—a 73-year-old man feeling very frisky on the day of his infringement. A breakfast regular for years, there had been nothing unusual in the man's behavior or in what he ate—the same bacon-and-eggs entrée every day. On one warm summer morning, however, the man became impetuously familiar with a waitress some fifty years his junior. When she bent over to lay down his bacon and eggs in front of him, he unexpectedly chomped into her left breast, partially exposed due to the heat of the day. The waitress yelled; the manager rushed from the cash register to render summary judgment: "Sir, you're banned for life from the Hy Ho." His breakfast untouched, the guilty man left immediately. He reportedly serves his life term at a nearby Hardee's.

Another veteran breakfaster parked his automobile near the Hy Ho front window and stepped out wearing a pair of hot-pink shorts. "Some of the regulars seated by the window spotted the man, who was in his seventies, and began to taunt and tease him," recalls former co-owner Mike Mercurio. Responding to the taunts, the man started to dance, increased his speed, and worked himself into parking lot rage by kicking at the window and shattering some glass. For that he received a one-year ban.

A six-foot-eight breakfast regular crosses the line as well. "After quarrelling with the cash register clerk about his bill, he went to our men's room, removed the lid from the toilet, and stuck it up inside the acoustic ceiling tiles. He got six months for that," says Curtis. The Hy Ho has never caught the customer who wrote a death threat to one of the owners for suddenly changing the ingredients of the restaurant's chili recipe.

A perennial morning favorite at the Hy Ho, besides the French Toast special and the three-egg western omelet, is the biscuits and gravy entrée. "I run into people wherever I go and they say to me, 'What do you do?' and I tell them I help run the Hy Ho restaurant," says Curtis. "You've got the best biscuits and gravy at 2 A.M. in the morning anywhere in the world,' they say. 'Whop' biscuits are what the patrons really like. By whop I mean we take a can of biscuits, whop one end of it on the counter, and they pop open." The restaurant serves its biscuits and gravy from 8 P.M. to 11 A.M. only because, as Curtis says, "we don't want our biscuits to dry out."

The Hy Ho has a good lineage. The first restaurant on the site opened in 1952 as Calavito's Spaghetti House. Then, one of the cooks bought it and renamed it Compton's Cafe. In mid-1965, Mercurio and his pal Fred Bohannon pulled into Compton's Cafe for a cup of coffee and found the door padlocked. They learned that the Compton people hadn't paid rent for six months. "Here's our chance to run a restaurant," Fred said to Mike. The pair named the new cafe "Hy Ho" because, when he was young and eligible, Fred would visit a girlfriend in Springfield, Illinois. On the way, he passed a restaurant called the HiWay Cafe. The transition from HiWay to Hy Ho was a piece of cake!

Hy Ho publishes a weekly menu and stacks it by the cash register. This creative menu also includes small news articles and occasional obituaries about regular customers. Curtis has added a Joke of the Week to the menu. "Our customers tell me they send the jokes all over the world over the Internet," Curtis says. One taboo subject is banned customers and their sentences.

Hy Ho Restaurant

20 S. Belt West, Belleville, Illinois

☎ (618) 235-1269

🕐 6 A.M. to 10 P.M. Monday
Open 24 hours Tuesday through Saturday
Closes at 10 P.M. Sunday

♿ Wheelchair accessible

🚭 No smoking

Kopperman's Deli

St. Louis

KOPPERMAN'S IS A renowned Jewish or "East Coast" deli in St. Louis's Central West End that serves salmon, lox, whitefish, cheese blintzes, matzo and eggs, and sides of Best Kosher salami or pastrami for breakfast.

But what sells over everything else in the morning are (1) two eggs over easy with bacon and veteran cook Martha Triplett's chunky hash brown potatoes; (2) French toast made with real French bread; and (3) potato pancakes with sour cream.

Kopperman's has resided on Euclid Avenue near McPherson since 1983 in quarters that once housed the 1930s Wakefield Tea Rooms and the 1940s Woman's Exchange. Kopperman's took root in 1897 as a combined butcher shop and smoked fish operation called M. Kopperman and Sons, located at Sixth and Cole in downtown St. Louis. In 1917 in a new address on Franklin Avenue, Kopperman's went beyond wholesale fish and meat marketing to add a modest Jewish deli. "There were only four tables there on Franklin, but we were fortunately across from the *St. Louis Post-Dispatch* building and until it closed in 1969 the deli averaged five hundred to six hundred sandwiches a day," reports Myron Kopperman, grandson of M. Kopperman. "My father, Henry, was in charge of operations then. Corned beef was the number one sandwich. That was really before delis were delis."

When Henry Kopperman died in 1973 the Kopperman deli ceased and lay fallow for a decade while Myron worked as a food broker. In 1983, yearning for more golden deli days, Myron struck a partnership with Sanford Rich—who is now sole proprietor since Myron's early retirement—and opened on Euclid Avenue.

"We were open a month or so," says Myron, "when Sanford came in wearing blue jeans and a bandana and said: 'I am going to fix breakfast (French toast) this morning and if it goes over I will fix breakfast until you find us a breakfast cook.' Although I had never hired a cook, a lady named Martha who was cooking at Bobby's Creole in University City was highly recommended. In our interview I told her that my favorite breakfast dish was matzo and eggs. 'Do you want it European-style or Russian-style?' she asked. I hired her immediately and she's still at Kopperman's."

Martha Triplett, who claims to be semi-retired, arrives at 5 A.M. She makes the potato pancakes (about one hundred orders a day) from an old family recipe. (Her family owned two Nichols barbecue stands in the 1930s and 1940s, one in St. Louis and another in East St. Louis.) She makes the celebrated Kopperman's homemade applesauce from a recipe she knew as a young girl. "I peel about a bushel of Golden Delicious apples a week and I season the sauce with the right amount of cinnamon and sugar," she says. She reminds me that Kopperman's menu has no pancakes or waffles, save for the specialty potato pancakes. "We let our French toast take the place of pancakes and waffles," she says.

Kopperman's corned beef hash is a heavenly presence to customers who are used to doctored canned corned beef at many breakfast places. "We process our one hundred percent pure corned beef along with sweet onions, parsley, and green onions," says Triplett. "Then we add potatoes, mix everything up, and roll it. There is nothing false about our corned beef."

On weekends, Kopperman's is constantly busy. "When I look out on some weekends, I see lines waiting to be seated and waiters and waitresses rushing around like they are on roller skates," observes Triplett. "It's like going west on Highway 40 in rush hour."

Triplett, being somewhat indispensable, has other duties beyond breakfast food supervision. "Come over here and see what else I do," she says, directing me to the twenty-eight-foot-long deli display case next to the open kitchen, near rows of non-smoking tables and chairs, and across from what Kopperman's calls the "garden area," a small enclave with a couple of tables, chairs, and a ficus tree. "Besides breakfast, I make two kinds of cole slaw, two kinds of potato salad—about sixty pounds at a time—tuna salad, egg salad, marzipan, tabbouleh, salmon croquettes, mac and cheese, quiche, spaghettini with broccoli, jambalaya, baked chicken, Greek pasta salad, and a lot more. We sell things in the case as take-out and we use it for lunch and dinner." In addition to its restaurant operation, Kopperman's is one of the Central West End's largest gourmet grocery and wine shops.

In Kopperman's front end—curtained off by deep maroon drapes—customers sit at tables and candy-striped booths and look through an enormous floor-to-ceiling window to the bustling patio. The front side, where smoking is allowed, also contains a mahogany bar with brass rails and an impressive collection of old and rare lithographed Ringling Brothers Barnum & Bailey Circus posters from the early twentieth century.

Another French touch at Kopperman's, beyond the French toast, is the restroom setup down a deep flight of stairs in the basement. "Les Toilettes," as they are called, are at the end of a long, curtained corridor and, unfortunately, are handicapped unfriendly, even though wheelchairs can be navigated on the main floor.

Kopperman's Deli
386 North Euclid, St. Louis

(314) 361-0100

7:30 A.M. to 4 P.M. Monday through Thursday
7:30 A.M. to 5 P.M. Friday
11 P.M. Friday through 4 P.M. Sunday

Limited wheelchair accessibility

Smoking

10

La Dolce Via
St. Louis

LA DOLCE VIA is a lunch and brunch scone-and-scramble-driven neighborhood café in the Gibson Heights section of St. Louis. It lies in the backyard of Washington University medical center.

Marcia Sindel, a trained social worker, runs the café-bakery. She opened the bakery part in 1990, mostly to produce fourteen different desserts per week for the Bar Italia restaurant a few blocks away; she added the café by popular demand in 2002. Since 1990, Marcia, her business partner, daughter Carli Issitt, and her spry and youthful staff that includes manager Jason Main, whose business card has a quote from a *St. Louis Post-Dispatch* review: "Delightful Counter Attendant," have operated this charming outpost in a neighborhood under rehabilitation by the Forest Park Southeast Development Corporation.

Sindel effusively describes her food business. "We have a sweetbread scramble and lots of veggie scrambles. Our biscuit gravy is to die for, not to die from. We make it from lamb sausage and we serve it over homemade cheese scones. We also have a cheese scone with eggs and bacon and we can cut it in half as an egg sandwich. It's our 'Egg McVia.' We make twenty-four scones weekdays and thirty-six on Saturdays. We have people who buy scones on Sunday so they won't be without them on Monday when we are closed. We use very little sugar in our scones, about one cup for all twenty-four of them."

"For brunch, we have fresh free-range eggs from a local farm. Farmers e-mail us and tell us what they have and then drop by. Just last week we had fresh tomatoes and fresh arugula; we made an egg scramble from that." Daughter Carli adds: "We have mixed berries and heavy cream which may constitute forty percent of our brunch orders. We get berries from farms in the summer, then from Chile, then from Mexico. We never use frozen berries or veggies."

Sindel is very possessive when talking about her neighbors, many of whom are regulars. "I consider you a regular if you are a stranger and you come back," she says.

One neighbor, Jim Halcomb, a financial executive, has been a longtime Sindel booster, aware that her business is a pivotal piece of the neighborhood. "Some of us neighbors said to Marcia (in 2002), 'What do you think of adding a café to your bakery?'" She agreed; the café quickly took shape. Halcomb donated tables, chairs, and a lamp and others contributed, too. "On the day the café opened," recalls Sindel, "twenty-five neighbors were on hand at 7 A.M. when I turned on the lights. They all cheered."

Sindel notes an impressive list of good deeds that her staff members have performed for neighbors.

"We took care of a 95-year-old lady who lives across the street," says Sindel. "She broke her leg and was waiting to go to a nursing facility. We bathed her, cleaned her home, and made breakfast, lunch, and dinner for her. We were her surrogate mothers.

"We learned that a woman down the street was fighting cancer. She told us she was on chemo and couldn't sleep. We started a campaign called 'Help Julie Sleep,' collected $1,200, and bought her a new bed.

"A while ago, a neighbor got her car stolen twice and couldn't get insurance for it. We threw a spaghetti dinner for her and invited all the neighbors. From the proceeds, we got enough money to pay her auto insurance premium."

Sindel has a special quasi-clinical fondness for children. She invites neighborhood kids in to help make—and consume—Christmas cookies. For young children of customers, she is the self-described baby whisperer. "When kids cry and parents can't eat, I come from the kitchen to find out what's wrong. Quite often, I take the kid into the kitchen where the lights are bright and I'm whispering gibberish to them. They usually stop crying immediately."

For the children, Sindel installed a makeshift dollhouse that resembles a big play kitchen. Parents and staff members alike are encouraged to play in the "kitchen" with the children. Not all parents participate. "We have some parents who sit away from their kids and don't play with them at all," observes Sindel.

In managing the café, Sindel has not abandoned her bakery roots. "We make three hundred loaves of bread weekly for Frazer's Brown Bag restaurant on Pestalozzi Street. And we make mostly non-traditional wedding and birthday cakes and sell them retail here. We have done cakes in the shape of an infant and space cakes with planets on top. We don't put candy flowers on our cakes—our tops are fresh flowers. The florist brings us an arrangement and we cut it up artistically and put it on the cakes. Whenever we do a special cake, we display it in the refrigerator in the dining room so people can see it for a while."

La Dolce Via

4470 Arco Avenue, St. Louis

 (314) 371-1926

 8 A.M. to 6 P.M. Tuesday through Friday
8 A.M. to 5 P.M. Saturday
10 A.M. to 4 P.M. Sunday

 Wheelchair accessible

 No smoking

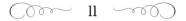 11

Lewis Café
St. Clair, Missouri

In 1843, St. Clair, Missouri was founded. Previously, the settlement was known as Traveler's Repose. "The name (Traveler's Repose) may have been derived from the word traveler … and the word repose, a catchy name for a wayside inn," explained Herman Gottlieb Kiel in *The Centennial Biographical Directory of Franklin County, Missouri.*

Kiel explained that Franklin County is one of twenty-five U.S. counties named for Benjamin Franklin. "He is one of the greatest names in the world," said Kiel. "He snatched the thunderbolt from heaven and the scepter from tyrants. A trustworthy biography of this man should at least be in the courthouse and every schoolroom of Franklin County."

Officially incorporated in 1859, St. Clair was an early stagecoach stop between St. Louis and Springfield, Missouri. In the late 1920s, the newly poured U.S. Highway 66 lapped the northern edge of St. Clair.

Ford Model As were still rolling along Route 66 in 1936 when Vergil Lewis, sensing a local mood for decent hamburgers and chili, took over a confectionary and opened the Lewis Café near the Frisco tracks in downtown St. Clair. Vergil's place had seven oak booths, including a corner booth with one seat called the "Cozy Booth" or the "Lovers' Booth." Vergil put in a 3.2 beer bar with fourteen stools and a traditional back bar with lace doilies along the shelves. The booths and back bar—elegantly refinished in 2004—remain, as do half the stools, but beer is only a memory. On her deathbed in 1950, Vergil's mother, Neva, exhorted her son to quit selling beer. When Neva died, beer sales stopped immediately, says Vergil's great-nephew, Chris Short, the café's current owner.

Vergil was a local character. He traded pocket knives with customers, sponsored softball teams, paid for their uniforms, and treated players to free coffee. During World War II, non-smoking Vergil sent cigarettes or money to buy them to customers and pals in the armed forces. And when the first U.S. 66 weigh station opened near St. Clair in the late 1940s, he learned that a restaurant owner needs a keen sense of humor

"The state patrolmen from the weigh station came in for meals all the time," recalled Hazel Crow, a longtime Lewis Café waitress. "The patrolmen kidded Vergil, who was a bachelor, unmercifully. Whenever one of them went out of town, he would mail Vergil a postcard signed 'Patsy.' Soon, practically everyone in town was sending Vergil 'Patsy' postcards.

"In one postcard, Patsy said that she would soon visit St. Clair and wanted to meet Vergil," continued Crow. "'I know Patsy is going to come to see me,' Vergil told customers. One day a bus stopped by the station a few doors down the street. When Vergil wasn't looking, someone slipped a suitcase inside the café's front door. Vergil opened the suitcase and found it filled with bras and panties. The next day, a good-looking lady, who happened to be the chief weigh officer's wife, entered the café to claim the suitcase. Vergil wasn't around to meet her and never learned the secret." On another occasion, prankstering weigh station officers brought in two excitable guinea hens and let them loose by the front cash register. The birds flew straight into the back wall, plunging to death by the Cozy Booth.

Nowadays breakfast customers savor the café's buttermilk biscuits and homemade milk and pork sausage gravy; in fact, half the café's breakfast business is biscuits and gravy. To produce his whole-hog sausage, Short has two hogs slaughtered weekly and two more in the summer to help meet customer demand for take-home sausage. "My food vendor tells me that we're just about the only restaurant in Missouri that does what we do with sausage," says Short, who also raises Angus cattle on his nearby farm, sacrificing two steers weekly for hamburgers, plate lunches, and dinner entrées. A sign in the front window says the café "serves our own farm-raised Angus beef."

At breakfast, sausage is king. "Number one at breakfast is our buttermilk biscuits and gravy with a side order of pattied, half-pound sausage," says Short, who sells a decent number of what he calls "the ultimate breakfast sandwiches" that include sausage, two eggs, hash browns, a grilled onion, and cheese. His hot cakes and French toast product lines sell nicely, too.

Customers take home orders of sausage, bottles of Vergil's poppy seed celery dressing, made from a recipe that Vergil clipped from a newspaper in the 1940s, and pies. "We make forty pies a day," says Short. "Thirty of the pies are sold by the slice and most are consumed here and the rest are bought whole, usually to take to the office in the morning." Coconut cream sells the most, followed by cherry, apple, and a handful of sugar-free fruit pies.

Short's three dining areas include the original counter room; the carpeted, no-smoking main dining room; and the three-table back room that is frequently reserved at breakfast time. The local Gideons come in Saturday morning and the local Church of the Nazarene preacher and some parishioners arrive late Sunday morning for either breakfast or early lunch. In mid-week, ladies' groups reserve the room for bridge or pinochle.

As in most small-town cafes, coffee is a big commodity. "We go through six hundred pots a week here," says Short, counting ten cups to each pot. Some customers, of course, come in and drink only coffee. Short observes how, on some days, "We can have up to thirty men sitting in the coffee counter room while thirty women are sitting in the main dining room doing the same. When the women are ready to go, they'll all come by to pick up their husbands and the place will suddenly be empty."

Lewis Café
145 S. Main, St. Clair, Missouri

 (636) 629-9975

 5 A.M. to 8 P.M. Monday through Saturday
6 A.M. to 8 P.M. Sunday

 Wheelchair accessible

 Some smoking permitted

Louie's Kampsville Inn
Kampsville, Illinois

THE NEW "MEETING of the Great Rivers National Scenic Byway"—one of America's treasured national scenic highways, as chosen by the U.S. Department of Transportation—starts along the Mississippi River at Alton, Illinois on Illinois Highway 100, the Great River Road. It rolls past chalky white bluffs, slender finger islands, barges longer than NFL playing fields, the flood-prone village of Grafton, Pere Marquette State Park, and some of the country's major archaeological digs. It then crosses the Illinois River at Hardin and officially ends at Illinois Highway 108 in Kampsville, Illinois near the free car ferry.

Near the junction of the two highways is Louie's Kampsville Inn, where you can find hot coffee, great breakfast BLTs and pancakes, and stories about the inn's tempestuous neighbor, the Illinois River.

Louie's is in a two-story, white-frame building built in 1888 as the Brenn Hotel. It accommodated passengers on packets and excursion boats that sailed in from St. Louis or Peoria. Brenn guests were met dockside by a live ensemble called "Our Boys Band." Around 1900, Kampsville was promoted "as one of the most popular summer resorts in western Illinois…a mecca of the anglers." Passengers approaching Kampsville on the steamer "Bald Eagle," for instance, leaned over the railing and saw enough fish "to start a market." After a weekend of fishing, anglers re-boarding the "Bald Eagle" often carried with them large baskets of bass and crappie. At the peak of resort season, the showboat "Cotton Blossom" stopped in Kampsville to perform "Uncle Tom's Cabin" and "Nine Nights in a Bar Room."

Way back in 1850, when Kampsville was still known as Farrowtown—years before Michael A. Kamp, a German immigrant whose occupation was barber-surgeon, came on the scene—the Illinois River was a major route for travelers from Springfield, Illinois and other interior spots to reach St. Louis or Peoria. One old ledger notes that 788 steamboats passed Farrowtown in 1850 en route to Peoria.

"Many of the early boats were very uncomfortable," wrote John Conger and William Hull in their 1932 book, *History of the Illinois River Valley*. "There was but one bedroom candle on board and this was made to serve the four ladies' staterooms in turn, one lady being obliged to go to bed, while the candle was then passed on to the next room. Of towels also there was but one, which had to go the round from cabin to cabin in the same way."

Mr. Kamp did so well barbering and running the local bank that the citizens petitioned to re-name Farrowtown as Kampsville. He lived in town for fifty-nine years, dying at age ninety-two in 1922. Reprinted in the centennial edition of the local newspaper was a story recalling the night that Kamp and a friend stepped into a saloon for a nightcap. The bartender was out; a young man was scrubbing the floor. This young man told Kamp that he was underage and could not sell them liquor, but he could offer them a nip from a decanter set aside for the owner's private use. Chatting a while, Kamp learned of the young man's background, darkened by poverty and loneliness. The young man said his name was Joseph Pulitzer. "The encounter resulted in the employment of young Pulitzer on the *Westliche Post* (a St. Louis area German-American newspaper), his start on the rise to fame," claimed the newspaper.

In Kampsville today, the Illinois River continues to command respect. "The inside of my restaurant has flooded six times since I bought it in 1984," says owner Louie Hazelwood. In 1993, the year of the most severe flood, Louie got hammered twice. "We were first flooded out in April, then the water receded and we got new carpeting in June. We reopened July 1. A second flood closed us down July 4 when the water reached eight feet in the dining room and we didn't re-open until October 9, so we were out of business for nearly six months."

Louie's presents a family-like feeling at breakfast. "Betty Boop," nickname for Louie's fiancée of twenty-plus years, circulates in the dining room saying hello. Louie's daughter, Tracy Hatfield, is the manager. Megan Hatfield, a granddaughter, is a waitress, and grandson Zach busses and works the cash register and sells Louie's T-shirts and white ballcaps. Easy-going Louie sits with customers and looks out the window toward the river. By the time the Illinois reaches Kampsville from its headwaters in Chicago 450 miles to the north, it has taken aboard tributary waters from the Chicago, Des Plaines, Kankakee, Fox, Iroquois, and Sangamon rivers.

Louie enjoys watching the free ferry, "Miss Illinois," make its five-minute run across the Illinois. Occasionally, automobiles waiting for the ferry roll into the river when their brakes fail or when the driver steps on the accelerator in error. When this happens, divers must hook up the car so it can be lifted from the water. Meanwhile, the Coast Guard closes the river to traffic and the ferry stops, anywhere from two to four hours. Louie then gets a surge in patronage from motorists waiting to get across the Illinois.

The restaurant is practically next door to the Center for American Archeology. Locals call Kampsville, a village of around four hundred, the "archaeological center of North America." That means there are "arkies" and tourists who come in for coffee, Louie's pancake batter waffles, his BLTs, his deep-fried breadsticks covered with brown sugar and cinnamon, his best-selling biscuits and milk sausage gravy, and hash browns. In the years before her recent retirement as a breakfast cook, local legend Millie Wirth would often walk over to the bar side of Louie's and snatch a can of Pabst Extra Lite beer to mix into her biscuit batter. "Customers preferred this biscuit recipe over all the others," says Louie.

Close to midnight on a rainy Kampsville Annual Old Settlers' Day in 1990, a possum dropped through Louie's acoustical-tile ceiling (no one knows how this happened) and landed on a slice of pizza sitting on the bar. The possum quickly scampered off the bar and plopped to the floor. He led a lively chase around Louie's tables and chairs before one Old Settler, still in his re-enactment costume, caught him, recalls Louie. "We hit the possum on the head, skinned it, cooked it, and the Old Settlers ate it. Later, we mounted the possum's head on a plaque over our bar with an inscription that says 'Dew Drop Inn.' Since then we have conducted tours showing where the possum fell, what his escape route was, where he was caught, and the club that we knocked him out with."

Dr. Jane Buikstra, Distinguished Professor of Anthropology at the University of New Mexico in Albuquerque and former board president of the Center for American

Archaeology, considers Louie's to be the Center's lunch spot, but many of her arky colleagues come in just for coffee to watch the Illinois River flow by with Louie.

Buikstra observes the Illinois River with a much different eye than Louie's. "This is the Nile River of North America," she declares. "Our archaeological mounds near here, like the Pyramids in Egypt, are monuments to the dead. And we both have the flooding that renders the soil fertile."

"Since this is a famous arky center," Wade Gibson, former Kampsville mayor, once stated, "people call me from all over the world to find out what's happening here. I tell them to take the new Scenic Byway to get here—and to not forget to come to Louie's when they visit."

Louie's Kampsville Inn
102 Second Street, Kampsville, Illinois

 (618) 653-4413

 7 A.M. to 9 P.M. daily

 Wheelchair accessible

No smoking

Majestic Restaurant
St. Louis

A FEW YEARS ago members of St. Nicholas Greek Orthodox Church voted against moving to the suburbs and to stay the course at South Kingshighway and Forest Park Parkway.

Undoubtedly a good many of those who voted to remain were among the "Greek Boys" who are Sunday morning regulars at the Majestic Restaurant, which is located several blocks from the church.

Every Sunday morning, several of the St. Nicholas males leave their wives and children at the church, park their cars, and walk to the Majestic. "The routine is that the men will drink coffee and chat while standing at the bar where we have our gyro rotisserie," said Bill Politis, the café's co-owner with his brother, Louis, since 1961. After an hour or so, the men will gulp down the last of their coffee, return to church, and find a place in the rear of the sanctuary for the final hour of the service.

Says Alex Politis, Bill's son and kitchen manager: "The priests at St. Nicholas have occasionally chastised the Majestic group for ducking the first half of the service." Indeed, said a priest with an understanding sense of humor, "I have called them 'bad Christians' for not being willing to sit through two hours of church on Sunday, but they don't listen to me."

"Someone said that we ought to run a collection bucket on Sunday mornings right here in the Majestic since a lot of the main church business is taken care of here," said a Greek Boy. "We see the Majestic as an annex of the church!"

On weekday mornings, more of the Greek Boys drop in for omelets and coffee. They sit in a red Naugahyde booth near a sign that says "No Parking—Greeks Only."

Gyro meat (a blend of lamb, beef, and spices) has proved to be a lure for the breakfast crowd. The biggest draw is the "Bill's Special Omelette," which includes gyro meat, feta cheese, tomatoes, and onions. If "Bill's Special" is too overwhelming then you should try "Aleko's omelette," with tomatoes, onion, feta, and diced chicken breast. There are fifteen other omelets to choose from on the Majestic menu, making the place just about the local omelet king. In addition, there are six egg specials, led by the popular Eggs Florentine.

Most of the artwork in the Majestic's two serving rooms is Greek-tinged. A poster of the Acropolis in Athens, given to the Politises by the Greek National Tourism Agency, is mounted in the bar area. Over the bar is an oil painting of Kefalari, Bill's hometown by the Sea of Corinth. He maintains a family home in Kefalari.

Bill encouraged his son Alex to carry on at the Majestic and he has—first by graduating from the Culinary Institute of America in Hyde Park, New York, and then by assuming the reins of the kitchen. From a narrow kitchen window, Alex can astutely observe the main dining area.

"You see a lot," says Alex, who describes the Majestic as an American regional diner with Greek underpinnings. "Most people at breakfast sit facing the kitchen. This could be that the sun is in their face—our window looks out to the east into a sometimes blazing sun—or maybe they choose to keep their heads down reading their paper so looking outside could be a distraction. At lunch, when the sun has changed its course, people prefer to look outside and not face the kitchen.

"I have observed that most of the breakfast regulars like to sit in two places: near the kitchen or by the cash register. People sit by the kitchen because, in a way, we keep them company with our loud talk and joking around. They see us bringing food orders out and see things they wish they had ordered."

Alex notes differences between occupants of booths and tables. "Booth people will not sit at tables; they'll wait for a booth. Table people will gladly take a booth if there are no available tables. I can stand here in the kitchen and tell you just about where half the people who enter the restaurant will sit—in a booth or at a table."

A couple sat in a booth one day; the lady was carrying a live rodent that looked like a squirrel, recalls Bill Politis. "Right after they sat down this animal escaped from a pouch the lady had. 'Jeez,' I said, 'we've got a rat.' The animal was about a rat's size and shape. We chased it all over the restaurant. The lady and her husband were hysterical because the animal, which I later found out cost about $1,000, was a loving pet, I guess. Finally we caught it and gave it to the lady, who stuck it back into the pouch, returned to the booth, and ordered a stack of blueberry hotcakes. We ordinarily don't allow animals in here but I decided to let that one stay. It's been our only squirrel-type animal since we've owned this place."

"A gentleman came in and ordered French toast and he asked that it be heavily sprinkled with powdered sugar," Alex said. "Unbeknownst to him and to me, one of our morning waiters had mistakenly refilled the powdered sugar jar with cornstarch. The customer unscrewed the lid of the shaker so he could liberally pour what he thought was powdered sugar on his French toast but what he really poured was a load of cornstarch. After the first bite, he couldn't open his mouth. It was shut tight. It was hilarious watching this from the kitchen. Gradually his mouth loosened and everything was back to normal. We saw to it that the man got a free meal.

"It's amazing," says Alex, "how some breakfast customers find it hard to tell us what they want to order. 'How do you want your eggs?' we ask them. 'Fried, over, up, easy, basted, scrambled, poached?' Maybe there's too much of a choice to make, but some people can't make up their minds. Same way with toast. 'What kind of toast do you want?' we ask. 'What kind of toast do you have?' they will say."

Majestic Restaurant
4900 Laclede, St. Louis

 (314) 361-2011

 6 A.M. to 10:30 P.M. daily

 Wheelchair accessible

 Smoking permitted

14

Mary Lou's Grill

Carbondale, Illinois

IN *ROADFOOD*, A book by Jane and Michael Stern that celebrates rural cafes, truck stops, and small-town restaurants, Mary Lou's Grill, a college hangout in Carbondale, Illinois, is compared to Mory's at Yale University and the famous beer hall at Heidelberg University in Germany. "Mary Lou will prepare a batch of 'poor boys' for you if you've got a problem she knows of, or she'll cook up a double-size omelet for graduates (of nearby Southern Illinois University) who return for one last look," wrote the Sterns. Genuine concern for student welfare continues at the restaurant although Mary Lou retired many years ago. "All food served here is with one hundred percent love," the Mary Lou's menu has stated since the first day of business.

Mary Lou's has been a popular breakfast joint since 1962 when Mary Lou Trammell took over Flossie's Restaurant on Walnut Street and renamed it for herself. In 1976, needing much more space, Mary Lou moved into the vacant Hewitt's Pharmacy on Illinois Street. Hewitt's left Mary Lou a wall full of sports photos that she expanded greatly with memorabilia of her own.

Today the restaurant is perhaps best known for its breakfast biscuits and made-from-scratch gravy, an offering that constitutes nearly fifty percent of breakfast orders. Omelets are also big at Mary Lou's. The "meatlover's" omelet, laden with ham, sausage, bacon, cheese, and optional veggies, is popular, as are Mary Lou's legendary chili cheese, ham, and jelly omelets. "One of our best deals," says manager Robert Martin, Mary Lou's son-in-law, "is the three hotcakes or the three slices of French toast for $4.39. The students love it."

What students like more than anything is the Pretty Legs Special for only $3.69. "Mary Lou named this special of two eggs, toast, coffee, and a half-order of biscuits and gravy for a railroad worker who came in here almost every day in Bermuda shorts and ordered the special," says Martin. "His legs were so ugly, Mary Lou nicknamed him 'Pretty Legs.'"

"On December 13, 1976 Coach Rey Dempsey and most of the SIU-C Salukis football squad, about fifty players, helped me move to Illinois Street, six blocks away," Mary Lou once recalled. "You should have seen them roll those big steam tables and refrigeration units and the ice cream cooler down that street. When they were done, the players helped me clean and get the place in shape for opening day. Coach Dempsey came in for breakfast regularly. I gave him a Mary Lou's Grill T-shirt and said to him 'If you don't wear it to every game, SIU will lose.'" The Salukis notched win after win the following season until the game that Dempsey accidentally forgot to wear his special shirt. SIU lost. "We're still feeding SIU football teams," said Martin.

Near Mary Lou's curvy counter area and adjoining dining room are photos and wall hangings that highlighted Mary Lou's culinary career and her wanderings. "In my first restaurant, I hung only one picture on the wall—Tony Orlando," said Mary Lou. "I was back stage three times to meet him. When my husband died in 1987, Governor (James) Thompson of Illinois got Tony Orlando to phone me with condolences.

"Some graduates of SIU who were my customers return and bring in politicians to meet me," said Mary Lou. "My first politician-customer gave me his picture and it's still hanging. He was attorney Ty Fainter of Carbondale. Mr. Skill still comes in. He was press secretary and advance man for Governor Thompson. We named a dinner item after him, a cheeseburger with chili." Thompson once remarked that Mary Lou's "has more politicians' pictures on her walls than there are in the state capitol or the local post office." "We're still noted for our politicians," says Martin.

Besides politicians, Mary Lou displayed photographs of notable SIU grads, family members, and country-western bands. "When I was running this place, I went to see a country and western band every Saturday night," said Mary Lou. "I always met the drummer first and he helped me get the band's picture."

Because of her deftness at the grill—one young customer said that "she can carry on a conversation with twenty people at the counter and get the orders out all by herself. I come in just to watch her"—Mary Lou made some unlikely connections. "Bob Hope called once to sing me 'Happy Birthday,'" she said. "The son of producer of *My Three Sons* was in here. John Wayne's son was here. Dennis Franz from the *NYPD Blue* TV show ate breakfast here all the time when he was a student."

"President Bill Clinton was in Carbondale one day and wanted to have lunch where the college kids go," said Martin. "Of course, they go here. Two Secret Service agents knocked on my door but it was Monday and we were closed. I was here and answered the door. I had to tell them we couldn't serve the president. We sent him to a competitor.

"On Saturday, our busiest day, we cook breakfast all day," says Martin. "We don't even serve plate lunches on Saturday. Most college kids get up at noon or 1 P.M. with hangovers and want to eat breakfast. Biscuits and gravy and ham and cheese omelets are the most popular orders on Saturdays. The kids also want lots of water or milkshakes; they're not big on coffee. We have Rolaids for them on the counter."

Back in 1987, Governor James Thompson issued a proclamation on Mary Lou's twenty-fifth anniversary as a Carbondale icon. It said in part that Mary Lou's had probably cured more good old-fashioned SIU hangovers than any medical personnel could ever hope to do, that more of her homemade pies have been eaten at breakfast than most places serve at lunch or dinner, and that Mary Lou herself is probably one of the state's best substitute parents—"nursing anxiety about homesickness, less than sterling grades, lost loves, and worries about the future." As noted, that attitude continues under a new generation of Mary Lou's family management.

Mary Lou's Grill
114 S. Illinois Street, Carbondale, Illinois

 (618) 457-5084

 7 A.M. to 2 P.M. Tuesday through Saturday

 Handicapped accessible

 No smoking

15

Miss Aimee B's Tea Room
St. Charles, Missouri

MISS AIMEE BECKER, a devoted alumnus of Lindenwood University (class of 1908) and active member of nearby Immanuel Lutheran Church, lived in the eleven-room red brick Marten-Becker home on First Capitol Drive in St. Charles from 1894, when she was four, to 1982. After eighty-eight years in the family homestead, illness forced Miss Becker to move to a nursing home where she died at age 94 in 1984.

Miss Becker left her National Historic Register home to the St. Charles Historical Society as a museum, which it inhabited briefly until it could no longer afford its maintenance. In 1987, the society leased the building to two imaginative women who opened Miss Aimee B's Tea Room there. Four years later, the society decided to sell its property; Judy Howell and Sherry Pfaender, the tearoom lessees, bought it.

Three small dining rooms and two separate kitchens—one downstairs for serving, the other upstairs for food preparation—support the enterprise. Other upstairs rooms contain gift and craft shops. Aimee's longtime maid, Miss Nully, lived in what is now the downstairs kitchen and her longtime boarder, Miss Hawkins, (nobody remembers their first names) lived upstairs. Aimee regularly walked up to play cards with Miss Hawkins.

Aimee, who never married, enjoyed entertaining her friends from the Bible Study Club, the Monthly Birthday Club, and the Women's Missionary League from Immanuel church. An organ, harp, and piano in her music room helped keep the meetings lyrical and lively. Aimee and her spinster sister, Vivien, often staged hymn-filled musicals there for friends and church people. (So talented was the pair that KFUO-FM, the Lutheran station in St. Louis, brought them in as a duet to sing standards such as "Jesus Calls" and "Let the Sweet Saints Repose.") During meetings at her home, Aimee would bring out a batch of her homemade chutney, her "Grandmother's Butter Cookies," her lemon cake, and her winning nut torte. "I like cooking and I like trying out new recipes," she told the *St. Charles Banner-News* in 1970.

On Sunday afternoons, Millie Heine and her husband, Reverend V. Paul Heine, then Immanuel's pastor, often strolled up Aimee's front walk and rang the doorbell. "Aimee made us feel welcome," Millie said. "She would say, 'Let's sit in the parlor and let 'My Lady'—that was Miss Nully, of course—make us some tea.'"

In the two decades that Pfaender and Howell have operated the tearoom, they have built a wide following, starting at breakfast. The partners serve dishes that Miss Aimee would have cheered: Dutch Baby Oven Pancakes; EGG-Strada, layered with bread, ham, artichokes, onions, mushrooms, peppers and Monterey Jack cheese with tomato chutney; Simply Delicious Scrambled Eggs; a three-egg Puffy Omelet that seems like a soufflé; eggs benedict without poached eggs and breakfast time's most consumed item, "Elegant Praline French

Toast with Bacon." Naturally, there's always a tea chest where customers can choose the tea they want.

A seasonal bestseller is a one-of-a-kind breakfast dessert called "My Neighbor's Peach Bombs," based on a recipe from Howell's neighbor. The menu describes a "Bomb" as follows: "Luscious whole peach carefully wrapped with pie crust. Baked and drizzled generously with almond butter glaze. Watch for the seed!" Peach Bombs are available from Memorial through Labor Day and are so coveted that customers order them in advance. "We start getting calls for them in April," says Pfaender. A Peach Bombs recipe is in Miss Aimee's *Cookbook of Divine Cuisine*, for sale at the restaurant.

"Men are intimidated by the name 'tearoom,'" suggests Pfaender. "Most men say 'Will you please put me in a room with another gentlemen?' But once most men come here and try our food, especially the breakfast meat pies and crepes, they almost always return."

With a home so old—it was completed in 1865—there is apt to be speculation about ghosts. In the early days, Pfaender and Howell hung an oil painting of Adelheide Viola Becker, Aimee's older sister who had died at age four. Breakfast patrons reported sensing "air" flowing over their shoe tops while seated near the oil painting, maybe some whispering from Adelheide's own lips. Pfaender says that she once heard Adelheide say "Mommy" straight out of the picture frame. "I was in the room next door and heard it distinctly," recalls Pfaender. Howell was calling names and seating guests when she heard someone call her own name, Judy. It was Adelheide, thought Howell. "We figure that Adelheide missed out on most of her life, so she's enjoying what's happening around here. The only problem is that our servers don't like Adelheide's portrait hanging near their work stations, so we have to rotate her from one dining room to another."

Local historians have noted that Aimee's mother had a teenage female slave named Harry. Aimee often showed her friends the framed deed to Harry. Although they have not engaged a paranormal to track down ghosts as has Donna Hafer, owner of the Mother-in-Law House on St. Charles's historic South Main Street, Pfaender and Howell concede that their place harbors gentle spirits that may include Harry, Adelheide, and other folks from long ago.

"On several occasions the upstairs cooks claimed to hear mysterious noises, usually muffled coughing or rattling," recalled Howell. "We were preparing breakfast one day when what I thought was a ghost floated by the kitchen door; it looked like a large sweater walking by," said cook Edie Hollander. "We came out in the hall with a knife," continued cook Brenda Rogers. "We were like 'Hello, who's this?' No one was there."

"At night, when we're gone, we leave the radio on for the spirits to enjoy," Pfaender said. "They prefer piano and guitar music almost exclusively."

Miss Aimee B's Tea Room
837 First Capitol Drive, St. Charles, Missouri

 (636) 946-4202

 Breakfast: 9 A.M. to 10:30 A.M. Tuesday through Saturday
Lunch: 11 A.M. to 3 P.M. Tuesday through Saturday

 Wheelchair accessible

 No smoking

Myrtle's Place–Backalley BBQ

Poplar Bluff, Missouri

WHILE CHOMPING THROUGH "Debbie's Special" breakfast at Myrtle's Place and Backalley BBQ in downtown Poplar Bluff, Missouri, it is reassuring to know that you're surrounded by family: Debbie Sliger's family. Even if you're a total stranger.

For background, Debbie purchased Myrtle's in 1996. It had been Myrtle's since 1986 when Myrtle Mitchell bought the place. Previously, the café operated under different names: Anna's, Sue's, Granny's. It first opened in 1936 as Willie's Chili. "Willie's real name was George Hill," says Debbie. "He was my father-in-law's third cousin. You should also know that Myrtle still comes in here to eat. Yesterday she had chicken strips. On Thursday she eats pork steak."

"Myrtle's is an institution in Poplar Bluff," says Joann Stricker, a prominent local resident. "There's nothing in town like it. A lot of business is transacted here and disagreements are smoothed over. It's a meeting place that everyone knows. Even the sports teams come here."

Breakfast, served all day, packs the house. The Debbie's Special—two eggs, choice of meat, hash browns or American fries, and biscuits and gravy on toast—is reasonably priced. There are breakfast wraps, egg scramblers, six omelets, pancakes, waffles, and the "Lady Special:" one pancake, two bacon pieces, and one egg for $3.75. There is a "Hashbrown Delight," described succinctly as "loaded hashbrowns" plus a brimming bowl of grits on the side.

One can't eat at Myrtle's without encountering at least two or more of Debbie Sliger's family on a daily basis. Debbie, who is chief cook but who knows how to take quick breaks from the grill to come out and greet her customers, supervises a staff of fourteen, nearly half of them on the family tree. "My daughter Leanna is a waitress who also does grocery buying and writes the checks," Debbie explains. "My sister Patricia Ingle is known as 'Pete.' She works sixty-six hours a week. She walks in here with me and she walks out with me. She'll be here when the last hog dies. My daughter-in-law Amy Hood is a waitress. Pete's daughter, Sarah Long, also waits. My mother Georgia Benfield, who's known as 'Granny' or 'Mom'—is eighty-three and is cashier and hostess. Mom and I spent eight years waitressing together when we worked for Myrtle. Another member of our family is Shauna Vaughn, who cooks. Her mother and Pete were best friends."

Myrtle's customers are "family," too. Consider Bill Luhn, "a gentlemen who ate here for twenty-two years before we lost him at eighty-four," says Debbie. "Bill always wore a hat to Myrtle's but removed it once inside the door. He told a lot of our customers that they should remove their hats, too, particularly baseball caps. Bill came here at 10:30 every morning and even though we serve breakfast all day he ordered roast beef, green beans, carrots, and applesauce. In the last three weeks of his life, when he was very ill, he was in the Cedar Gate Nursing Home where I shipped food to him the whole time. After he died, Bill's daughter brought me his old brown hat, a gentleman's felt hat. We remember Bill by displaying his hat in our lighted corner cabinet in the main dining room along with our sports trophies."

Another Myrtle's regular is Jay Githens. "He's at Myrtle's most every day sitting by himself with the *Wall Street Journal* and his soup," reports his sister, Joyanne Githens. "Talk about a place that cares for its customers! If Jay's soup appears too hot arriving from the kitchen either Debbie herself or a daughter will come over and personally fan the soup until it's cool enough to sip."

Myrtle's, like downhome cafés elsewhere, is most hospitable to sports teams, especially winning ones like the Poplar Bluff High School Mules, state basketball champions in 2004 and 2005. Tyler Hansbrough, maybe America's best-known college player today—for the University of North Carolina Tarheels—was the high-scoring power forward who led the Mules. "Tyler and the whole team ate breakfast here the day they drove to Columbia, Missouri to win the state title," says Debbie. "Tyler's family members come here regularly. His father in an orthopedic surgeon and his mother was once Miss Missouri and placed real high in the Miss America contest. And the Poplar Bluff high school football team meets here for breakfast every Friday morning during football season."

Another breakfast cluster is the "coffee table group." The group, at Myrtle's from about 7:30 to 10 daily, includes a dentist, the retired city manager, a retired schoolteacher, a truck driver, a retired UPS driver, an insurance agent, and a city detective who has appeared on a *CSI* episode on television. "The coffee table group sits in the rear of the main dining room," says Leanna Sliger. "Every day, each of them puts a quarter in a slot in a ceramic pig that they call 'Hog Ringer.'

At Christmas time, when they have collected $400 or $500 or so, the men open the pig and divide the money among us five waitresses. They use a different ceramic pig every year. Last year's pig was 'Slop the Hog' and it is now in the lighted display case in the dining room along with Bill Luhn's hat."

Myrtle's is physically organized as follows: the main dining room where smoking is heavy and where most people sit anyway; the Big Room; the Apple Room where laptop use is encouraged; and the No Smoking Room which once was the office for a Standard Oil service station. Out in the alley is Stella, the old hickory grill. Guarding the front door is Queenie, a 350-pound concrete pig. Mrs. B is the fiberglass pig just inside the front door. Priscilla is the ceramic pig by the cash register. "We change Priscilla's clothes four times a year including the Fourth of July," Debbie says.

Myrtle's Place–Backalley BBQ
109 N. Broadway, Poplar Bluff, Missouri

 (573) 785-9203

 5 A.M. to 3 P.M. Monday through Friday
5 A.M. to 2 P.M. Saturday

Wheelchair accessible

 Smoking permitted

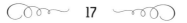

Pioneer's Cabin

Percy, Illinois

DAN VALERIUS AND his wife, Mary, run Pioneer's Cabin restaurant down in Percy, Illinois and make a specialty of "family style." "Everything comes in bowls—biscuits, toast, scrambled eggs, bacon, sausage, potatoes" says Dan. "It's just like Grandma's house—we bring it out in bowls and they're large portions, too. No buffet line here."

Dan and Mary got their idea for a log cabin setting while thumbing through *Farm and Ranch* magazine. "There was a piece about a Kansas farm that had an authentic log cabin from frontier days. That's for us, we said."

The Valerius clan and friends built the cabin themselves. "It was like a community barn raising," recalls Dan. "If you had a strong back and were willing enough to answer my call for help, we got together a group that put up the roof and the shell in seven days." Later, the family added a room used for weekend overflow and meetings

Dan and Mary were prescient enough to add a long front porch to their cabin and a gazebo as another waiting spot. "With our St. Louis people—there are carloads of them—they will eat and pay up," says Dan. "You think they are gone but an hour later they are still sitting on the front porch or in the gazebo."

Three of every four customers order the family-style breakfast, though some opt for biscuits and gravy only. If you bring your kids, this place is a bargain. Children up to six are free; from seven to twelve are half price. "We're cheaper than McDonald's," Dan boasts.

Pioneer's Cabin serves all-you-can eat lunches, too, especially fried chicken. "I had a lady sitting by the fireplace one day," Dan remembers. "I saw that she had a leather briefcase that was full of plastic bags. My server told me that she was stuffing our all-you-can-eat fried chicken into her plastic bags. I approached her and said 'Our chicken is all-you-can-eat right here and now and not how much you can pack out of here and eat all next week.' She threatened to sue me for my remarks but I said 'the county sheriff will be here before you hit the main road out of here.' We retrieved our fried chicken from her briefcase and, of course, never saw her again. I also saw a man who came in out of the blue and ate twenty-one pieces of our all-you-can-eat fried chicken. He kept saying 'That's good chicken. You can bring me some more.' He literally cleaned the bones off each piece. He never showed up again either."

Customers bring in keepsakes, trinkets, signs, and souvenirs that they hope the Valeriuses will post or mount on their yellow-pine walls. "We hung a bull harness with blinders over the door to the back room," says Dan. "We get asked about this harness more than anything on our walls. Some people think it is a chastity belt."

Dan, a park ranger at next-door Pyramid State Park (largest in Illinois) for fifteen years before turning to restauranting, is active in the Denmark Baptist Church down the road. "I am Sunday song leader and Mary plays the organ. As soon as the final amen is said, we leave church, get in the car and open the restaurant. We serve from 11:30 to 3 on Sunday and then we return to church Sunday evening for a relaxed worship service. If the Lord didn't take care of us, this restaurant wouldn't be here. Did I mention that I married the preacher's daughter?"

Dan is often asked to say the prayer at meetings and family gatherings in the restaurant. "When that happens, it is a most humbling experience for me," he says. His prayer giving has caught on. "I have many tables of two or four people in the main dining room ask me if I can do a blessing for them. I always start off by saying: 'We'll have a blessing on the food at this time.'"

Mary, who operates the cash register, particularly on weekends, writes tracts that can be purchased for a nickel but which are usually handed out free to those who ask. "I cut the plywood for her and she sits out in the yard and paints and letters her signs," Dan explains. "She's a reader. She makes signs about things she's read or heard."

Among Mary's signs are: "Discover wildlife. Teach school" and "Endangered species—people who have bad manners." The latter sign may speak to patrons who abuse the Pioneer's Cabin all-you-can-eat policy.

Pioneer's Cabin

1162 School Street, Percy, Illinois
(From Chester, Illinois, follow Illinois Highway 150 about 15 miles ortheast to Percy.)

 (618) 497-2380

 8 A.M. to 9 P.M. Tuesday through Saturday
11:30 A.M. to 3 P.M. Sunday

 Wheelchair accessible

 No smoking

 18

Spencer's Grill
Kirkwood, Missouri

IN THE LATE 1940s when Spencer's Grill stayed open around the clock to capture business from the U.S. Highway 66 bypass out front, a down-and-out architect named Art came in regularly to mooch coffee. "He was as full of stuffing as the Christmas goose," recalled the late Kirkwood photographer and unofficial historian Francis Scheidigger.

"Art would walk into Spencer's when coffee was a nickel a cup and ask for half a cup and lay down three pennies," said Scheidigger. "He'd spy a couple sitting in a booth and compliment the lady's good looks or her clothes. Then he'd say 'I'd like to buy you both a cup of coffee but I left the house with only enough for one cup.' Then the man or his wife would invariably say 'Please join us and have a cup on us.'

"Once while in Spencer's, Art met an affluent couple who lived in a magnificent home where the Grace Episcopal church in Kirkwood is today. He told the couple that he'd always wanted to see the inside of the place, that he admired its grandeur. 'Stop by anytime,' they said. So, Art drops by in midweek and says to the missus: 'I was in the neighborhood and wonder if I can use your bathroom.' She said: 'Yes, it is upstairs on your right.' Well, he was up there for a long time and the Missus heard water running. After an hour or so, he came downstairs and walked out the front door without saying a word. She went up to the bathroom and found the tub and towel wet. Art had mooched a bath!"

Spencer started business in 1941 by taking over Lee's Grill in what is now The Hobby Shop, just south of the present location. He moved into the existing Spencer's, then known as Hugo's restaurant, in 1947. Spencer's new domain was an 1860 building that once contained shoe shops and a grocery downstairs and a justice of the peace upstairs. Spencer retired in 1973; since then the business has had six owners, though the breakfast menu hasn't drifted much from the original Spencer's.

In the years that Spencer's was open 24 hours a day, the place drew people from all walks of life. Spencer said his biggest crowd arrived on the first Saturday night he was open—the crowd from the local Lion's Club dance dropping by for coffee and breakfast. On nights when big fires occurred, the Kirkwood fire chief came in to buy hamburgers (called "Spennyburgers" then) for his hard-working firemen. Even a local gang or two hung out at Spencer's. "One night, in the lot behind Spencer's," says David Jones, a lifelong Kirkwood resident, "there was a knockdown fight between Kirkwood policemen and gang members. The police straight-out went in fighting with no guns! I learned about this years later from the police chief himself."

In his new location, Spencer decided to install a phone booth. The phone company demurred, contending there wasn't enough revenue potential. Spencer won out; the booth went in. Four days later Spencer found the phone to be out of order. "So I called the phone repairman and asked him to check the booth because it wouldn't take any money. After the man had finished, I asked him what was wrong. 'Nothing much,' he told me. 'It was just full of coins.'"

In 1948 the phone company replaced the original booth with a newer model that has occupied the same corner ever since and has become a relic of curiosity for children. "One day," recalled Spencer, "I overheard a little boy ask his parents: 'What is this little house? It's got a phone in it.' Kids now like to go inside and play. Most of them have never seen a phone booth before."

Spencer was always keen on customer retention. "In 1950 I had a contest where people guessed how many cups of coffee I sold in one year. The barber next door won. That year I sold 263,000 cups at seven cents apiece—with pure cream from the Woodlawn Dairy in Kirkwood. We gave the barber a coffee server for his prize."

The grill's 24-hour presence on the 66 bypass attracted tourists heading for Florida, California, or the East Coast. "One day Gig Young, the movie star, stopped by for breakfast at three in the morning," said Spencer, who was there. "Mr. Young was driving a new sports car from New York to Hollywood. A Kirkwood policeman was in the restaurant and spotted him 'I know you—you're Gig Young,' the policeman said. 'Yes, I am,' said Mr. Young. The policeman got his autograph but I was too shy." Later, hometowners swore that Clark Gable had stopped by, but confirmation is lacking.

In his later years, Spencer recalled Gig Young, the wrestler Gorgeous George, and other well-known customers: the moochers, "Old Spoon in the Glass"—the man who stirred the cream and sugar in his coffee cup and then parked the spoon in a glass of water—and an official of the Chrysler assembly plant in nearby Fenton. "That man ordered the eggs and bacon breakfast special every day. Just as soon as the waitress took his order and headed for the grill, the man took his fork in one hand and knife and spoon in the other and raised them to the ready position and held them there—staring intently toward the grill—until his order was delivered, which could be a while on busy mornings. Our employees were so intrigued by him that they never got around to giving him a nickname as they did other eccentrics. But they still talk about him."

Spencer decided he needed to advertise his restaurant, so he hired a pilot and a Waco bi-plane in 1948. Attached to the plane's tail was an eight-foot banner that said "Eat at Spencer's Grill." "We put a siren on the plane and flew it low over Kirkwood Road blowing the siren loudly hoping people would look up to read the sign," said Spencer. "The only response I can recall is a lady who told me she had heard my plane fly over. Shortly afterward, the FAA came out with a regulation that said a person is not allowed to advertise his restaurant when flying so low; they told me never to try this again or I'd get a big fine. I like to think that I was America's pioneer aerial restaurant advertiser."

As if a flying banner weren't enough, Spencer installed a neon sign and clock in front of his place, but neither had functioned adequately for years until Chris Powers bought the grill in 2005. The new owner illuminated the long-unlit sign and, with help from loyalists from the Saturday Morning Breakfast Club that meets in Spencer's back room, got the clock running for the first time since 1972.

In its latest incarnation, spruced-up Spencer's continues to draw dozens of regulars who savor most entrées with eggs, ham, bacon, or sausage as well as the popular scrapple. A former owner introduced scrapple in 1979 and it's been through several versions since then, all of them without the liver that is a key ingredient of the more traditional Philadelphia scrapple. The Powers recipe, as the menu explains, consists of "sausage and grits dipped in pancake batter, cooked on the grill, and served with white gravy on top." It's worth a try.

Spencer's Grill

223 S. Kirkwood Road, Kirkwood, Missouri

 (314) 821-2601

 6 A.M. to 2 P.M. Saturday through Monday
6 A.M. to 8 P.M. Tuesday through Friday

Not wheelchair accessible

Smoking permitted

19

Uncle Bill's Pancake and Dinner House
St. Louis

ON WEEKEND MORNINGS at Uncle Bill's Pancake and Dinner House, the pancake and waffle parade that marches on trays into the dining area from the kitchen definitely attracts the notice of customers who are undecided as to what to order. "People are impressionable," said Debbie Henson, a former Uncle Bill's manager, reflecting on a situation that exists to this day. "When a chocolate Alaskan waffle topped with vanilla ice cream and our pure fudge sauce comes out of the kitchen and the waitress brings it into the dining area, people see her walking past and you immediately get a landslide of orders for that same waffle. People ask the waitress, 'What is that you are carrying?' then say 'I'll have one of those, too.' One day I thought we were having chocolate Alaskan waffle day from hell around here. If you walk through the dining room with our Crepes Pee Chee, blueberries, or strawberries, or anything smothered in whipped cream, the same thing happens."

Uncle Bill's waitresses not only must be able to carry plates of showy food through the room, they must learn to balance a fixed number of loaded plates on their left arms, walk unassailed from the kitchen, and reach their target table without spillage. "There are only two ways to serve customers:

arm or tray service," said Henson. "You bring customers their orders on a plate that is balanced on your arm or you bring them on a tray. We use the arm method here.

"My cooks used to call me the 'She-Man,'" continued Henson. "I could balance eight full plates on my left arm. It has to be the left arm because you serve on the right. Orders like plates of ham and eggs, or bacon and eggs, are usually the bottom plates on your arm; the chocolate Alaskan waffle or pancakes, the blueberries or strawberries, or the whipped cream orders are on the upper levels of your arm. It's like a platform that you build with your plates and then you go up your arm. You want to be sure you have the flat foods on the bottom and the fluffier foods on top. Eight full plates will take care of a table of four or five. The hardest thing a waitress has to learn is arm service. If she has had prior experience, it takes about a week to refresh her memory and learn our version of arm service. Timing is everything, of course."

At Uncle Bill's, sixty to seventy percent of the day's sales are for breakfast items, including fourteen kinds of pancakes and five of waffles. Most of these entrées were introduced in 1961 when Bill Ernst, a used-car salesman, converted his moderately successful Fireplace Bar that had once been Medart's restaurant into a new venture that he noted was St. Louis's first pancake house. In the process, Ernst yanked out the bar but retained the tilted martini glass neon sign out front. In the early 1970s Ernst added "the lower porch" dining area accented by stained glass windows facing South Kingshighway. That's where Uncle Bill's directs customers who smoke.

"On his opening day in 1961, Bill Ernst came to me and said 'I don't have money for my cash register,'" said Joe Charleville, a legendary coffee dealer in St. Louis. "I gave him $700.

Bill's word was always good. It was typical of many car dealers who operated out of their pockets." Ernst fretted that he didn't have enough parking space for his pancake operation. "I happened to know that the chef at the Mayfair Hotel owned the lot next door to the north," said Charleville. "That night I took Bill to the chef's house and Bill bought the lot for $10,000. Bill said it was the best investment he ever made."

Although Uncle Bill's pancake list is stable, there are exceptions, points out veteran manager Betty Kraus, who started as a waitress in 1964. "The apple pancakes and apple crepes are fairly new. We discontinued our corn pancakes because of poor sales. We get calls for them occasionally so I will run out and buy a small can of corn. We also discontinued our coconut pancakes. We do get requests for customized pancakes. People want us to put pecans and bananas and pineapple and what-not into our batter; we charge them 90 cents for each additional ingredient not listed on the menu. People will mix their pancakes with everything imaginable—they'll put eggs, sausage, sauce, and bacon on their cakes and then chop the whole mixture up and eat it. One lady always wants mustard for her buckwheat cakes."

Some Uncle Bill's regulars are "self-seaters," a manager told me. "They walk in, pass by the hostess, pick up a glass of water from a tray, and go directly to their customary table. Then the girls come by and take their order. Self-seaters are like family—we know them and they know us. There are about twenty of them every morning." A well-known self-seater was Elaine Viets, a longtime humor columnist for the *St. Louis Post-Dispatch* who came to Uncle Bill's most weekday mornings, ordered one scrambled egg, whole wheat toast, and coffee and read several mystery novels a week while breakfasting.

"Readers knew I hung out there and would stop by with stories and gossip," said Viets who now writes mystery novels herself. In her first novel, *Backstab*, the setting was a place called "Uncle Bob's," which, of course, was Uncle Bill's in disguise.

Uncle Bill's has its share of breakfast characters. "One man ordered three distinct kinds of pancakes which came to six cakes an order so he received eighteen pancakes every morning," said Kraus. "There was the nickel lady who tipped us with nickels. There was the man who only ordered a potato pancake and a glass of milk. We remember him and the lady named Grace who eats everything well done. On our tickets, for example, we simply write 'For Grace' and turn them in. The cooks know what to do which, in Grace's case, is to make sure her food is almost burnt."

Uncle Bill could be moody and temperamental at times, Henson recalled years ago. "His wife, Betty, who was a hostess at the restaurant for years, kept him upstairs in his office most of the time. He was our threat in case a customer situation got totally out of hand. If we got too much flak from someone, we would say, 'Would you like me to take you up to see Uncle Bill?' That would calm the party down."

Uncle Bill's Pancake and Dinner House
3427 S. Kingshighway, St. Louis

 (314) 832-1973

 11 A.M. to 3 A.M. daily

 Wheelchair accessible

 Smoking permitted

20

Vandalia Drug

Vandalia, Missouri

TODAY A MODEST small-town pharmacy fills a patch of land where antelope and deer leaped, roamed, and played; where wild rabbits rollicked 140 years ago when the endless prairie was high enough to nearly swallow ex-president Ulysses S. Grant, who picked his way through the tall grass on his horse. A county historical society publication quotes Grant as stating that the area was and probably always would be uninhabitable. Grant, of course, was wrong.

To keep some of the life force flowing in what is now Vandalia, Missouri, Vandalia Drug, Inc. is doing its part, mostly through affordable coffee.

At Vandalia Drug where everyday regulars prefer to sit on stools at the old and still functioning soda fountain, coffee costs five cents a cup. The price hasn't changed since 1953 when then pharmacist John P. Fitzgerald decreed to happy townspeople and Main Street denizens that he'd never raise the price of his coffee.

But wait! On two out of every three weekday mornings you can save your nickel because someone very kind has bought your coffee for you and everyone else in the place.

Vandalia Drug regulars and former Vandalians who remember old times at the drugstore counter literally line up, even in absentia, to buy coffee for the house, says Fitzgerald, who in retirement remains a strong presence at the pharmacy. The system works as follows: You tell pharmacist Joe Salois that you want to buy coffee for everyone and to find a day on the calendar that isn't already spoken for by other humanitarians. Then you either deposit $10 with Salois or you come in the day after your beneficence to find out how many pots of Folger's Special Blend coffee were sold and how much you owe.

"Buying everyone coffee was a spontaneous decision on the customers' part," says Fitzgerald, who volunteers weekdays with half a dozen others who stand behind the counter and make new pots, pour coffee, wash dishes, wipe the counter, and greet regulars and newcomers.

Volunteer Patsy Clithero, a widow for many years, says that Vandalia Drug "is a basis of needs. Numerous people here have lost their mates. This place gives us a reason to get up in the morning. In Vandalia, all you need to do is reach out a hand like we do here. I love coming here and standing behind the counter and getting fussed at and watching my friends bang their cups for service."

On a day that I visited, Fitzgerald said that a "Mr. Betts mailed in the money for today. He's been in poor health and lives with his granddaughter over in Bowling Green. We've got one gentleman in Florida who left $10 to buy coffee anytime we designated a date. Mack Teague of the Veteran's Home over in Mexico, Missouri came through a few days ago and left us his coffee money. All these people are former Vandalians who once drank coffee with us in person. One customer, by the way, died before his date to buy. His estate still owes us!"

A full breakfast is not a possibility at Vandalia Drug, although one can buy doughnuts at 55 cents each that Joe Salois picks up at the Vandalia IGA store several times a week.

Until recently, Vandalia Drug faithful walked down Main Street to the now-closed B & F Café to use its restrooms, since the drugstore bathroom was small and hard to access. "I got a big bang out of seeing those characters from Vandalia Drug come quietly in our back door to use the restroom," says Betty Blontz, who ran B & F with her husband, Floyd. Many drugstore customers would take lunch at the B & F, which was famous for its Big Liars' and Little Liars' tables. "Did you know that our Liars' tables are a big attraction to tourists who come to Vandalia?" Betty Blontz once said to me. "They all want to take our Liars' table idea back to their own hometown restaurants so they can adopt them." With the B & F's demise, most Vandalia Drug coffee people either return home for lunch or continue on to the local Dairy Queen.

"We have what I'd call 'a poster person' for the soda fountain industry who comes in here every day for coffee," says Salois. "Her name is Rosie and she is 103 years old and I think she still drives. She started coming here regularly when she was 97. Someone came in and took her picture with a couple of friends and it's been appearing all over America. We may be the only place in the country where you can buy a nickel cup of coffee—if you're not lucky enough to get it free."

Vandalia Drug
112 N. Main, Vandalia, Missouri

 (573) 594-2136

 6 A.M. to 8 P.M. except Thursday afternoons and Sunday

 Wheelchair accessible

 No smoking

LUNCH
RESTAURANTS

21

Acapulco Restaurant
St. Ann, Missouri

ACAPULCO'S ENCHILADA PLATE offers a choice of ground beef, cheddar cheese, or chicken wrapped in soft corn tortillas and is priced at $7.50. For an extra 75 cents, you can request "Mexican beef" in your enchilada.

"Mexican beef is something that tells people our food is really Mexican," says Ernestine Zeger, who founded Acapulco in 1976. Zeger created the Mexican beef offering that her daughter, Madi, describes as "chunks of shredded beef that just fall apart."

Rice and refried beans is a staple at Acapulco, as it is at most Mexican places. "For a meal, you have to have rice and beans and then let the other things roll," says Zeger. "We have five lunch specials every day until 4:30 P.M." As for the rest of the menu, "We can make ten dishes out of our Mexican beef. Every day we cook up ground beef, pork, rice, beans, and chicken and from these basic ingredients we can produce thirty-one different dishes."

Half of Zeger's recipe collection reflects her native state of Oaxaca in Mexico from which she emigrated around 1960, speaking no English. "The other menu items are Tex-Mex," she adds.

Since day one, Zeger has listed a permanent Daily Special, always announced in a box at the top of the menu. It consists of two tacos plus rice and beans and a choice of crispy corn, soft, or flour tortillas. "This accounts for nearly fifty percent of our daily lunch trade," says Zeger. "And you have a choice of ingredients in your tacos, such as beef, pork, Mexican beef (for which there is no extra charge), chicken, or cabesa. Cabesa is meat from a cow's head, but it's only for Mexicans to eat."

Charbroiled steaks and burgers share the menu with seven plate dinners; half a dozen entrées from Mexican-style chicken dinners to huevos rancheros, and Ernestine's special (a charbroiled ribeye plate), Madi's special (chicken in mole), and Sergio's special (a combination plate named for Ernestine's son, Sergio, who owns an Acapulco restaurant in downtown Alton, Illinois.)

Another special is Acapulco's hot chicken wings. "We serve the whole wing—not pieces," says the menu. "It's the chicken itself that makes the wings so good," states Madi. "We get our chickens from a longtime distributor and add secret spices. We go through two hundred to five hundred pounds of chicken wings a week. People come from all over for them. Some folks on their way to the airport come in and get their wings here."

A Macho Platter posts some challenges, especially to male customers. It brings together a burrito, tamale, enchilada, Mexican beef burrito, and a beef-and-bean tostada and dares them to conquer it. "Many men feel pressured to eat everything on the Macho Platter," says Madi. "If you can't finish it, it means you are not macho. But not everyone can finish the platter. For some unknown reason, they usually leave the tostado untouched."

Acapulco is lodged in a double-storefront building in a modest strip center in what locals call "downtown St. Ann." Zeger owns all the buildings in the center including Cristina's (mostly Latino) Videos and More next door, which she operates. The restaurant is divided into two large rooms—the main dining room-dance hall and the more informal barroom where lunch is available. Customers can eat at the long bar with a strikingly impressive red neon sign above it that says "Acapulco." For folksiness, there is a glamour photo of Ernestine Zeger by the end of the bar, a jukebox that plays tuneful Mexican music, and a couple of pool tables off in a corner. On certain evenings, neighborhood Latino boys come in to watch Mexican soccer on television. In the more formal, non-smoking dining room, there is dancing from 9 to 1 every Friday, Saturday, and Sunday night with an authentic local Latino band.

Acapulco celebrates May 5 (Cinco de Mayo) in a festive way with piñatas, balloons, and special foods. It also celebrates Ernestine's birthday each November 11 and is open on Christmas day from 11 to 2. "One Christmas several years ago a regular customer knocked on the restaurant door; we happened to be there," says Madi.

"Our mother died and this is our first Christmas without her—she loved this place," the customer said. "Can we come in for something to eat as it would help us to remember our mother?" The plea was successful and twenty family members arrived for a meal prepared by Ernestine and Madi. "That family returns every year and now others come too," says Madi, happy that Acapulco has established a Christmas tradition.

Acapulco Restaurant

10114 St. Charles Rock Road, St. Ann, Missouri

 (314) 428-5621

 11 A.M. to 11 P.M. Monday through Saturday
Noon to 12 A.M. Sunday

 Handicapped accessible

 Smoking permitted

22

Acropolis Greek Café
Belleville, Illinois

IF YOU LUNCH at the Acropolis Greek Café and Import Emporium in downtown Belleville, you will automatically enter the culinary realm of Big Papou.

Big Papou, ("papou" is Greek for grandpa), was Louis Hages, proprietor of the onetime Toddle Inn and 400 Club nightspots in East St. Louis, places that thrived in the 1940s and 1950s. Sharon Noblitt, Hages's grandaughter and her daughters, Stephanie Dahm and Heather Noblitt, are in possession of recipes and secret sauce formulas from Big Papou and his wife, Stella, and run Acropolis.

Unless otherwise specified, all luncheon plates, including the Monday through Friday daily specials, come with the Deluxe Greek Salad topped by Big Papou's dressing. In his salad, Big Papou combined lettuce, carrots, red cabbage, cucumbers, tomatoes, a Greek olive (which comes with a pit, the owners warn on the menu), and feta cheese.

Stella, who died in 1988, contributed to the current menu, too. Acropolis serves Stella's spinach pies and cheese pies as well as her baklava, which most dessert-seeking customers tend to order. Stella was called Yiayia, grandma in Greek.

"We have had customers who tried to get recipes out of us," says Stephanie. "We ask our staff to leave the kitchen when we make family recipes such as Big Papou's Toddle Inn dressing. Our people say 'What would we ever do with that recipe even if we knew it?' but we send them out anyway. We hide our recipes. They're all in our heads."

The owners have created plenty of their own entrées. An example is the Apollo plate, which consists of Texas toast (an item Big Papou never knew), melted feta cheese, cooked eggplant, tomatoes, and lettuce. And there are the gyro and pastitio plates, the mazithra (Greek cheese) pasta dish, Greek spaghetti, and the Greek pork chop plate. "In the morning we're all in the kitchen cooking," explains Heather. They do the appetizers, the plates, the Sloppy Joe mix, the chicken dishes, the soup, the noodles, and the sides, which include unusual menu items like baked squash and beets.

"We make our own breads but we get pita bread from Chicago along with our gyro meat," adds Stephanie. "The food broker is from our church, St. Constantine and Helen, a Greek orthodox church in Swansea."

Louis and Stella Hages married in the church in 1945 when it was still located in East St. Louis. "So many people came to the wedding—about 2700 of them—that they had to remove some pews," says Sharon. Father Dimitri Macaila, the current priest, comes in annually to bless the Acropolis.

Among memories of Big Papou, who died in 1974, are the Toddle Inn wooden tables toward the front of the long and narrow Acropolis, formerly an ice cream shop. Photographs of family members cover walls in the booth area. A picture of Big Papou in his Greek navy uniform is in booth A5. Sharon is shown as a girl at the old church in East St. Louis in booth A4.

Louis and Stella are seen in booth A7. A photo of the Toddle Inn is near the front door, as is the Greek flag Big Papou brought with him as an immigrant in 1918.

Acropolis opened on B Street in 1993, then moved to West Main adding a side operation that sells wine, cheeses, olives, pita bread, noodles, and coffees as well as Acropolis T-shirts. "There are some three hundred Greeks in Belleville proper," states Stephanie. "We love being the only Greek restaurant in Belleville. The town is not big enough for two of us."

Acropolis Greek Café
200 W. Main, Belleville, Illinois

 (618) 234-5883

 7:30 A.M. to 9 P.M. Monday through Thursday
(to 10 P.M. Friday)
4 P.M. to 10 P.M. Saturday; 11 A.M. to 4 P.M. Sunday

 Handicapped accessible

 No smoking

23

Adriana's
St. Louis

ADRIANA'S ON THE Hill abounds in Sicilian specialties. "We have no white or cream sauces or Chianti bottles on our tables," says ebullient owner Adriana Fazio. "If you talk Sicilian, you talk tomato and basil."

Fazio usually sits at the cash register. "The ambience here is comfy and cozy and my job is to make sure everybody feels cozy when they come in. We have our traditional red-checkered tablecloths and plenty of green and white (colors of the Italian flag) going for us on the walls."

Adriana's is extremely popular; it has been since it opened in 1994. Lines for lunch form most every day. "I get worried when people come by and see lines and a few people out the door. Most people eat here between 11:45 and 12:45, but we move the line quickly," says Fazio.

Until recently, Adriana's offered—among its mostaccioli dishes, hearty salads, and homemade soups—nine bounteous sandwiches, each named for a Fazio grandchild. Fazio admits that nine sandwiches with her grandkids' names attached to them was quite enough for the menu. "I said that after nine sandwiches, we don't need any more sandwiches. I'd run out of creative ideas for them," But, alas, two more granddaughters came along and they required equal billing.

"When baby Clare came, we decided that she'd be the baked ham and pepperoni cheese sandwich on toasted bread with lettuce, tomato, and Italian dressing. Then baby Grace was born and at first we thought 'Let's make a big salad up for her,' but, no, we reasoned, she's got to have a sandwich named for her like everybody else. So Grace is our very last new sandwich. She's a sausage and pepperoni, on Italian bread with provel cheese and tomato sauce. And I have to say that Grace is climbing to the top of the sandwich list."

Clare and Grace joined other notable cousins including the Big Jack (because he weighed eleven pounds, three ounces at birth) hot mortadella and provel cheese sandwich; Sunny's veggie sandwich (because granddaughter Domenica's name means "sunny" in Italian); the Carlo (who is Sunny's older brother) roast beef and salami sandwich; and Joe's special which combines salami, pepperoni, and provel cheese. "Joe is special because when he was born I was so happy that I built him a throne for his baby crib," says the doting grandmother of her eldest grandchild, now in his early twenties.

Not to be upstaged, Fazio named the hot roast beef and salsiccia sandwich "in our own Sauce topped with Provel cheese" after herself—the "Nana's Favorite." "Our roast beef sandwich is the best on The Hill in my opinion," Fazio claims. "Most places use vacuum-packed beef cooked to perfection. We get our own rounds of beef and leave the fat on. We add Kosher salt and seasonings, roast them for four-and-a-half hours, cool them overnight, and the next day trim and slice them and add our gravy. We also make our own sausage and meatballs."

Adriana's mostaccioli wins applause. Fazio explains: "In California and on the East Coast, they don't call it mostaccioli; they call it penne. In St. Louis, it's a traditional pasta dish served on holidays and at weddings—you couldn't have an Italian wedding without it. We serve it here every day. When we first opened, we served linguini, but few people ordered it. They all wanted mostaccioli."

On Fridays, Adriana's offers Papa's Sicilian Slice, a deep-dish, meatless pizza named in memory of her father, Ben, who ran Fazio's Bakery on The Hill. "We often can't keep up with the demand for this pizza," says Fazio.

Fazio's daughters are integral to Adriana's success. Dianna Guimbarda is manager, Tia Zanti handles front-of-the-restaurant operations and promotion, and Suzanne Miramonti is the head chef who cooked with Mario Batali when the Food Network came to town and cooked in Adriana's kitchen.

A frequent customer is Metropolitan Opera soprano Christine Brewer, who lives in nearby Illinois. "When Christine and some of her friends from Opera Theatre of St. Louis are here they might just break into arias at lunch," says Fazio. "At Christmas time once, they did 'Oh Holy Night' and brought down the house. The same thing happened later when they sang 'You Are My Sunshine.' They will sing 'Happy Birthday' for anybody in the house with a birthday that day. I usually introduce them by clinking two salt shakers together."

"Sometimes," says daughter Dianna, "my mother will ask Christine and her group to start singing 'Happy Birthday' without the slightest idea if anyone around is having one."

Adriana's

5101 Shaw Avenue, St. Louis

 (314) 773-3833

 10 A.M. to 3 P.M. Monday through Saturday

 Handicapped accessible

 No smoking

The Airliner Bar & Grill
E. Alton, Illinois

THE AIRLINER BAR & Grill, "your friendly neighborhood pub" in East Alton, Illinois invites folks to 'stop in and see our antique toy collection.' That's it! Not their Airliner Zing Wings, their Airliner Sizzler, or their Alaskan White Fish Sandwich, but toys.

Airliner is located in the Rosewood Heights area of East Alton, about half a mile from Illinois's fourth largest airport, St. Louis Regional, a fixture since 1946. The airport's presence has definitely impacted the restaurant.

Things are airplaney at Airliner, which is housed in a building about the size of a hangar. A 1930s model airplane called "The Airliner Plane" is suspended from the high ceiling over the long bar. A leather-framed jet plane sculpted in leather is on a wall by a string of blue-and-white booths. "A guy in Oklahoma made it for me; the jet looks like some of the business planes that fly out of St. Louis Regional," observes Richard Tite, restaurant owner.

Some of the toys up near the ceiling are antiques; some aren't. Tite's daughter, Michelle, once sat in the rocking chair; daughter Ashleigh had the Barbie dolls; Ashleigh and son, Jordan, rode the tandem bike that hangs on high. With Tite on a tall ladder arranging the unusual decorations, the toys were hand-me-ups rather than hand-me-downs. Puppets, a punching bag, pedal cars and a stuffed parrot are from the family toy archives. Tite has installed a carousel horse with a life-size Woody doll sitting on it over the front door. It's his favorite toy.

Tite says that he was the first to bring [chicken] wings to the area. You can order Airliner Zing Wings as a luncheon appetizer—hot, medium, or mild—or wait until after 6 P.M. Tuesdays when they come free with the purchase of food or alcohol. "One night, we gave away four hundred pounds of wings," recalls Tite.

At lunch, the Alaskan White Fish Sandwich, not seen on many local menus, sells well. The menu describes it simply as "Two pieces of fish served with bread, pickles, onion & chips." When it arrives, the battered fish are lying atop two pieces of white bread from which one can build a sandwich. It's best to accompany your fish with a bowl of homemade chili. Tite's family recipe for this mild chili won the restaurant four first-place awards from a local booster group. Chili is always delivered on a saucer with a solitary white paper napkin under the bowl.

Tite calls his half-pound hamburger seasoned with his secret herbs and "grilled to perfection" the best in town. He says the same for his Airliner Sizzler, a ribeye sandwich, and his Philly Cheese Steak, which is served on a hoagie roll with chips. At Friday's lunch, the fish is more often than not salmon or mahi mahi, items that aren't generally offered at most pubs

The Airliner was built as a Quonset hut, then torn down and replaced by the present brick building. As owners have come and gone, the restaurant has always had airplane-related names: The Red Baron, Amelia's, Tarmac's.

The Airliner Bar & Grill

573 E. Airline Drive, East Alton, Illinois

 (618) 259-9781

11 A.M. to 2 A.M. Monday through Friday
11 A.M. to 3 A.M. Saturday

Wheelchair accessible

No smoking

25

Almond's Restaurant

Clayton, Missouri

WHEN HE FIRST pondered the start-up of a restaurant of his own in Clayton, pals asked Tony Almond, "Just what kind of a nut are you?" It turns out that he is a genuine Almond.

In 1996, Tony and Kelli Almond strolled into the "woods" to discover a challenging culinary adventure—they purchased the former Woods Restaurant with its signature hardwood-burning stove and three once-thriving poplar trees.

"When we opened Almond's, we had a chef, a sous chef, and Tony at the front door," remembers Kelli. Nine months later, the chefs, tired of long hours, walked out of the kitchen. "This turned into the happiest day of my career," says Tony, who, chronically happy, often dons black T-shirts with messages such as "Phantom of the Okra" and "Fennel Retentive." "I was left without anybody (except Kelli) to help me. It was very scary, but challenging, since I had never been a chef. And when you have an open window kitchen and I'm the guy under the microscope, it's intimidating."

Long before becoming a restaurateur, Tony was an X-ray technician, then a certified public accountant and, finally, a recruiter of medical executives. Kelli has a degree in education from the University of Missouri and a master's in social work from Washington University. Neither had much culinary experience save for Tony's teenage stint as a busboy at the Howard Johnson's in Hot Springs, Arkansas.

"I remember the chef standing by the grill at HoJo's," says Tony. "'Oh, my God,' the chef would say, 'there's a Greyhound bus in the parking lot and it's full of people.' All of us scrambled to our posts. We would get over one hundred people and they would wipe out everything in the buffet. I really got a buzz when the buses pulled in. I remember going home and telling my mother that someday I would open a restaurant of my own."

In 1995, Tony edged into the food business by becoming a partner in Parker Almond Wine and Food, a few doors down from the Woods Restaurant. "I walked past the Woods place and nobody was ever there; the tables were set but the lights were off," he says. "Then a guy from Decatur, Illinois bought Woods and called it Robbie's Grill. Six weeks later, Robbie walked into Parker Almond and said he wanted to sell his place immediately. I made an offer that he rejected. Six weeks later, Robbie came in soaking wet from a rainstorm and said: 'Just make me a damn offer.' I said, 'My old offer stands.' He said, 'We'll sign the deal on Monday.'" Days later, Robbie's (née Woods) was Almond's.

Almond's is essentially two rooms—the bar side and the old (original) side. Pressed wood or chipperboard (typically used as new home insulation material) is employed in the floors, reception stand, wainscoting, and bar. "I built the bar myself one Sunday afternoon after waiting for a carpenter who never showed up," says Tony. When the bar debuted in 2000, the Almond's revenue tripled.

The Almonds designed their maiden menu around "things we liked to eat that weren't readily available in the St. Louis area." For instance, the recipe for Creole gumbo is from Kelli's folks back in New Iberia, Louisiana. "It has a dark roux," says Tony. "It's filled with green pepper, onion, and okra and very authentic. On a cold day, we sell sixty-five percent of our customers gumbo, which comes in a cup or a bowl. We don't put crabmeat or other seafood in our gumbo because they don't hold up well. We use chicken and sausage."

The inherited wood stove has worked to the Almonds' advantage, notably with their popular quesadillas. "Most restaurants do their quesadillas on a flattop grill, but I like the wood oven because there's very little grease," observes Tony. Almond's baked quesadillas can be filled with sausage and jalapeño, black beans and chicken, cheese or veggies—or you can build your own. "Our customers have two choices," says the ebullient Tony. "They can go home and make their own lunch or stay here and get something crazy and pay us for it." What borders on craziness? "It's what people want us to fill their quesadillas with," Tony continues. "One guy wanted a barbecue pork sandwich but not on a bun. He wanted it folded into his quesadilla along with cole slaw. Another customer wanted spicy crawfish tails with mushrooms and pickles and we cheerfully accommodated him."

Tony follows just about the same practice with his noonday pizzas. "Our policy is that whatever people want on their pizza, we give it to them. Artichokes, anchovies, whatever! Now we're getting requests for pizza without cheese, which, of course, is not pizza at all. So we serve a tomato pizza without cheese and a garden patch pizza with no cheese but with mushroom, peppers, and tomatoes. Incidentally, most every place in town uses a red sauce on its pizza, but we use a basil pesto instead," says Tony. "If you set yourself apart, you'll be well received. And we have been."

Tony proudly boasts that Almond's is the only place in town where customers are served mesquite barbecue Zapp's chips from Granmercy, Louisiana along with their sandwiches and salads.

Almond's displays posters, photographs, collages, watercolors, and Bud Lobdell's fish art that covers half the wall in the old side. "Bud had his painting stored in his garage before I rescued it," says Tony. "Its major feature is the swarming goldfish but within the painting is a photo of the pond at Missouri Botanical Garden and the shape of the state of Missouri and also of Texas. I had it on loan for years but later I bought it to make sure it stays on our wall." Five photos, all showing rainbows in various colors, line the black (west) wall in the barroom. "All the photos have a silver almond hidden in them except one," says Tony. "It drives people crazy when they can't find the one without the almond." (The orange rainbow is almond-less.)

Almond's regulars who lunch at the restaurant three or four times a week are well recognized. "Occasionally I approach a regular and say 'How's about I buy you lunch today?'" says Tony. "Every year at Christmas time we give gifts to our regulars. We have given boxes of almond clusters, wine openers with rosewood handles with our name on them, boxes of white chocolate-covered pretzels, leather-bound Day-Timer organizers with our logo, and a kitchen grater to get the zest off oranges."

The poplar trees (a fourth was added when Almond's expanded into the vacated Mister Guy's men's furnishings space in 2003 and a fifth later on) are secured with metal plates screwed into the floor and ceiling. They have to be sprayed and wiped down with Pledge every three or four weeks to forestall a dust storm. "One day," recalls Tony, "a lady named Mary, who has since died, came in and said to me 'Do you know where your trees came from? My backyard in Creve Coeur!'"

Almond's Restaurant
8127 Maryland Avenue, Clayton, Missouri

 (314) 725-1019

 11:30 A.M. to 2 P.M. Tuesday through Friday
6 to 10 P.M. Tuesday through Saturday

 Wheelchair accessible

No smoking

26

Anthony's Bar

St. Louis

ANTHONY'S BAR IN the downtown Equitable Building "is all based on service, good food, a simple menu, and interesting architecture," said local architect William Bowersox over a bowl of the restaurant's daily pasta special.

"I think Anthony's Bar has the best lunch around because we serve what people want to eat today," says Vincent Bommarito, owner of both the bar and the esteemed Tony's restaurant diagonally across the building lobby. "We have no greasy, precooked, skinny hamburgers here. We broil our nine-ounce ground chuck hamburgers and serve them on a light egg bun because fewer people today like heavy bread with their sandwiches. We roast fresh turkey every day. We offer simple salads. Our romaine-based Caesar salad, where we substitute Italian tuna fish in oil for anchovies, is maybe our best-selling lunch item."

Wednesday is the bar's busiest day. "We have what I'd call a Merchant's Lunch on Wednesday," says Bommarito. "That's really a plate lunch, a term that isn't used much anymore. People who live far away make special trips here Wednesdays. We might have a roast pork open face sandwich or veal Parmesan with saffron sauce or chicken piccata with garden vegetables or barbecue pork tenderloin on focaccia bread. Wednesday specials are not repeated again for a whole year."

Bommarito's daily pasta special leans to marinated red meat sauces rather than whites. "People don't use as much white sauce with their pasta these days, so we have it only with the Monday special. The red sauce we make every day. Our homemade soups—there's a different one daily—are hearty soups like beef barley or chicken, rice, and spinach. We don't have consommés." Lunches come with Italian bread and a generous mound of fresh butter. Former *St. Louis Post-Dispatch* food reviewer Patricia Corrigan once said the bar's bread "may well be the best in town."

Anthony's Bar usually offers a catch-of-the-day such as salmon, walleyed pike, cod, or grouper. "We get fish flown in fresh three times a week for Tony's, so Anthony's Bar is a beneficiary of that," explains Bommarito, who points out that his staffers can wear different hats at lunch. For example, the lunchroom's sole server since 1992, Everett Lancaster, tends bar on weekends and takes shifts as cashier in Tony's gigantic kitchen. "We are open for only three hours at lunch so our people work both sides of the kitchen," says Bommarito. "We have a chef, cooks, salad makers, and vegetable people, and all of them participate in the lunch hour. We couldn't sustain Anthony's Bar at lunchtime and offer great food and service without this arrangement." (A sign in the kitchen says: "Cooking is an art, a noble science.")

The restaurant operation is smooth and precise. The bartender phones in each lunch order using the intercom phone that he keeps in a drawer at the bar. With the information he provides, the kitchen can tell him exactly how long the order will take before the "runner" brings the tray across the lobby from the kitchen. For the last decade Rogelio Hernandez has been the devoted runner—and he's obviously racked up impressive mileage. "I made about ninety round trips today," he says, "and it's not even Wednesday, our busiest day."

Bowersox, and his architectural partner, Fred Powers, are frequent Anthony's Bar customers who marvel at its spectacular interior design. "The consistency of what they do here with food and the consistency of the space in which it is served hasn't changed since the day the original Anthony's restaurant opened in 1972," said Powers. (Anthony's closed in 1991; Tony's replaced it in 1992. Anthony's was the namesake of Vincent's brother, Anthony, who is now in the wine business in Brentwood.)

"This restaurant is a two-story room with great vertical proportions," observes Bowersox. "The window drapes hang from the ceiling, which is about 24 feet high; so do the pendant lights over most tables and at the bar. This is basically a dark room just like the main dining room in the old Anthony's was. When you dined there, the hanging lights brightened your table, but the rest of the restaurant appeared to be much darker. It's the same here at Anthony's Bar. And look at the crystal glassware hanging upside down in the rack in the middle of the bar. Those glasses are both a source of light and a source of interest for visitors."

Powers and Bowersox admire the bar's black leather and chrome chairs and are impressed by the Shaker coat hooks protruding from the walnut south wall (there is no coatroom). The black bar stools, they explain, are immovable and the bright green carpeting that covers the undersides of the bar date back to 1972. "This is all a timeless design," says Bowersox.

Anthony's Bar

10 S. Broadway, St. Louis

 (314) 231-7007

 11:30 A.M. to 2 P.M. Monday through Friday
5:30 to close Tuesday through Saturday

Handicapped accessible

No smoking

27

The Anvil Saloon

Ste. Genevieve, Missouri

THE DOWNTOWN HISTORIC district of French colonial Ste. Genevieve, Missouri's oldest town, is a constant lure for tourists.

Another lure is the onion ring platter at the Anvil Saloon, the full-service restaurant and bar off the main square in Ste. Genevieve. "Onion rings are the most popular item on our menu," says Madeline Jett, the place's fifth owner in 150 years.

"We bread all our onions and go through four hundred to five hundred pounds of jumbo yellows a week. Almost every ticket has onion rings. People drive miles for them.

"Peoples' eyeballs nearly pop because they can't believe the size of our rings. We have lots of chain reactions when platters of our onions parade by in the dining room. 'Are those small or large rings?' people ask. 'Whatever, they say, send me a platter, too.'" Large platters serve four or five people, Jett advises.

Patrons also drive miles for Jett's liver dumplings. "I asked the mother of a friend if I could please use her liver dumpling recipe," says Jett," and she said 'Yes'. About twenty-five percent of our customers order them; they're available every day at lunch.

"We have lots of regular customers who drive here from St. Louis at least once a month," Jett continues. "They go for the liver dumplings because you can't find them in St. Louis and nobody up there has onion rings as big as ours. I try to warn people about the size of the rings."

Jett's lunch specials never seem to change because they have proven too popular to tinker with. Monday's special is meatloaf, which Jett claims is popular with older men because it reminds them of their mothers' recipes. "That was a time when burger meat was cheap," Jett says. Tuesdays bring chicken strips, Wednesdays are pork tenderloins, and Thursdays are country-fried steaks with milk gravy. Shrimp and catfish make Friday lunches special.

"On Saturdays during lunch this place will be full of people and I won't know a soul here," says Jett. "Almost every table will order onion rings and burgers. The people will say 'We stopped at a gas station and they told us this is a good place to eat.' On Sundays, most customers order the fried chicken dinner, although it's available every day at lunch and dinner."

Jett says that the Anvil has been a saloon since 1855 and first began serving food around 1950. Floors in her building are original maple. The hand-carved bar is solid oak; a solid piece of mahogany covers the entire bar top. "Visitors are amazed that we have this unsliced piece of mahogany on our bar," she says. Jett doesn't know the provenance of the iron anvil that is displayed mid-bar. "It was here when I bought this place in 1993," she says.

"Because we're a tourist town, I have kept the theme of the restaurant intact," Jett explains. "I've kept the lace curtains hanging, kept the striped awnings out front, and added some benches by the sidewalk." She hasn't touched the ancient radiators inside near the rustic brick walls and hasn't removed the old coal chute out front either.

St. Genevieve has changed considerably over the years. Antique and crafts shops now thrive near the square while retail shops have moved to strip shopping centers near the town's edge. "There are now more Germans than French people here and, unfortunately, the last French restaurant closed more than a dozen years ago. Wineries have sprouted up in the west part of the county and bring a lot of people in. They've really helped our business."

The Anvil Saloon
Third Street—On the Square, Ste. Genevieve, Missouri

☎ (573) 883-7323

🕐 11 A.M. to 8:30 P.M. Monday through Thursday
11 A.M. to 10 P.M. weekends

♿ Handicapped accessible

🚬 Smoking permitted

28

Ariston Café

Litchfield, Illinois

NICK ADAM, SPIFFY in a dark suit and patterned tie, stood by the front door as I entered The Ariston. He shook my hand and said, "Welcome." He does this for everyone. "Some people say that they have never seen a man in a coat and tie greeting them at the door and handing them the menu," says the jovial Adam.

(Lou Mitchell, who owned what may be Chicago's most popular breakfast spot, greeted customers at the door in expensive suits and handed out Milk Duds candy to women and kids. At Geno's 140 Club in Bethalto, Illinois, owner Dennis Cooper likes to stand at the door and thank customers as they leave.)

Adam admits that there is a price to pay for proprietors who like to be visible. "People want to talk to me; they want to talk to the owner. Even when they phone in take-out orders or make reservations, they want to talk to me." Fortunately, Nick is now assisted by his similarly attired son, Paul, who subs for his dad at the door and on the phone. "The Ariston policy is that us two bosses—Paul and I—are usually always here," says Adam. But there is a caveat, says Paul. "If no one sees my father, they ask me, 'Where's Nick?'"

There has been an Adam at the cafe since 1924 when the first Ariston was opened in Carlinville, Illinois by Nick's

Greek immigrant father, Pete, who dubbed his place the "St. Louis-Springfield, Ill." restaurant because of its location on Illinois Highway 4, then a major artery with connections to both cities. Two years later, U.S. Highway 66 debuted and came through Carlinville. But in 1931, the highway department re-routed 66 through Litchfield; the Adam family soon followed. Pete built a modest café-filling station then replaced it in 1935 with the Streamline Moderne-style yellow and ochre-tweed brick building that exists today. The building was loaded with Art Deco furnishings, many of which remain: the six birds-eye maple booths with vertical wall lights that appear to be fluorescent, but are incandescents; chrome tables now covered with Formica, the back bar and the neon sign above it that says: "Remember When Good Food is Served." In earlier days there was a piano and a bandstand. "I remember when the M.O. Clodfelter Band played here," says Adam.

"A Better Place to Eat" has been our slogan forever, says Adam. "Dad created it and printed it on the menu and put it on the neon sign that can been seen on the back side of the restaurant. It's definitely worth a walk around to view it."

Ariston's lunch menu has changed but one item, the "All American Favorite Hot Beef Sandwich, served open-faced with real whipped potatoes and gravy," survives from the 1924 menu. Ariston's first menu touted a lettuce, peanut butter, and bacon on toast sandwich (35 cents) as well as a lettuce, tomato, and sliced egg on toast sandwich (same price). A "young onion" side dish cost a dime.

Ariston's current lunch menu contains a best-selling chicken salad, chicken enchiladas, "Our Special Taco Salad," the daily special, the "endless soup and salad bar," the "Athenian salad with shredded longhorn cheese, homemade beef stew and meatloaf, Polish sausage and sauerkraut, fried chicken (you can order all you want on Thursdays), Buffalo-style chicken wings, Greek-style chicken livers, toasted ravioli, and the "classic burger— a Route 66 tradition of pure ground beef." The Ariston Greek influence is obvious, but some customers forget the Mexican influence. The family sold the restaurant in 1960 to a new owner who favored Mexican recipes then re-purchased it five years later, removing the inverted sombrero that hung prominently from the main dining room ceiling. It retains to this day some favorite Mexican recipes.

Desserts are shelved in a display case by the front cash register; waitresses in official Ariston uniforms bring dessert display trays to customer tables. "It's another of our policies," says Adam, whose other policies include no smoking and fresh flowers and American flags on every table.

Adam is amazed by the surging curiosity about Route 66 among foreign tourists who pop into The Ariston. "The love Europe has for Highway 66 is mind-boggling," he says. "We get hundreds of tourists every summer, people who start at Chicago and follow the old Route 66 through Illinois and then out West. Once most foreign tourists reach Litchfield, they are so happy to be truly on their way. Most of them have researched Highway 66 and know exactly where they want to stop."

Ariston Café
413 Old Route 66 North, Litchfield, Illinois

 (217) 324-2023

 11 A.M. to 9 P.M. Tuesday through Thursday
11 A.M. to 10 P.M. Friday, 4 P.M. to 10 P.M. Saturday
11 A.M. to 8 P.M. Sunday

 Wheelchair accessible

 No smoking

29

Balducci's Winefest
Maryland Heights, Missouri

BALDUCCI'S WINEFEST IN Maryland Heights is the only St. Louis County restaurant with its own winery, the Louis P. Balducci Vineyards near Augusta, Missouri. This fortunate situation gives veteran chef Joan Balducci Shinall license to pour some of the vineyard's premium wines into her famous pasta dishes and sauce concoctions, almost all family recipes.

Richard (Rick) Balducci, Joan's brother, owns Balducci's Winefest and the vineyards. His father, Louis P., was a local wine pioneer. "Dad was one of the first real wine people in St. Louis," says Rick. When Louis started his wine distributing company after World War II, "wine was considered a low-class drink, with lots of lowly jugs of California wine. Dad was convinced that the country was going to get educated and drink more and better wine. As a distributor, Dad introduced Reunite Lambrusco wine to Missouri and brought in the first Blue Nun Liebfraumilch and Lancers rosé and crackling rosé. A brief story about Dad is on the back of our wine label."

Good wine has had its grip on the Balduccis. After Rick played football at Kansas State and piloted an Army helicopter in Vietnam, his dad said: "Come and sell wine with me." So Rick toured California and Europe and fell in love with the business but with a warning. "I didn't want to remain in wholesale. I wanted to open a wine bar or boutique." To get some experience, he bartended at the Red Onion and Garage bars near the St. Louis riverfront; later, he managed a place called Scotty's Playpen. "Then I wrote a prospectus for a restaurant of my own which I called "The Festival" and took it to the bank."

When the bankers okayed Rick's loan proposal, he found an empty basement in a strip shopping center near the 1803-unit West Pointe Apartments, Missouri's largest apartment-townhouse complex. "You can have it cheap," the landlord said. Since opening in 1975, Rick has remained in the same spot but has transformed it into a kind of warm and cozy European wine cellar with a bar constructed from wine barrels.

Rick outfitted the Winefest with ten church pews he found at Father Jim's Charities. "We cut the pews in half and put in ten booths. Over the booths we put flags from wine-producing countries. We took our tabletops to Brother Matthew at the Black Madonna Shrine in Eureka and said to him 'Could you paint the tabletops for my wine restaurant'? I told him I wanted each tabletop to represent a month of the year and show what winemakers do in those months, such as spraying and harvesting. Brother Matthew painted them beautifully, but after a while they wore out so now they are stored at the vineyards. The tabletops we have now were painted in somewhat the same fashion by my cousin. He is Richard Balducci, the same name as mine. He signed them all. Now people come in and say to me 'You did a good job with the tabletops.' I tell them I am not the same Richard Balducci."

Joan Shinall prepares food in what is known as Joanie's Penthouse near the top of the stairs leading down to the restaurant. Rick says his sister is a "natural cook." "Joan makes soup every day. She does crab bisque, beef burgundy, French onion, baked potato, and beer cheese soup that sells like crazy. She makes white bean chili, and chicken and black bean chili. She makes the pasta of the day that could be the tutti de mare, Mediterranean with vegetables, or the chicken and artichoke. Her Alfredo sauce is terrific and so are her red and white marinara sauces.

"Sometimes I call this place a glorified pizza parlor since people rave about our pizza and salads. We don't do California-style pizza or anything exotic, but we can produce on demand both an excellent deep-pan pizza and a thin crust pizza. Our house dressing for salads is a creamy Parmesan that I got from my Aunt Judy with her permission. Joan makes all our dressings from scratch. And did I tell you that she prepares all the roast beef, meatballs, and marinated chicken from scratch, then carries them downstairs so that Allen Isadore, our kitchen manager, can assemble them into salads, sandwiches, or pasta plates?"

Shinall, the Balducci's cook since 1976, is a high-energy booster of the restaurant. Nothing in food preparation fazes her. "I make lasagna con spinach every day because people demand it," she says. "I make five or six salad dressings, the daily quiche, and I'm designing pasta recipes that go well with the Balducci Sonata wine and six or so other Balducci wines on our menu. At least forty to fifty percent of our customers go for the pizza and soup or salad at lunch, however."

Balducci's is a place to meet people, Rick says. "I met my wife, Carol, here. Phil, our manager, met his wife, Rhonda, here. Phil's brother, George, met his wife, Stephanie, here. Joan met her former husband, Greg, here." During tornado or severe thunderstorm watches or warnings, people tend to find their way down the stairs into the safe haven of Balducci's.

Customers can buy wine and beer aplenty at Balducci's, but not cocktails. "Originally, the place next door was Tully's," explained Rick. "Pat Tully said to me 'I'll be the tavern with little or no food and you be the restaurant which serves less booze.' Now Tully's is called The Brew House, but we still have the same arrangement."

Balducci's Winefest

12527 Bennington Place, Maryland Heights, Missouri

☎ (314) 576-5024

🕐 11 A.M. to 9 P.M. Monday through Thursday (to 10 P.M. Friday), 5 P.M. to 10 P.M. Saturday; 5 to 9 Sunday

No wheelchair access

🚭 No smoking

30

Bare Foot Café
Hardin, Illinois

To ENTER THE Bare Foot Café from its monster gravel parking lot, you walk up the covered handicapped ramp to the front door of the Stransteel building and read the sign: "Please seat yourself at any clean table."

I sat at a table by one of nine eight-foot windows that look out toward the Illinois River and beyond to a line of trees where bald eagles perch and reconnoiter for fish in the cold months. Moments later, in came Scott Isringhausen, head naturalist and interpreter at nearby Pere Marquette State Park, leading an entourage of mostly elderly birders, many from St. Louis. Most of them found window tables; others set up telescopes to scan for eagles. "I've come here at least seventeen times this year with around sixty people each time to have lunch and watch for eagles," Isringhausen said. As the birders gripped their binoculars and trained their long scopes, Isringhausen proclaimed Bare Foot as "the best place to view wildlife from indoors in Calhoun County. It's on a par with the Wild Goose Saloon in Grafton down in Jersey County." On this day, unfortunately, no eagles were seen so birders had to focus on lunch.

Bare Foot's menu is worth a good scan itself. Like other small-town or rural eating spots, it carries ads on its menu. A favorite of mine is from Calhoun Collision Center in Hardin with its not-uncommon slogan: "Highly Wreck-O-Mended." For some inexplicable reason, car repair shops and towing outfits find restaurant menus ideal places to tout their services

The Bare Foot features boneless buffalo out of the Mississippi River, but, ironically, nothing from the Illinois on whose banks it sits. Its popular catfish platters and fritters are pond-raised. Pork chops and chicken dishes are signature items along with the hamburger steak platter. Thick, moist, sprawled on the plate, the steak is embroidered with a tomato slice, lettuce, onion, pickle, and a bowl of coleslaw.

Lunch specials are available Tuesdays (baked chicken and dressing), Wednesdays, and Thursdays ("You'd better call me to find out what they are," says Bill Herter, co-owner) and Fridays (catfish fillet with slaw and potato salad, boneless buffalo, or taco salad). Chicken is perennially popular. "We get praised a lot about our chicken," says Herter, "especially the way we bread it." How do you do it? "I can't tell you. If another restaurant picked up that information, they'd start doing it themselves."

Herter and his brother, Ed, bought four-year-old Melody Trail Harbor restaurant in 1962. The name change was uncomplicated. All the barefoot boaters who tied their vessels to the restaurant's dock and came in for lunch made an impression on the new owners; thus, Bare Foot. Over the subsequent decades, boaters still patronize the Bare Foot but the river has been most unkind. "The 1969 flood was two feet shorter than the 1973 flood which almost ruined this place," says Herter. "In 1993 I had nearly paid off the damage from 1973 when we got flooded again. We had 18 inches of water in the main dining room and that put me a quarter-million dollars in debt."

Despite its plundering by the river, the Bare Foot remains a welcoming place in a quaint, often overlooked patch of western Illinois. Bare Foot's spacious dining room has around fifty tables typically inhabited by locals, St. Louisans, motorcyclists, and the boating crowd that wanders up from the dock, bare feet and all. Inside Bare Foot's front door is a small retail section that sells T-shirts, ball caps, and other merchandise.

Crew-cut, jean-wearing Herter sits on a stool at the cash register wearing a large green pullover. He is a fan of the neighboring Calhoun Senior High School football team that plays its games on the athletic field across the street. "Before each game, Coach brings the boys over here to eat," says Herter. "For $4.50 each (at the time of writing), I sell them two hamburgers, fries, a salad, ice cream, and orange juice. When the team has an undefeated season, I go to local merchants and get their contributions so we can give the team a free steak dinner. The boys do tip the waitress, however."

Bare Foot Café
Highway 100, Hardin, Illinois

 (618) 576-9012

 10:30 P.M. to 9 P.M. Tuesday through Sunday

 Handicapped accessible

 No smoking

31

Barney's Bar-B-Q

Ellisville, Missouri

BARNEY'S STAFFERS LIKE to boast that their barbecuing process is different. "We don't use a gas-fired rotisserie like some of the BBQ chains and there are no commercial smokers here. We make our own charcoal and we don't use any gas. Our style—especially with our ribs and chicken—is the open pit," says Don Toone, whose son, Trent, is sole owner of the Ellisville landmark.

Founder Barney Carver liked to tell friends that his take on the natural process, principally making his own charcoal, came upon him one Sunday while in church (the Ellisville Methodist). Barney's background had included coal mining, a Depression-era stint as a cook in Kentucky restaurants, honing his barbecue skills in Evansville, Indiana, then migration to St. Louis in 1960 to work the assembly line at the Chrysler plant in Fenton. In 1963, Barney took early retirement to plunge into barbecue full time and on his own. He opened a stand on Manchester Road, then moved his growing business to where Barney's is today: in the one-time detached garage of the brick home that lives on next door as a jewelry store.

Barney died in 1986 not long after giving the restaurant to Trent Toone, a reward in many ways for a warm and loving grandfather-only grandson relationship. "They were extremely close," says Trent's mother, Brenda.

Visually, Barney's looks like this: a linear graveled parking area by the street, an order window near shelves of family and former employee photographs in a covered patio with Adirondack chairs, a picnic table that the Toone family calls "Out Front," the kitchen where sandwiches are fixed and the pit resides, a back room that contains the kiln and smoker, and the screened-in "Old Hickory Room" with red-checkered table cloths on four old tables, woodchips on the floor, old Western throughout. "This looks like a cowboy's house," a little boy once told Don Toone. If customers find the outside picnic tables in Barney's side yard too sunny, they can retreat into the Old Hickory Room. Scattered around the complex are potted red geraniums, Barney's signature plant.

In the back room, staffers build between twenty and twenty-five fires daily in the kiln, using rejected oak barrel staves. The resulting charcoal is transferred to the barbecue pit where meat for the sandwiches is grilled well above the burning coals.

Pork is the meat of choice at Barney's, outselling beef two to one. On the sandwich list, pork is tops. All sandwich meat—beef and pork—is smoked ten to twelve hours and infused with Barney's no-ketchup, no-tomatoes, subtly sweetened vinegar-based sauce. On the plate list, the rib and Barney's Special are most preferred. Trent devised the combo plate (ribs, chicken, and pork steak) about ten years ago; it's the only new item on Barney's perennial menu.

Barney-Q-Beans head up the side dishes. "When Barney was alive, a four-year-old girl named Janice would come over from pre-school to talk with Barney, who was kind to all children. She loved his beans and called them her Barney-Q-Beans. Barney liked what she said and put Barney-Q on the menu," says Trent. "Don't forget to add that we put our vinegar-based sauce in the beans," adds Brenda. Barney's only dessert item, pumpkin cake, was originally a gift brought to Brenda's mother, Carmon Carver. "Mother loved it and thought it was complementary to our barbecue and began making it here. Now, some people come here for the pumpkin cake alone," says Brenda.

Barney and Carmon were churchgoers who fretted about being open on Sundays once they opened their BBQ place. "Lots of prayer went into whether to work Sundays," recalls Brenda. "Eventually, my parents thought that they had done the right thing and that their prayers were answered."

On some Sundays, says Brenda, "people come and witness to other customers. One Methodist church pastor was here and got around to almost all the customers. Some people say they joined the church because the minister came here to Barney's."

Barney's Bar-B-Q
16011 Manchester Road, Ellisville, Missouri

 (636) 227-2300

 10 A.M. to 8 P.M. Friday, Saturday, Sunday and holidays
Memorial Day through September

 Handicapped accessible

32

Beffa's
St. Louis

"On our old building, which was across Beaumont Street from our present building, we had window signs that said 'Beffa's Buffet.' But not here! I never thought about a sign or a phone listing for this place. To hell with it, I say," Francis Beffa, then owner of Beffa's, declared years ago.

In its "new" building that opened in 1966, Beffa's is run by Francis's son, Michael, and his wife, Nancy. The latter-day Beffas hold steady with Francis's thoughts about no phone book listing and no exterior signage. But, with respect to the wildly competitive restaurant business, Michael has breached family sentiment by publishing a take-out menu that prominently displays Beffa's phone number.

It is not that unusual for some restaurants to shun immediate identification.

An example was Mrs. Isaiah's Busy Bee Café in Oxford, Mississippi. "There is no listing in the phone book, no sign out front, no advertising anywhere—nothing but a faded painting of a buzzing bee above the porch of the ramshackle building," wrote John Egerton in *Southern Food—At Home, On the Road, In History,* in 1993. In 2007, *The New York Times* reported that some of New York's trendiest cocktail lounges and nightclubs are unmarked save for some distinctive artwork out front, a development mindful of the speakeasies of the 1920s. So maybe Beffa's is a trendsetter of sorts right here, the difference being that any distinctive artwork is to be found inside Beffa's in its colorful wall murals.

Beffa's serves breakfast, lunch, and dinner from its short steam-table cafeteria line. At lunch, Michael stands behind the line and wields the knives he inherited from his father. "I slice the roast beef, ham, corned beef, pork, meatloaf, and sausages, most of which go into sandwiches" Michael says. He learned his craft by standing next to his dad for years as the "sandwich finisher and condiment guy."

Breakfast at Beffa's is profoundly relaxed. Customers come in—starting informally at 5:30, half an hour before official opening—pour themselves some coffee and wait for the cook to turn on the grill. All breakfast orders are custom-prepared; most consist of traditional fare: bacon, eggs, toast or biscuits, homemade fried potatoes, pancakes or waffles. "Nobody cares about fat content at breakfast," Francis used to say. "They still order what they want." Francis sensed that breakfast customers "aren't very happy in the morning. When they have to get up and face the prospect of work, people are naturally less happy." Francis and his staff tried to cheer them up.

What's unusual is that seventy-five percent of Beffa's breakfast customers return for lunch.

"I remember everyone's name and I remember what they eat at both meals," says Michael. "Dad was like that, too." "Michael has a recall of people that is phenomenal," adds Ed Beffa, a cousin who takes over knife-wielding when "the Maestro," as he refers to Michael, is on vacation.

Beffa's customer spread is pretty special. It's the "Who's Who Café," wrote John M. McGuire of the *St. Louis Post-Dispatch* in 1998. McGuire cited mayors, lawyers, politicians, athletes, media notables, and business leaders as regular patrons. The late senator Thomas Eagleton was a luncheon mainstay. Playing his trademark harmonica and dispensing autographed baseballs, superhero Stan Musial marked his eighty-sixth birthday at Beffa's. "Stan comes in about twice a month and often brings several dozen baseballs to sign," reports Michael. "He is very generous with his time."

The original Beffas were among seventeen sons and daughters of Carlo and Lucia Beffa from Madrano, Switzerland in the heavily Italian-Swiss canton of Ticino. Sixteen of the Beffa children came to St. Louis in early 1898 as immigrants and all of them eventually were connected to taverns or food establishments. Two of the siblings, Sam and a brother whose name has been forgotten, opened Beffa Brothers tavern at Beaumont and Olive on St. Patrick's Day 1898. A year later, Attilio, known as "Tilly," joined his two brothers. When Prohibition arrived in 1920, the trio introduced free sandwiches at lunch. After Prohibition ended in 1933, the Beffas continued their limited food service. In 1948, when Tilly's sons Francis and Robert came on board, full food service, including breakfast, began in earnest.

"In the late 1940s and 1950s, every block on Olive had a restaurant," Francis recalled. "The phone company, with 3,500 employees, was across Olive and a lot of them were breakfast regulars. Our neighbors were a big book bindery, the Premium Cap Company, a huge three-story insurance company, auto parts houses, and A.G. Edwards (now Wachovia Securities), which was lodged in a small building back then. Since 1948, we estimate that more than 10,000 workers have moved from this neighborhood. We have no big customers anymore. Even Wachovia has two large cafeterias of its own, though we get many of their employees anyway."

Some fetching memorabilia are posted on or near Beffa's back bar. There's a picture of Carlo and Lucia, who raised the seventeen Beffas; the family coat of arms; an artist's rendition of St. Patrick; an autographed Stan Musial photo; and the stuffed head of a chamois, a deer-like animal that a Beffa cousin shot in the 1930s and that requires frequent dusting.

Murals banded high on Beffa's walls focus on the Swiss Alpine village of Madrano, all the Swiss cantons, especially Ticino, St. Moritz, and Lake Madrano. The late muralist Joe Jasinski from Kirkwood added his rendition of the Arch along with another view of Madrano in the mural he painted in the 1960s that now resides above the cafeteria line. Jasinski's original commission was to do murals for the old Beffa's. When the present restaurant opened in May 1966, the murals were transferred over. Beffa's is open one Saturday a year but only if there is a downtown St. Patrick's Day parade. "This place probably serves the best corned beef in town on St. Patrick's," Ed Beffa boasts.

Local lore says that if you happen to be in the cafeteria line at Beffa's with a policeman or a priest, you may get stuck with the bill. Not entirely accurate, says Michael. "We have customers who spot a policeman in line and volunteer to buy their lunch. And people will come up to me and say: 'I see a priest in line—I'll take care of Father's meal.'"

Beffa's is the only restaurant included in this book with a guarded parking area out back (although the guard is paid mainly to observe the sprawling lots that belong to Wachovia, Beffa's giant neighbor) and a corner display in the dining room acknowledging the Last 2 Man Club from old McBride High School in St. Louis. On display is a bottle of 1977 Smith Woodhouse vintage port that the last two men alive from the class will share. The classmates, including Francis, come for lunch on the first Tuesday of each month.

Beffa's
2700 Olive Street, St. Louis

 (314) 652-7429

 7 A.M. to 9 P.M. Monday through Friday

 Wheelchair accessible

Smoking permitted

33

Best Steak House

St. Louis

IF YOU'VE EVER asked a friend to give you a line on a different or unusual restaurant, one sure recommendation is Best Steak House, where the cafeteria line comes alive. The place is *all* line!

Best patrons must be forewarned that once you take your place in line, you must be savvy and alert. Your best bet is to quickly scan the menu up on the wall in front of you and pick out a steak or chicken platter, sandwich, or gyro offering (Best is Greek-owned). Since Best has no waitresses, the only way to communicate your order is to shout it to the broilerman way up front. When the broilerman looks your way and yells, "Next," you shout.

"Broilerman is the best job we have here," says owner Dean Kases. "Not too many people can handle the job because you have to remember faces of people in line. We've brought employees here in the past and they couldn't do it. They have to understand the rhythm of the line. Our current broilerman, the guy who yells 'Next,' is Terrence Crawford, who's been hollering 'Next' for fifteen straight years at lunchtime. He started here as busboy, then did toast in the kitchen, and then moved to broiler."

"These days, people come in here just to hear the man say 'Next,'" says Dean Kases, Jr, day manager.

Best opened in 1964 in the spot that once contained the original Flaming Pit restaurant. Back then North Grand was cafeteria city. There was Garavelli's over on Olive, the Southern cafeteria in the Missouri Building basement, and Pope's next door.

"I was just getting started," says the elder Kases, "and had to find my first customers. So I talked to people waiting in line outside Pope's and said 'Come over to my place—there's no waiting.' It also helped that the 1964 World Series between the Cardinals and New York Yankees was playing up the street in Sportsman's Park. That crowd spilled all over North Grand and many of them came in here to celebrate."

You never know who's going to be in line to order a sirloin or a chicken dish (lunchtime's top favorites of regulars who never need to look up to see what's on the wall menu). "When we first opened, the boxer, Archie Moore, was in line," recalls Kases, the elder. "Ann-Margaret, the movie star, came in while playing at the Fox Theatre across the street. So did Red Skelton, who gave me his autograph. Chuck Berry has been here and so has Leon Strauss, who owned the Fox. Minnesota Fats, the famous pool player, was in here and came to the cash register. 'Do I get a discount? I'm Minnesota Fats,' he said to my wife, Irene, 'I don't know who you are,' she said, so he had to pay full price. Irene stays home now and makes our baklava for dessert. I bring it down here every morning."

Best Steak House

516 N. Grand Boulevard, St. Louis

 (314) 535-6033

10 A.M. to 9 P.M. Monday through Friday
11 A.M. to 9 P.M. Saturday; 11 A.M. to 8 P.M. Sunday

Wheelchair accessible

Smoking permitted

34

Bill's Toasty
Taylorville, Illinois

BILL'S TOASTY, HALF a block off the city square in Taylorville, Illinois, is a six-decades-old 24-hour café about as wide as two pickup trucks parked side by side. On the right as you enter, you see ten burgundy stools facing the off-white flecked laminate counter. "Today's Menu" is posted on the wall above the grill. All the storage cabinets, the pie and bread containers, and the woodwork are original. "None of the owners changed any of this place," says former manager Pam Thunhorst.

Bounced checks made out to Bill's Toasty as well as detailed take-out orders from people who never showed up for them—and their names—are posted on a corkboard by the cash register. "We have Caller ID, so we know who calls to place their orders," says another former manager, Donna Strunk. In plastic sleeves fastened to the far wall are Bill's Toasty T-shirts. Waitresses are encouraged to wear Bill's T-shirts. If they wear their own shirts, no liquor or cigarette advertising is to appear on them—that's Bill's Toasty policy.

Bill's Toasty has been a Main Street denizen since 1938 when Bill Vaughan and his brother, Ivan, opened it. All current employees seem to know the lineage of Bill's. Pam Thunhorst rolled off the ownership bloodline perfectly in the pint-sized kitchen where loyal regulars are invited to sit when the counter is filled. "First, Bill went off to World War Two and never came back, so Ivan, he had it for years. Frank and Glenda Kalka bought it from Ivan. Orville and Ina Griffin bought it from the Kalkas. Mamie and Hiram Pedan bought it off the Griffins. In 1982, Calvin Scallions bought it off the Pedens. Patty Scallions, his wife, worked alongside us here in the restaurant until she died in 1998."

Because Patty Scallions was such a special person—she would, for example, pass platters of cookies and candies along the counter at Easter, Christmas, and Thanksgiving and would faithfully attend ill or troubled regulars—her death was a painful blow to the staff. "When I got the phone call that Patty had died," says Thunhorst, "I walked over to the front door and locked it shut. We were closed for a week out of respect for Patty. But, because our employees had no place else to go, we would come in around 6:30 in the morning and just talk about Patty and laugh and cry. We did invite a few of the regulars to join us. We had a pot going."

Before the final rites, employees wrote their farewell thoughts about Patty on small slips of paper. "The family left those messages with Patty in her casket," says Thunhorst. At Patty's funeral, she recalls, people came up to Calvin and his relatives to offer condolences, then they drifted to the long pew where the entire employee force sat and "they paid their respects to us as if we belonged to the immediate family."

Occasionally, Calvin Scallions sits on a stuffed brown sofa in a small second-floor room atop a stairway covered in faded Astroturf. He studies three TV monitors trained on the downstairs counter and stools. "I have guys who come in here and steal my (plastic) salt and pepper shakers and my mustard and ketchup containers," he says. "Some guys come here directly from the tavern. I usually make an eight-hour tape. I'll take it out and run it backwards if the waitress says such and such happened around a certain time. If so-and-so is suspected of foul play at 3 A.M., I run the tape real fast backwards until I get close to 3 A.M. We have caught quite a few stealing. Two guys from out of town picked up a mustard container and a ketchup jar and they did it on my tape. On a hunch, I called the cops and they caught them at a tavern. We charged them $30 each for the jars and warned them that next time they could go to jail. Once the swimming lake at the edge of town opens for the season, our salt and pepper shakers and our mustard and ketchup jars—even our sugar containers and napkin holders—seem to end up in trailers of people who have lake lots. That's why we have to have these surveillance monitors—so we can prevent all the theft."

Scallions leans forward, peering into his monitors. "Look, there's Ken, who's here to fix our cooler," he announces. Later, he rises to his feet. "There's a guy buying a T-shirt," he exclaims.

The Taylorville police station is a few doors away from Bill's. Some of its officers occasionally review Scallions' tapes when searching for criminal suspects. "A local man got killed," says Strunk. "The police knew he was in here eating shortly before his death because of two things—the videotape and the autopsy results. They claim they could identify an order of Bill's hamburgers and fries in the man's belly. All our regulars know about the tapes. Some wave 'Hi, Calvin' at the cameras."

Opinions differ as to the name Toasty. "Some say it was because of Bill's toasted cheese sandwich (which regulars call cheese toasties)," thinks Scallions. "Because everything on the grill is toasted," puts in a waitress. Nobody has dared to tinker with the name, Bill's Toasty, even though Bill was gone by the early 1940s. "Calvin had it fixed in court so no one ever will change the name," says Thunhorst.

Horseshoe sandwiches are endemic to cafes in central Illinois. Bill's offers breakfast horseshoes that are more heap than horseshoe: Texas toast is on the bottom and is smothered by a tower of hash browns, scrambled eggs, breakfast meat, diced onions, and a generous dollop of cheese. Kids love horseshoes, says Strunk.

College students who have been away at school often check in at Bill's before going home to see the folks, says Thunhorst. "When Taylorville Senior High School has class reunions, returning alums will drop in for a visit. Even wedding parties in tuxes and gowns come in here. In the old days, people would show up after dances at the Moose, Eagles, or Elks."

The late Irene Bennett was Bill's most famous waitress. She worked the 10 P.M. to 6 A.M. shift for thirty years before a brief retirement and death at eighty-two in 1995. "If I ever quit work, that will be the end of me," Bennett told Thunhorst, and it pretty much was.

Bennett was notorious for her off-color jokes. "Those college kids would return for the holidays and come here first and pay Irene $5 or $10 to tell them jokes," says Thunhorst. "Lawyers and bankers and other professionals would do the same. Some of them would pay her in advance so she would be prepared with a real clever one the next time they came in. Irene was such a tradition in this town that there has been some activity toward making Bill's Toasty a national historic landmark."

Bill's Toasty

111 N. Main Street, Taylorville, Illinois

 (217) 824-4022

 Open 24 hours daily

 Wheelchair accessible

 No smoking

35

Billy Goat Restaurant and Bar
St. Louis

BILLY GOAT IS "the only place in the city that is doing gourmet bar food," says chef-owner Brian Roth, who apprenticed at Old Warson Country Club then went on to the former St. Louis Steakhouse. "We treat our burgers, which constitute about thirty-five percent of sales, as if they were done in an upscale restaurant. We use gourmet ethics. We hand-grind our burgers using Angus beef top round, a more expensive cut than chuck."

Roth's BBQ pork steak, chicken club, cold chicken and ham, and grilled vegetable sandwiches have plenty of devoted patrons. So do his salads, particularly the grilled salmon, house, and Caesar.

Manager-owner Rob Lyons says that "Everything you can do with food has already been done. We use no secret recipes or ingredients here. There is nothing to kill or die for. We're dedicated to the way we assemble our ingredients and that is our real secret, if you will."

Roth is unusually inventive. "I make my own salt and my own seasoned butter. We mix the raw ingredients of our special seasoning which we call 'Billy Goat Dust.' We make our own soup from scratch with no starters or base. We dry-rub our chicken wings, poach them, blanch them in a fryer, and season them with our own wing dust. Our balsamic vinaigrette salad dressing is by far the most popular here; we sell pints of it to go. We make our own chili and sell around five gallons of it every week. All the ingredients are fresh, including the beans and ground pork. Every July on the restaurant's anniversary we sponsor a chili cook-off."

Billy Goat inhabits an 1892 brick building at Vandeventer and Boyle in the city's Forest Park Southeast neighborhood. Anheuser-Busch, Inc. owned the building, used as a tavern, until 1954. "The woodworking here matches four or five other bars of the same vintage in the city," says Roth. Support pillars have wooden boxes around them; wood panels form unusual patterns on the walls.

Roth purposely put in an open kitchen at Billy Goat. "Years ago I was the St. Louis team captain in the Junior National Hot Foods Competition sponsored by the American Culinary Festival. It was then that I learned the value of performing in front of people. I decided that customers should see everything that goes on in the kitchen. Our customers often walk up, see something they like, and place their orders right there. People sit across from our kitchen simply to watch us work. Since we don't have a door on it, some diners attempt to come in but we politely block them."

Billy Goat is mostly a word-of-mouth business, but the restaurant once briefly advertised in the bulletin of St. Cronin's Catholic church up the street. Roth says that the St. Cronin's priest often brings his visitors in for meals. "They seem to come from all over the world," observes Roth.

(Billy Goat had a predecessor with somewhat the same name at Thirty-Ninth and Chouteau. Billie Goat Hill saloon and restaurant operated from about 1977 to 1990, offering items such as Mexican goat soup, brain sandwiches, and the Billie Goat and Nannie Goat super sandwiches. My sons and I often ate the $2.49 breakfast special on our boys' mornings out. Revival, formerly King Louie's Restaurant, now occupies the space.)

Billy Goat Restaurant and Bar
1449 S. Vandeventer, St. Louis

 (314) 371-4628

 10:30 A.M. to 8 P.M. Monday through Friday

Wheelchair accessible

Smoking permitted

~~~~~~ 36 ~~~~~~

Blue Owl Restaurant and Bakery
Kimmswick, Missouri

THIRTY YEARS AGO the village of Kimmswick, Missouri, its population negligible, its water supply undependable, its housing stock on the fritz, languished on the right bank of the Mississippi River, 25 miles south of St. Louis. Previously Kimmswick was an outlying nineteenth-century resort destination for fun-seeking and roistering St. Louisans. Two main resorts, Montesano Springs Park, the centerpiece along with Crystal Spring, were steamboat and Iron Mountain Railroad stops for big city folks who came to picnic, drink, frolic, pitch horseshoes, sip clear spring water, and play softball on a hill above the river.

Spoken of as the second-oldest town in Missouri, Kimmswick had been generally torpid since its 1859 founding by German immigrant Theodore Kimm. After the Civil War there was a brewery, some greenhouses, a flour mill, the resorts, and a peak population of 1,500. The town itself had no restaurant until 1901 when the Dohack family opened a cafe for steamboat and rail customers.

It wasn't long after Dohack's debut in Kimmswick that Ma Green's Tavern opened. At Second and Mill Street, Ma Green's was also the home of Ma and, presumably, Pa and had a pool hall on the side. It offered beer and whisky and sandwiches from 1901 to the 1940s when the Greens closed the place and it reverted to a private home. Later, Wayne Kroner, the Green's grandson, and his wife Sugar (Dolores) and George Crow re-opened it as The Blue Owl. Why an owl? There's not much known about owls in Kimmswick but Darlene Spink of the Kimmswick Historical Society once told me: "We get up at 4:30 A.M. and it's great to hear the owls here."

When the original Blue Owl closed, the town again sank into limbo until 1969. That year a longtime summer resident, Lucianna Gladney Ross, widow of the founder of the Seven-Up Company and former daughter-in-law of Charles Ross, the popular press secretary to President Harry S Truman, decided that the town could use a battery charge. Her plan of gradual refurbishment led her to buy some fifteen dwellings, hire an architect and contractor, move in fixable log cabins from neighboring towns, and start the reshaping.

When the makeovers were completed, Mrs. Ross rented the buildings to private or business occupants. One notable log cabin restoration was a place called The Old House, a one-time trading post, tavern, and stagecoach stop located up the road in Arnold, Missouri. During the Civil War, General Ulysses S. Grant visited The Old House, declaring its food the best in Missouri. As part of the Kimmswick restoration, Mrs. Ross's group moved the building into Kimmswick where it has been, until recently, a restaurant. Mrs. Ross also bought the old Ma Green-Blue Owl building. She brought in a repair crew, redid the place, and rented it in 1985 to Mary Hostetter to re-open it as the reincarnated Blue Owl.

Mary had just recently moved here from Austin, Texas, ostensibly to work for Southwest Bell Telephone Company. She landed in south St. Louis County but soon discovered

Kimmswick. With a flair for cooking and baking, inspired by her Texas grandmother, Selma Rothfuchs, who labored for the most prominent bakery in Galveston, Mary and her family shared a home in Austin with her grandmother. "Every day my grandmother called up the stairs to say that the dinner rolls were ready; they were yeast rolls. It was her tradition. She also made cinnamon rolls, oyster soup, and plum kuchen with dark purple plums," recalls Mary.

Mary's Blue Owl began with Mary and three employees. "My first goal was thirty customers a day. On the first day we had thirty-seven. After two months, we had to remodel and enlarge one of our two dining rooms." In 1988, Mrs. Ross helped finance a new kitchen for Mary after she saw lines of people coming in to eat breakfast and lunch. In 1991, Mrs. Ross, expressing great confidence in Mary's managerial and culinary skills, agreed to sell the building to Mary. "It was the first building Mrs. Ross ever sold in Kimmswick," Mary says.

In 1995, Mary added another space, "Lucianna's Tearoom," in honor of Mrs. Ross. "We gave up our driveway and back parking lot to put in the tearoom," Mary explains. Two local landscape paintings by Mrs. Ross now hang in the tearoom near the antique fireplace. "The room always fills up first," says Mary. Late in 1995, Mary opened "Grandmother's Bakery" in memory of her grandmother Mrs. Rothfuchs. The Blue Owl now sells rolls, pastries, cakes, and its famous Levee High apple pie.

In the summer of 1993 when the Mississippi River encountered a five-hundred-year flood, "Fifty percent of our customers either helped sandbag or they prayed for us," says Mary. With such divine intervention the restaurant and most of the town was saved while nearby towns were pummeled by the unrelenting waters.

Today, with at least sixty-five fulltime employees—all women—the Blue Owl complex consists of the tearoom, The Blue Room, the main dining room, the bakery, the Owl's Nest, the Texas Tearoom, and Miss Mary's Veranda with its twenty-six French doors.

Mary is a rigorous entrepreneur. She conducts cooking schools for the Dierberg grocery chain in St. Louis. "There are pretty long waiting lists for my classes," she says. "People like to hear the history of our restaurant and about the mistakes we've made. I also do speeches at mothers' clubs and churches."

Mary has six cookbooks in circulation including *Creation for Sharing*, which had a printing of five thousand copies. "Our best-selling book was *Treasures from the Heart,* in which readers can find our recipe for white chili," she says.

Mary encourages her customers to bring in their favorite recipes to try out. If the kitchen staff likes a recipe it may appear on a future Blue Owl menu or even a cookbook. "We're excited when someone brings in a recipe," says Mary. "A man just made a reservation for Valentine's Day. 'I'm going to bring you a pie you've never tasted before,' he said. We can't wait to taste it. People also come by to bring us cookies and things. Frankly, it's nice to taste someone else's goodies."

Blue Owl undergoes seasonal decoration changes. The restaurant's main seasons revolve around St. Patrick's Day, Mother's Day, July 4, and Christmas. The really busy stretch for the restaurant is from May 1 to December 31. "The quiet season, which includes sub-seasons such as Valentine's Day and Easter, is our time to make repairs and arrangements for the busy season," Mary explains.

Breakfast-seeking customers (please note that breakfast begins at 10 A.M.) tend to prefer the "fluffy homemade biscuits with our delicious homemade milk gravy and crumbled pork sausage," Mary reports. Others opt for the quiche of the day, country ham and eggs, pancakes, or French toast. If you are late for breakfast, you may decide to order a bountiful Blue Owl lunch. The lunch menu is teeming with homemade soups, tempting salads such as the Tossed Strawberry or The Tropical, croissants, sandwiches, daily specials, the quiche-of-the-day, and desserts such as the mile-high pie.

On off days Mary enjoys visiting other restaurants. How does she judge a restaurant to be competitive? "Is the tea fresh? I don't like places that serve instant tea or tea that's been sitting around, old tea. I want it brewed after I walk in the door."

Mary was recently named the Greater St. Louis Restaurant Association's Restaurateur of the Year. One reason was her dedication to customers. Mary usually stands by the front entrance, at least on busy days, to say hello to customers. "As long as you recognize and give them a smile," she insists, "they know you know them. It's even better than calling them by name."

At a restaurant seminar, Mary learned that she will lose one percent of her customers each year to death. "We attend countless funerals," she says. "We are sometimes among the first to know when a cherished customer dies. We get lots of calls from relatives when that happens."

Blue Owl Restaurant and Bakery
6116 Second Street, Kimmswick, Missouri

 (636) 464-3128

 10 A.M. to 3 P.M. Tuesday through Friday
10 A.M. to 5 P.M. Saturday, Sunday

 Wheelchair accessible

 No smoking

37

Booche's Billiard Hall

Columbia, Missouri

BOOCHE'S BILLIARD HALL has occupied the same location on South Ninth in the center of downtown Columbia for around seventy-five years—hence the mirrored mahoghany back bar, antique pool tables, weathered dining tables, Mizzou football team photos from the turn of the last century, and locked-up pool cues in dusky wall cabinets.

Students tend to patronize Booche's evenings; business-people, Mizzou alums, and curious travelers and townies order cheeseburgers for lunch. On most weekday mornings, before Booche's officially opens at 11, the Kaffee Klatch holds forth at a long table near the brass rail bar.

Kaffee Klatcher John Hunt says "I sold the *Columbia Tribune* in here in 1965. They gave me ten minutes to sell my papers, then get out." Mac McCluskey, a retired sign painter, says "I'd rather be in Booche's than in any country club. It's cheaper and has a better class of people." Hunt is a local three-cushion billiards champion; McCluskey is a decent snooker player.

A regular since the 1950s, McCluskey remembers a former customer who would leave Booche's after lunch but linger outside. "'Why do you stick around so long after telling us you have to be somewhere at such-and-such a time?' we asked the man. 'I'm not leaving here until my meter expires,' he said. He did this all the time."

Until the 1970s, Booche's banned women. "Before then, my mother would come to the window and motion to me to come outside and talk to her," says McCluskey. "When I was a Mizzou student in the early seventies, my girlfriend at the time crossed the barrier at Booche's and even smoked a cigar at the bar," says John Robinson, a former Missouri director of tourism. "Patrons stared, stunned."

McCluskey painted many signs on Booche's walls. "I drew the 'No Sniveling' sign which they put on their T-shirts here for a while," he says. "I drew another sign that says 'Parents of unattended children will be asked to leave or will be put down the basement to play with rats.' I hand-lettered the menu on the south wall (Booche's only menu) for which my pay was a gift certificate and a T-shirt." "If our food, drinks and service are not up to your standards, lower your standards" is another McCluskey masterpiece.

Most Kaffee Klatchers usually exit by 11 but some stay for lunch. Retired fireman Ron Blaylock says his favorite food at Booche's is not the cheeseburger, perennial recipient of national acclaim, but the grilled pork loin sandwich with a slice of onion, pickle, and horseradish. Terry Prince, a former University of Missouri medical center manager, prefers the King Tut sandwich with two eggs, ham, sausage, and cheese on rye. "That sandwich was named for a customer who was so huge we called him King Tut," reminds Prince.

Most Booche's lunchtime customers order the cheeseburger, a quarter-pound patty topped with Swiss cheese and served on waxed paper—or "patty paper" as co-owner Charlie Kurrie calls it—instead of a plate. The cheeseburgers are pretty small, so most customers opt for a pair plus a cup of Kurrie's soups—sausage, potato, and kale on one of my visits—or housemade chili. The Double Dog (two wieners on a bun), the Fast Freddie (chili cheese dog with kraut), the Knockwurst, and, of course, the pork loin and King Tut sandwiches are constants on the menu board.

On its dining tables, Booche's bestows some clever nicknames. Co-owner Rick Robertson knows the lore: "Your table was named for the guy we called the 'Thief of Baghdad,' who stole things from Booche's, so we call it the 'Baghdad Table.' The 'Deer 1' and 'Deer 2' tables are by the wall where we once had two deer heads mounted. The heads suffered from nicotine, grease, and dust and are now retired to the attic. The 'Phone Table' is self-explanatory since it is next to the phone booth. The five-top table near the back is called 'The Hook.' It is named for a General Telephone Company manager who came in here looking for GT workers who were goofing off. The 'One and One Table' is named for an old guy who always ordered one beer and one shot. The table closest to the window is, naturally, the 'Window Table' and the long 'Ballpark Table' is near the picture of a ballpark. Another long table is the 'Scoreboard Table' next to the 1950s baseball scoreboard on the south wall. By the way, there are two snooker tables, one three-cushion billiard table, and three 8-ball tables but you can't eat at them."

A committee of longtime Booche's regulars meets in secret to determine if a recently deceased customer might warrant a brass plate, either moored under the bar by that customer's usual stool or on a wall somewhere. One bar stool plate reads: "Billy Rader, 1921-2005. Hat's Off, Billy." Another plate is wall-mounted directly above the 'No Sniveling' sign. It memorializes Hank Hartley, 1912-2005 and repeats Hartley's favorite request: "How About a Cool One, Mama?" A line of empty Budweiser bottles, each with a clear beer glass slipped over the neck, tops a hutch along the north wall. "Those are more memorials for deceased regulars," explains Robertson. A large whiskey bottle next to them commemorates the life of Mick Jabbour, a former co-owner whose three-cushion billiards cue is on permanent display near the pool tables.

In 1884, Venable's, a high-toned gentlemen's pool parlor, opened in Columbia. Paul Blucher Venable (1867-1912) was the now-revered founder who operated the place for twenty-eight years. Its present location is its fifth in central Columbia. Venable did not call his parlor Booche's; that moniker came only after his death as a kind of memorial by new owners. Local legend has it that seven-year-old Venable encountered poet-to-be Eugene Field ("Little Boy Blue," "Wynken', Blynken' and Nod"), a Mizzou underclassman. Field supposedly asked the boy's name. "Paul Blucher Venable, but most people call me Blucher," the lad replied. Field allegedly responded: "Blucher is no nickname for a kid. From now on your name is Booch." Venable's elderly daughter visited Booche's seventy-two years after her father's death and vouched for the story.

An oversize brass plate inside the entrance is a shrine to Venable. A catchy inscription has long adorned the front door. "Closed on Sunday. See You In Church," it says. "That sign has little significance," a Kaffee Klatcher concedes.

John Robinson recalls floating on the Eleven Point River in southern Missouri. "I got my canoe at the 11-Point Canoe Rental in Alton, Missouri where one of the owners is a former Booche's bartender. When the screen door into the office slammed behind me, it sounded familiar. It's the same door which, in an earlier incarnation, had slammed a billion times at the threshold to Booche's."

Booche's Billiard Hall
110 S. Ninth Street, Columbia, Missouri

☎ (573) 874-9519

🕐 11 A.M. to midnight Monday through Saturday

♿ Handicapped accessible

🚭 No smoking

38

Carl's Drive-In

Brentwood, Missouri

NO PLACE IN metropolitan St. Louis can match the Carl's Drive-In building, originally erected in 1918 as a filling station. It's pretty much a square box with entrance doors on the east and west sides, two separate counters with eight stools each, and the "kitchen" in between. A customer can't walk from one side of the place to the other, so he usually picks his favorite side.

Back in the more ferocious days of sports rivalry between Webster Groves and Kirkwood high schools, Carl's, in all of its innocence as a Brentwood neighborhood drive-in, was sometimes a victuals battleground. "I once saw a food war here when I was in high school," says owner Frank Cunetto. "There used to be filled pie cases on each counter back in the 1960s. Kids from Kirkwood High would sit on the west side and kids from Webster Groves High would be on stools on the east side and they would reach forward, take out pies, and throw them at the kids on the opposite counter. The same was true with kids from Maplewood High who would would sit on the east side and people from Brentwood High who sat on the west side. People from Kirkwood who know the history of this place probably never sat on the Webster Groves side. You always stayed on your side, not theirs, even when this place was empty. The same is true with people from Brentwood and Maplewood." To restore calm, Carl Meyer, Jr., who bought the joint in 1959, finally removed the pie safes.

Carl's could well be the area's double cheeseburger king. "We sell more of them than anything else," says Cunetto, who bought out Meyer in 1987. "There's nothing in our burgers but pure ground beef—no seasoning or anything. We are consistent so the burgers taste the same every time. To make it complete, we put on American cheese.

"These days," says Cunetto, who attentively stands behind the counters in the tiny kitchen where three or four waitresses and grill persons toil, "we're selling double- and triple-cheeseburgers without the buns because people are calorie-conscious. Once in a while we serve a quadruple cheeseburger, again with no buns—you just eat it with a knife and fork off the plate. Yes, we get vegetarians who request a burger but ask us to 'hold the burger.'"

In earlier days, the business was known as the Foot Long Hot Dog Company, one of six regional outlets. When Meyer bought the place, he named it Carl's and added curb service. Under Cunetto, the foot-longs remain, curb service doesn't, and the official name of Carl's in the Brentwood City Hall register continues as the "Long Dog Drive-In."

"We still sell a box of hot dogs every day—that's sixty of them—but we sell ten-to-one more hamburgers than hot dogs," says Cunetto. Carl's is one of few local purveyors of foot-long dogs. If you want chili on your foot-long you must know that it was made by the same man who once stirred up the chili for the long-gone Hodge's chili chain in St. Louis. Carl's also offers a normal-size curly-q hot dog. "The curly-q here is truly unique," wrote *Southern Living* magazine in February 2002.

"You take a hot dog and cut slits in it. If you drop it into a french fryer it curls up and gets real crisp on the outside." End result is a dog so rounded that it comes on a hamburger bun.

A few furnishings from the past remain in the old building. One is an old-time penny gumball machine that still works; another is a huge root beer barrel. When he owned Carl's, Meyer acquired the recipe for IBC Root Beer from a one-time IBC distributor after IBC went out of business. Today Cunetto mixes syrup and carbonated water in the barrel to make up to fifty gallons of root beer a day, far and away his most popular fountain beverage.

Cunetto says that nearly ninety-five percent of his customers are regulars. That means that with only sixteen stools the place can get jammed. "Some days the east side has people standing three-deep and the west side, which is narrower, two deep. One day I told all the customers to stop and hold still so I could get a good count. I got forty-two, the most I ever counted." For several years, Cunetto awarded a plaque with a spatula on it to the customer of the year, chosen by employee vote. One year, the top customer won a Carl's counter stool with his name on it. Another lucky customer had his face imprinted on T-shirts, which Cunetto sold for several years.

"One of our customers who worked for the Frank Blair Shell Station near Brentwood and Manchester came in every day for nearly forty years," recalls Cunetto. "This guy would order one of three things for lunch—two plain hamburgers, a chili dog, or two hot dogs with mustard. After a while our employees would bet on what the man was going to order that day—we'd all throw in a buck or so. When the customer found out we were betting on him, he came in one day and ordered a fish sandwich. We were stunned. All the betting stopped and we kept serving him one of his three favorites for many years afterward."

Cunetto recalls that at least five motorists have somehow left Manchester Road and crashed their vehicles into the side of Carl's. So he has erected two concrete-filled steel pipes, sunk deep into the ground, to prevent any re-occurrence. "The last crash we had was when someone tried to back into a parking space, hit a parked car, and drove it into the building," recalls Cunetto. "It sounded like an explosion to us and broke the wall completely free. A lady who was a regular customer was sitting at the far end of the east-side counter. She looked up from the counter for a second and went right back to eating her burger. You had to be here to see that."

Carl's Drive-In
9033 Manchester Road, Brentwood, Missouri

 (314) 961-9652

 11 A.M. to 8 P.M. Tuesday through Saturday

 Wheelchair accessible

No smoking

39

Charlie's Drive-In
Wood River, Illinois

CHARLIE'S DRIVE-IN, A midtown Wood River, Illinois fixture since 1950 when it debuted as Narney's, is open from April through Halloween. Coincidentally, the drive-in stand has been painted pumpkin orange since day one.

Two-carhop Charlie's traditionally used Sherwin-Williams orange paint for the building exterior until Sherwin-Williams discontinued its orange at a time when the stand needed a new coat. "We finally found a painter in Bethalto who mixed us a perfect Charlie's orange," said a relieved Teresa Tweedy (daughter of Charlie Tweedy, proprietor from 1976 to 1991) who runs the place with partner Michelle Garin. Once, word around town was that Charlie's was about to be painted white and you'd better run over there to see it. "But it was a coat of primer," explains Michelle, "and it lasted only one day."

The orange menu has two sections, one for sandwiches, the other for some pretty dazzling sides. It headlines its sandwich section: "Whaaz up in great sandwiches." Whaaz up principally is the quarter-pound hamburger on a large sesame bun. "We smack our quarter-pounders on the grill with a spatula," volunteers Teresa. "It makes them more homemade." The hamburger is delivered to your car by a carhop who carries a standard aluminum tray. The hamburger rests on an orange towel in a red plastic basket lined in foil. The whole package looks so meticulous and proper that you may momentarily hesitate to attack it.

Smaller burgers, called "Our Little Burgers," are also dubbed "Charlie's Special Burgers" because Charlie, in his heyday at the stand, called them "My Special Burgers," are sellouts all year. "They come ten to a pound and we can average four hundred sales a day," says Teresa of the eighty-cent burgers. Among other sandwiches are competitively priced hot dogs, Coney Islands, grilled cheeses, corn dogs, and barbecued hams with a secret sauce that Michelle says "we get cussed over it's so good." Quite often the sandwiches and sides are joined on the tray by a glass of Charlie's own root beer. "We still have the original root beer equipment working, but if something isn't functioning properly—like the carbonator—we're in trouble," adds Michelle. "People will pull in, place their order, and then, if we say 'The root beer machine is down,' they may just start their car and drive away."

Charlie's "delicious sides" include cheese fries, deep-fried mac and cheese wedges, fried cheddar cheese cubes, and crab Rangoon. "We figure that there are people around here who don't always want to go to a Chinese restaurant and who might like their crab Rangoon here," says Teresa. "You wouldn't believe how they move."

In Charlie's early days, students from Wood River Senior High School directly across the street would come in droves during the lunch hour and stick around until the bell rang for classes to resume. "All those kids hanging around made us look so busy that people would drive past us because we looked as if we couldn't accommodate them," recalls Charlie Tweedy.

"Then the school decided to have a closed campus where the kids could eat in the school cafeteria only. It was then that the teachers and staff would come over for lunch. So we traded the kids' trade for the adult trade, including all the people who used to drive right past us."

(After Tweedy sold the drive-in, he worked for a local funeral home "dressing the dead and helping to place them in caskets." He said he helped lay out some of his former drive-in customers. "Occasionally I'd look at one of the bodies and remember the person. 'That guy used to eat a lot of Coney's at my place,' I'd say.")

Teresa and Michelle usually put in 14-hour days, except for Sundays when the stand is shut. Late Saturday night they bleach out the concrete apron that surrounds the prim stand with its screened-in porch and the orange awnings. "We never get home until 2 Sunday morning," says Teresa. "When we're out their scrubbing, people drive by and honk. One van drove past and someone screamed, 'Get a life!' I loved that."

After winter hiatus, the partners return in March to clean and ready their stand. "April and May are prime time for us," Teresa says. "People are ready to eat your food again. They haven't had it for five months."

Charlie's Drive-In
762 Wood River Avenue, Wood River, Illinois

 (618) 254-6416

 11 A.M. to 10 P.M. Monday through Saturday April through October, 11 A.M. to 9 P.M. September and October only

Chuck-a-Burger

St. John, Missouri

CHUCK-A-BURGER IN ST. John, Missouri opened as a drive-in restaurant in 1957, first of a chain of eight. Though vigorously enduring the teenage cruisin' era that fizzled around 1970, it alone of its original brethren survives. Relishing its past, it bills itself "Cruisin' Capitol of the Midwest."

In its first decade, Chuck-A-Burger was a pre-eminent area stop for cruisers, mainly on weekend nights when boy carhops wore white shirts, white ice cream pants, red bow ties, cummerbunds, and money pouches and "curb girls" wore colorful poodle skirts. Cruisers arrived in family sedans or in jazzed-up supercars, tailored to capture the attention of female cruisers. "Back then you cruised from one drive-in to the next, from one hot spot to another and then maybe returned to some of the places to check out the crowd one more time," the late Ralph Stille, manager-supervisor in the cruisin' period and later, Chuck-a-Burger's sole owner, once told me. "They'd drive from a Steak 'n Shake to a White Castle to the Parkmoor on Clayton Road and to us," says Ron Stille, Ralph's son and current owner. "The problem was they spent little money."

Here's what the Chuck-A-Burger parking lot, which has barely changed, looked like to Ralph Stille on heavy cruise nights: "People with no dates, the nerds, and anybody over thirty-five parked in the row closest to our building. In the middle double row were youngsters with dates. In the outer row were cruisers who arrived in cars filled with all girls or all boys. After ordering a 15-cent Coke or something like that, they'd leave their cars and gather to talk and kibitz between cars. After a while they'd take off and another car would drive into their place. Our curb boys hated to go out there mainly because the studs in the supercars never tipped and they talked rough. On weekends we stayed open until 2 A.M. I dreaded those nights."

(Once-monthly gatherings of retired cruisers and car buffs and their now-ancient vehicles still occur at Chuck-A-Burger. "We play fifties and sixties music on our loudspeakers," says Ron Stille, who drives a 1957 Chevy Bel Air race car to work in good weather. "When we bring in crowds of five hundred to twelve hundred people, that is a good night for Chuck-A-Burger.")

When Ralph Stille died, Ron made a fundamental change. He dropped breakfast, including the popular "Little Cruiser Breakfast"—five silver dollar pancakes and one bacon strip—and the popular "Breakfasts #1, #2, #3, and #4" to focus entirely on lunch and dinner. Ron retains his dad's recipe book crammed with secret sauces and mixes. "If I told you the secret of our Chuck Mix, (basic formula for his trademark Chuck-A-Burgers), I'd have to kill you," Ron says. So the methodology for the popular pizza burger, a product with mozzarella cheese and homemade sauce; the Barbecue Chuck-A-Burger with the creamy coleslaw on top; the basic Chuck-A-Burgers; the Super Chucks; and cheeseburgers—even the homemade chili—is in Ron's little brown book and for his eyes only.

Chuck-A-Burger is rare among local restaurants in that it, along with Sonic, the national drive-in chain, and Charlie's Drive-In in Wood River, Illinois, employs curb girls and has done so continuously since 1957. "Our eight girls work in all kinds of weather," says Ron. "We have two on the lunch shift; in the old days, we had five at lunch. Look at the artwork on our sign out front—there's a female carhop dressed in a poodle skirt that my mother hand-tailored for the girls in the cruisin' days."

Inside Chuck-A-Burger, decorated in red, white, and yellow under a freshly painted ceiling (once coated with nicotine stains before Ron banned smoking), lunchers can sit in booths, at tables, or at the low Formica counter where one can order cherry Cokes, Ron's "real malts" and shakes, or root beer in big mugs. Ron is serious about no smoking. "Generally, when smokers finish eating, they usually sit around and have a cigarette and visit—and we run a fast-food restaurant. My dad was usually blunt with lingering smokers; he'd make a point of gathering up their plates and telling them 'We need this table.'"

Most small restaurants put up art and bric-a-brac and keep them up forever. Not so Chuck-A-Burger. "We spend a lot of time going to garage sales and flea markets on the lookout for nostalgic 1950s and 1960s art and photos," says Ron. "I'll put up the good stuff in the dining room, but remove it in three or four months for something new. One item remains on permanent display, however. I have a picture of Marilyn Monroe at a drive-in eating a hamburger in her car with a curb service tray in the window. My dad always told people it was photographed here in 1957. I've been offered hundreds of dollars for it. I've had to have it wired to the wall."

Chuck-a-Burger

9025 St. Charles Rock Road, St. John, Missouri

 (314) 427-9524

 10 A.M. to close

 Wheelchair accessible

 No smoking

Joe Clark's Restaurant and Bar

Fenton, Missouri

AT JOE CLARK'S Restaurant and Bar in old town Fenton the setting is pure 1950s. Early 1950s. The food is retro, too, and is offered cafeteria-style. There's an elderly steam table where you can select a daily special platter, salad, sides, and dessert. Three permanent sides are available every day by popular demand: freshly mashed potatoes, corn, and green beans. Joe Clark's weathered bar is near the cafeteria line; many customers head that way to select a luncheon beverage.

"When he was around, Joe Clark was picky about too-large servings being dished out on the cafeteria line," says longtime chef Douglas Nitzsche. "When Joe saw an employee giving out too many green beans or carrots, he would snatch the plastic serving spoon from the server and saw the top of the spoon's head off so the stunned employee would learn a lesson and serve less food." From behind the steam table, Nitzsche grabs a Clark-modified spoon and holds it up as living proof.

Clark lived upstairs and was a constant presence until the day he died at eighty-nine in 1989. "One day, a customer came in complaining of a sore tooth. Joe looked at it, then reached in and pulled it out," says Sandy Seemayer, restaurant co-owner with her husband, Mark.

Albert Wallach stops by Joe Clark's daily to read the paper and sip lemonade. Wallach said he complained to Clark in 1975 about unevenness in his false teeth. "Take out your lower plate," Clark told him. "Joe went to the back room with my teeth. He put them on his meat saw and filed them on his sanding wheel. My teeth have felt great ever since." Others recall Clark putting Super Glue on customer's chairs, Saran-Wrapping toilet seats, or slipping hot sauce or shaving lotion into brimming cups of coffee.

Since Clark's passing, the restaurant continues to thrive. Mondays and Wednesdays are the busiest days on the cafeteria line; Fridays are slower, although an active paycheck-cashing window is open off the barroom. Clark's fried chicken, available Monday and Thursday, is the best around, chef Nitzche hears. "I put on a lot of fried breading with spices." It's this combo that does it, he believes. Ham and beans (Monday), meatloaf (Tuesday), BBQ pork steaks (Wednesday), and pork tenderloin (Thursday) sell consistently right behind the fried chicken, says Nitzche of his daily specials. To ensure that your favorite lunch special or entrée is available, however, you had better phone Joe Clark's since "Menu items are subject to change at chef's discretion," as a sign says.

Joe Clark's is divided into three parts: the barroom where most people sit on black chairs at aging Formica tables, a smaller dining room, and the Buggy Room which exhibits a century-old doctor's buggy, a ten-gallon Sieveking Oil Company gasoline pump from a 1940s High Ridge, Missouri service station, and stuffed animal heads that give the restaurant the appearance of a taxidermy studio. Among the stuffed heads is a ram that Mark Seemayer shot; a mountain lion that Joe Clark's son, Dick, shot; a six-point deer that was a gift to Mark from the Fenton city attorney; a Texas longhorn that Mark bought from a pal; an elk that someone gave to Joe; and a boar that was donated by a local taxidermist who lacked space to display it himself.

Clark started his operation as a tavern in 1951, added breakfast in 1953, then followed with lunch and dinner later on (breakfast was discontinued long ago). An early menu sits in a display case. It says: "Clark's Dining Room. Your host, Joseph G. Clark."

As a Fenton alderman for twenty-two years Clark supposedly lent the short-of-funds city $1,000 so it could purchase land for what is now Fenton City Park. Joe was married to the former Eileen Opp, whose parents ran a popular restaurant called Opp's, a few doors east by the old bridge across the Meramec River. Caviar was on the Opp's menu, but its specialty was fried chicken. Some Clark's customers liked to joke that Joe married Eileen for the fried chicken recipe. Opp's is now an American Legion post that features fried chicken dinners.

According to Della Lang's 1992 book, *The Story of Fenton, Missouri*, a crawfish plant occupied the space that became Opp's. It shipped 7,400 pounds of crawfish from the Meramec River in 1909 alone, she wrote. By 1925, when the Meramec Bridge was dedicated by Governor Sam Baker, the plant was history and so were the crawfish. Miss Irene Koch was chosen to christen the bridge—which closed in 2007—but, Lang writes, "the bottle of christening wine mysteriously disappeared before the ceremony. If that sounds a little strange, remember the country was in the midst of Prohibition at the time."

Joe Clark's Restaurant and Bar

42 Gravois Road, Fenton, Missouri

 (636) 343-2177

11 A.M. to 2 P.M. Monday through Friday
4 P.M. to 10 P.M. Monday through Thursday
4 P.M. to 11 P.M. Friday, 11 A.M. to 11 P.M. Saturday
Bar opens at 8 A.M.

Wheelchair accessible

Smoking permitted

42

Crane's Country Store
Williamsburg, Missouri

CRANE'S COUNTRY STORE in the village of Williamsburg, Missouri is swaddled in "accumulation." Since 1926 the Crane family has collected Americana—lamps, airplanes, toy cars, lanterns, dolls and wicker doll buggies, pulleys, pocket knives, coffee grinders, kettles, arrowheads, bear traps—that it hangs, mounts, shelves, and displays in its weathered, patterned-pressed-tin building just north of I-70 in northeast Callaway County. Co-owner Joe Crane calls his vast Americana antique holdings his "accumulation." And speaking of Americana, a stretch of the original U.S. Highway 40 lies in front of Crane's long front porch; two blocks north is County Road 184, which, 200 years ago, was known as the Boonslick Trail, the pathway frequented by Daniel Boone and his peers.

Specializing in men's work clothes, Crane's rooms are jammed with hats, work socks and boots, work and Buzz Off shirts, hardware, feed, hunting and fishing gear, and provisions. The aged store in the middle of Nine-Mile Prairie is the local grocery, polling place, and the spot to buy white Wonder Bread sandwiches cheap.

"Here's the deal," explains Joe Crane, sitting in a well-used, orange-yellow-brown easy chair near the 1927 wood-burning pot-bellied stove in mid-store. "See my cap? On the front is 'Crane's Country Store' and on the back (he removes the grey cap) are the words 'One Meat, One Cheese, One Dollar'. That's our sandwich offering, something we've had for at least fifty years."

On a good day Crane's runs through fifteen loaves of fresh white Wonder Bread and on better days, fifteen loaves more. "The important thing is that we don't vary from our offer," said Joe. "You get a choice of lunch meat such as ham, turkey, roast beef, or 'Williamsburg round steak' which is actually baloney. You can choose the cheese you want; most people pick Colby. And you know what kind of bread you'll get. You do have a choice of mayo or mustard—most people want the mayo. After that: no variation."

"We make little money on our sandwiches because costs have risen so much," states Joe's son, David, a co-owner. "We sell sandwiches to get people in the door. Hopefully they'll buy a coat or a pair of shoes as well.

"We serve our sandwiches on wax paper," David continues. Customers eat them standing by the stove on the worn yellow-pine floor, wandering the showrooms, or sitting on the front porch. Longtime customers sit on chairs by the stove and chat with Joe or David on their breaks from sandwich making.

"To make things clear," says Joe, "we sell no coffee here, no beer, no guns, or no lottery tickets." For coffee, customers must walk up the street to Marlene's Restaurant where, Joe points out, "there is hot food." Marlene is Joe's enterprising wife who also writes *The Williamsburg Villager*, an illuminating gazette of area news, history, and philosophizing.

"We get college teams and buses that stop by for sandwiches; it doesn't faze us," says David. "We tell people not to get in a hurry. We are a slow store, not a quick store. Trucks come off I-70 for sandwiches, sodas, and chips. So do farmers, retirees, junkmen selling scrap steel, sale barn guys, and college students from Mizzou and Westminster. Edward D. Jones, the famous stockbroker, had a home nearby in the 1930s. He was a regular customer, as was his son Edward, and his daughter-in-law, Pat, who still comes in almost every day. This place is kind of a country shrine for Edward Jones employees."

Williamsburg was founded in 1828 and for some unfathomable reason was first called Fruits, a name that thankfully gave way to a more acceptable Williamsburg in 1835. Located nine miles from Loutre River and nine miles from Auxvasse Creek, Williamsburg rests on flat prairie land. Local historians say the village peaked in either 1859 or in 1920 when its population hit one hundred-twenty both years. It now teeters between fifty and sixty.

The store debuted in 1898 as the Harrison and Crane Country Store in nearby Mineola. In 1921 the operation moved to a building in Williamsburg and in 1926 to a second building (the present one) to coincide with the opening of U.S. Highway 40 out its front door.

"When I was a child in the 1930s, we'd come here Saturdays and men sitting on the porch would give us dimes to buy grape or orange soda," says Fay Oden of Auxvasse, sitting on a stove-side chair. "We'd bring in arrowheads we found and the store would give us dimes for them. I'd make dresses from 100-pound bags of chicken feed they sold at Crane's."

As its reputation rose, Crane's attracted wide-eyed tourists from all over. "I took Winston Churchill's daughter, Lady Mary Soames, to Crane's in 2006," says John E. Marshall, a former Westminster College executive and one-time interim president. "She said that she'd never been to anything quite like it."

"Over the years, when international scholars and distinguished guests came to visit the University of Missouri, I often picked them up in St. Louis and drove them to Columbia," says Ron Turner, executive vice president emeritus and founder in 1985 of the University of Missouri South Africa Education Program. "I typically involve a stop at Crane's Store and find my guests enjoy the unique nature of the store and like to compare it with stores in their own countries. One professor from South Africa purchased a nice leather hat and wore it out the door. When I saw him later in South Africa, he told me how much he liked his hat and how he guarded it from his teenage son who wanted to wear it. I also stopped by one day with the provost of Magee College in Derry, Northern Ireland. He liked the quirkiness of Crane's; we often speak of his visit there." (No telling what the visitors thought about what Crane's calls its restrooms—Reuben and Rachel.)

For the record, Crane's Museum (located in the building that contains Marlene's) houses the bulk of the Crane antique accumulation. It includes a life-size 1930s filling station complete with a 1923 Chevrolet touring car and a 1930 Ford Model A. Although the museum is a true gem and worthy of repeat visits, never take your Wonder Bread sandwich there. It's definitely not allowed.

Crane's Country Store
10675 Old Highway 40, Williamsburg, Missouri

 (866) 254-3311

 8 A.M. to 5:45 P.M. Monday through Saturday

 Handicapped ramp in back

 Smoking permitted

43

Dandy Inn

Fairview Heights, Illinois

DANDY INN, THE Irish-operated restaurant on Lincoln Highway in Fairview Heights, Illinois, is the St. Patrick's Day destination for hundreds of Metro-Easters, but if you want to get a sense of this place's heritage and sample the Dave's Fat Man Burger or the Dandy Deluxe pizza in relative peace and quiet, come here any day but March 17. And bring the kids.

"We hand out M&Ms to little kids," says owner Mark Daniel. "If we don't personally give out the M&Ms, the kids who come here regularly know where they are and head straight for the plastic container on the waitress stand.

"A mom and dad brought in their two-and-one-half year-old with a pacifier in her mouth. I said to the kid: 'I'll trade you an M&M for your pacifier.' She said no. I said: 'two M&Ms?' She said no again. I said 'three M&Ms?' She said yes. Later on, her mother called to tell me that after I gave the kid three M&Ms she never used her pacifier again."

During lunch, Dave's Fat Man Burger is wildly popular as are the well-spiced chicken wings, chosen best in the area by the *Riverfront Times* several years ago. "When the waitress asks if you want the wings dipped in the Dandy's sauce, think of it as a declarative not an interrogative and for God's sake, say

Yes," wrote the *Times*. Made-to-order pizzas and wraps (notably the chicken, turkey, and ham and cheddar cheese) are in much demand. Leading the menu's sandwich list is what has become a Metro-East standby—cut-up codfish with "chunks of codfish breaded in our own secret seasonings." "I guess no one around here ever drove over to St. Louis to show them how to cut up cod," says Mark with a grin.

Like other family restaurants, Dandy Inn offers daily lunch specials except on Fridays, "when we are busy with the fish," says Mark. "We have meatloaf, lasagna, roast beef and mashed potatoes, deep-fried pork cutlet, and deep-fried turkey specials." The turkey offering, he adds, is "very unusual in this form."

The Dandy Inn has significant historic footing. When Phyllis and David Daniel bought it from Kate Becherer Roach, last member of the Becherer family that had operated on this patch of land since 1850, they asked Ms. Roach repeatedly: "Are you sure you want to sell and transfer this place out of your family for good?" "It is time," was the seller's reply.

Long after the sale, Kate made one final "visit" to the Dandy Inn. "Kate's funeral procession happened to proceed past the restaurant," says Mark. "Coming through the intersection, the hearse with Kate in it was hit by a car. So, she had to stop temporarily right in front of the restaurant."

In 1850 this corner, known far back as "The Crossroads," was a combined stagecoach stop, general store and tavern run by Henry Becherer (pronounced Becker). Ninian Edwards, first territorial governor of Illinois, may have been the original owner of the land and Edwards's brother-in-law, Abraham Lincoln, may have been an overnight visitor, local lore maintains. The east-west roadway in front of the Becherer business was probably known as the Vincennes to St. Louis highway, according to scholars at the Illinois Public Library in Springfield.

Becherer's original nineteenth century log cabin operation was called Ridge Prairie Saloon. In 1900, Henry Becherer's son, Adam, changed the name to Becherer's Tavern, adding a deli and post office and offering dancing in the pasture out in back for 10 cents a person. On New Year's Day 1934, following the end of Prohibition—during which Adam and his bartenders would gladly pour whiskey into the house drink, root beer, if so requested—Adam opened the present red-brick building with upstairs family living quarters. During World War II, when Adam was in service, his children Adam Jr. and Kate gradually took over the management.

When the Daniels purchased the property in 1976, they renamed it the Dandy Inn, added a beer garden with a fireplace and thirteen oversized picnic tables with green Formica tops, and decided to emphasize St. Patrick's Day.

A digital clock in the barroom counts down the months and days before St. Patrick's Day when Mark sets up a huge tent in the parking lot, makes sure all his food products and beer—he sells a month's worth of beer on this one day—are sufficiently green. "I sometimes get up on the roof and throw T-shirts, hats, and beads to the sea of people on the parking lot," Mark told a reporter. Ironically David Daniel died on St. Patrick's Day, his favorite day of the year. "The priest wore green presiding over Dad's funeral," Mark recalls.

Beyond the St. Patrick's Day tradition, regular customers of Dandy Inn are invited to the restaurant on New Year's Eve, when the place is normally closed. "Everything is free that night," says Mark. "Before we bought this place from the Becherers, they had a policy of inviting all their regular customers in for free hot Tom and Jerrys on Christmas Day."

Dandy Inn
1030 Lincoln Highway, Fairview Heights, Illinois

 (618) 632-8881

11 A.M. to 2 P.M. Monday through Friday
4 P.M. to 10:30 P.M. Monday; 4 to 11 Tuesday through Friday
4 P.M. to 10 P.M. Saturday; noon to 9 P.M. Sunday

Wheelchair accessible

No smoking

44

Ted Drewes Frozen Custard

St. Louis

THE TED DREWES custard stand on Chippewa Street in St. Louis is, in its own scaled-down way, just as much a tourist attraction as is the Arch, the baseball Cardinals, or Forest Park. Beyond a doubt, it is a mandatory stop for aficionados of old U.S. Highway 66 because its location on Chippewa is on a surviving section of the original highway that coursed through St. Louis in the 1940s.

Food and feature writers gravitate to Ted Drewes. *Bon Appetit* magazine in 2004 listed the operation as one of America's ten favorite places for dessert. "Customers retrieve their orders from the walk-up window and then dig in while standing in the parking lot," it commented. America's once most-celebrated food writer, the late R. W. Apple, Jr., of the *New York Times*, said his favorite Ted Drewes offering was the butterscotch sundae, even while acknowledging that the house special is the "concrete…a gravity-defying, extra-thick shake so thick you can turn it upside down without losing a spoonful." In his 2005 book, *Apple's America*, he listed Ted Drewes as "a local eating place of choice."

The owner's business card reads: "Ted Drewes, Inc., Frozen Custard and Christmas Trees. Theodore R. Drewes,

Jr., President." The original red-and-blue neon sign in front of the white clapboard super stand reads: "Ted Drewes Frozen Custard." Ted Drewes, Jr., son of the founder, often hangs out inside the stand cheering on his staff of mostly young and spirited high schoolers; sharing thoughts with son-in-law Travis Dillon, his trusted general manager since 1976; or appearing at a serving window to chat with customers or helping fill take-out orders. Nobody knows how many customers the Drewes operation has accommodated since its 1941 opening on Chippewa. "At least a couple million, more or less," Drewes told the *St. Louis Post-Dispatch* years ago.

Much of the original 1941 building remains, its signature wooden icicles still hanging below the roofline—icicles, writes Quinta Scott in *Along Route 66,* meant "to attract (hot and) sticky summer travelers to the cool, rich taste of (Drewes') frozen custard." "The wooden icicles are originals," Drewes explains, "although we've had to repair them when they started to decay. There were no icicles on our original store on Natural Bridge Road in Pine Lawn when we started in 1929, but we did hang them on our (still existing) Grand Avenue store in 1931. Dad (Ted Drewes, Sr.,) may have been the originator of icicles on custard stands or maybe he copied someone else. I don't know." Drewes' mother, by the way, was the company's first carhop. Back in 1930 she had to compete with tuxedo-clad black male carhops from Ed's Whitefront Bar, located just across the street on Natural Bridge. The Chippewa stand discontinued *its* drive-in service in 1978 after thirty-seven years.

Ted Drewes is not a lunch destination per se, but it does qualify as a lunch spot once removed. "People come here who somehow skipped lunch," says Drewes. "We have a lot of people who have lunch elsewhere and come here for dessert. Other folks come in for an early afternoon snack or a mid-afternoon reward, which I've heard people call 'the Drewes run.'" And people who regularly take the ritual one-mile hike around nearby Francis Park or live in the surrounding St. Louis Hills savor the walk to Ted Drewes to cap their days. Some folks swear that the reason they moved to the neighborhood is its proximity to Ted Drewes.

Up until 1959 the Ted Drewes vanilla custard—totally creamy and abundantly rich—had been dispensed mostly in cones, dishes, sundaes, and shakes. "In 1959 Steve Gamber, a neighborhood kid who was an eighth-grader at Nottingham School came to the window and said 'I want a thicker shake.' So one day I just used straight custard and lots of chocolate and I really made it thick. When I handed it to the kid, I turned it upside down and the kid went nuts. He said, 'Hey, guys, look at this! Ted, what do you call it?' I said, 'Some may call it cement but we'll just call ours concrete.'" And thus was created the concrete milkshake, which now constitutes from forty to fifty percent of sales.

Among the more popular concretes are the plain chocolate, chocolate Oreo, and chocolate chip, which had an intriguing beginning. "In 2003, when Itzhak Perlman was announced as the musical advisor to the Saint Louis Symphony Orchestra, we said: 'Let's introduce a concrete in his honor and use some of the proceeds to donate money to the Symphony.' So we came up with a new flavor, caramel, called 'the Perlman,' and sent one over to him. He said 'I like chocolate chip better.' So the Perlman has become our famous chocolate chip concrete. We still don't have a caramel."

Concretes are so popular—on summer evenings, there are lines ten or twelve people deep at every window with an in-house staff of nearly forty—that Drewes and his crew once decided that it would be a keen sales promotion idea to purchase a big black tub, buy some mix and make real concrete concretes. "We got to making up around four thousand concrete concretes around Christmas time a few years ago." said Drewes. "Our purpose was to wrap a Ted Drewes gift certificate around a real concrete and people could buy them to give as gifts. Once we made up some concrete canoes for the University of Missouri-Rolla rowing crew and put gift certificates around them, too. Nowadays, we make a thousand big concrete concretes and five hundred of the small ones around Christmas time."

Another practice is the Ted Drewes Hall of Fame that recognizes customers who have come to Ted Drewes for decades or who have helped to create favorite dishes. "Most every year we take the twenty-five or so members to lunch at places like Spiro's or Bevo Mill and award them Ted Drewes gift certificates, mostly for concretes," says Drewes. For years, names of Hall of Famers were printed in the *Post-Dispatch* comic section!

Celebrities and politicians have long found Ted Drewes to be a magnet. "Dick Gephardt (the former U.S. congressman) has been a regular here for years," says Drewes. "The late Missouri governor Mel Carnahan stopped by a few nights before his fatal plane crash in November 2000. At the time he was running for the U.S. Senate against John Ashcroft. Later Ashcroft called and said he wanted to come in and learn how to make a concrete. He said that his first job ever was working for a Dairy Queen. One of our managers got hold of John as if he were a young kid applying for a job here. He made John wash his hands, taught him how to scoop the ice cream and so on. In less than five minutes, John got all the concretes right! I said, 'If you don't win, your starting pay will be $9 an hour.' As it turned out, he won."

In early December, Drewes and Dillon turn their attention to Christmas tree sales. Drewes grows its trees on more than 500 acres it owns and manages in Nova Scotia. Drewes has remarked that he began selling trees in the early 1950s when ice cream sales were foundering. "Now, our trees are a tradition," he says. In fact, he adds, some of his regular tree customers don't realize that he also sells ice cream.

Ted Drewes Frozen Custard
6725 Chippewa Street, St. Louis

 (314) 481-2562

 11 A.M. to midnight daily
(Limited winter hours)

 Wheelchair accessible

45

Failoni's Café

St. Louis

ROSE FAILONI, BLESS her memory, lives on at Failoni's Café. Her black-and-white, no-nonsense 1950 photograph is mounted behind the bar where her grandson dispenses beer, booze, and Frank Sinatra songs. Her lunchtime pasta and salad recipes are still followed by her daughter-in-law, Rosemary. Stories about Rose—those printable—are still told.

"Rose, of course, was a staunch Catholic," says Rosemary. "She refused to sell anything but fish on Friday. When someone ordered beef, she approached them with the question: 'Did you forget that this is Friday?' She also refused to serve French fries because they created too much grease and dirtied up her kitchen.

"When a man came in with what may have been his girlfriend," Rosemary continued, "Rose would sometimes rush from the kitchen and say to the man: 'What are you doing with her? Your wife is much prettier than she is.'

"On Tuesdays, Rose always had a meatloaf special. When someone ordered hamburger, she wouldn't serve it. 'You can't have hamburgers because meatloaf is just the same,' she told people. So if you really wanted hamburger you'd get meatloaf on a bun. Rose didn't know the difference."

Failoni's, then as now, has held to high moral standards. Rosemary remembers when Joe Failoni, her brother-in-law, ran the bar. "If a woman came in and stood at the bar and if she was not escorted by a date or her husband, she was asked to leave. That policy was intact for years."

Failoni's has a special niche in St. Louis restaurant history. It is the restaurant that has been in the same spot longer than any of its peers—since 1916 when ancestral Failoni's bought the tavern from Lemp Brewing Company. Hearsay has it that the tavern was first named Muldoon's.

During Prohibition, Failoni's operated as a soft drink parlor but derived its main revenue as a speakeasy. "We served food at the beginning at a cost of about 25 cents," Joe Failoni told the *St. Louis Globe Democrat* in 1945. "But we often gave away more food than we sold. Food was the draw for the beer and liquor sales."

When Prohibition ended in 1933, Failoni's lengthened its lunch menu, attracting workers from Scullin Steel Company and St. Louis Rolling Mill across the street. Business flourished for decades until 1980 when Scullin Steel closed down. "Suddenly Failoni's became a very quiet place," says Rosemary.

After sixty-four years in business, Failoni's had to reinvent itself. Rosemary's husband, Alex, hired Don Kotzman, an accordionist, to play during the lunch hour. "Sometimes the place was so quiet that Don played for free, pretending he was merely practicing," says Rosemary. Kotzman, it turns out, was pivotal to Failoni's resurrection. "He told us all that we should be singing to our customers," says Rosemary. "My brother, Alex Jr., didn't know he could sing until Don badgered him," says Victor, the non-singing Failoni. "I am now the Frank Sinatra of St. Louis," Alex told me one day.

On Thursday afternoon during Failoni's now-legendary "Four-Hour Fantasy" from 1 P.M. to 5 P.M. and now stretched to 10 P.M., Alex Jr.—from behind the bar—will do two or three sets of Sinatra ballads. His father, Alex Sr., will most likely render the Julius La Rosa 1953 gold-record hit, "Eh, Cumpari" (meaning Hey, Neighbor!) and Rosemary, who has church choir and a cappella experience, will sing a few pop tunes of her own. The Failoni clan is joined by vocalist Cindy "Beno" Ankelman who follows former Failoni's popular chanteuses Mary Daly, Anita Rosamun, and Zoe Ann Eidson. Over many years, salesmen, sportsmen, retirees, and Failoni lunchtime regulars made up the audience, laughing, singing along, drinking beer, ordering barbecued ribs and pork steaks produced by Alex Sr. on the patio grill or lunch specials produced by Rosemary.

Failoni's Café
6715 Manchester Avenue, St. Louis

 (314) 781-5221

 11 A.M. to 2:45 P.M. Monday through Friday (lunch)
7 A.M. to 9 P.M. Monday, 7 A.M. to 1:30 A.M. Friday

 Wheelchair accessible

Smoking permitted

46

Joe Fassi Sausage & Sandwich Factory
St. Louis

SUNDAY IS MOSTLY a day of rest and churchgoing for residents of St. Louis's acclaimed Italian district, The Hill. Most of the popular restaurants and cafes are closed around Sunday noon, but not the Joe Fassi Sausage & Sandwich Factory.

"The people who come here on Sunday are mostly tourists who drive around The Hill and discover that we're open," says owner Tom Coll, Jr., Joe Fassi's grandson who took over the tavern and market in 1992 and renamed it. "Ninety percent of our Sunday customers are from out of town. We sell a ton of meatball and Italian sausage sandwiches on Sunday plus a lot of pasta."

Inside the rejuvenated Fassi's is a wall of fame that honors two baseball legends, Yogi Berra and Joe Garagiola, who were raised on nearby Elizabeth Avenue in the 1930s and 1940s. On most evenings Yogi and Joe would walk to Fassi's Market to fetch cans of beer for their fathers when they returned home from work. "As soon as they heard the whistle from the factory, kids would hustle to Fassi's for beer. We filled about fifty pails a day," recalls Tom's dad, Tom Coll, Sr.

"When we decided to put up our wall, Joe gave us a baseball bat and Yogi signed a ball," says Coll, Jr. "Yogi's sister gave us a 1956 World Series plaque. We added news clippings, trophies, and other things. On the day the wall was unveiled, sportscaster Bob Costas came in for lunch and so did Joe and Yogi. We made them risotto and served it with red wine and garlic sausages and a salad on the side."

Fassi's menu lists twenty-three nine-inch hot and cold sandwiches. Among them, the meatball sandwich, assembled with Mrs. Joe Fassi's recipe, sells the most. "We go through nearly ninety pounds of meatballs a week," says Coll. "The secret to their success is the garlic. For every ten pounds of meatballs, we put in six ounces of garlic."

Second in popularity, the salsiccia (Italian for sausage) sandwich is "The Best in St. Louis," says the menu. Butcher Louis Fassi, Tom's great uncle, wrote the original recipe for the sausage mix. Coll personally cuts, grinds, stuffs, hand-ties, and pressure cooks his sausages. "I can pop out about two hundred pounds a week," says Coll. "Our neighbors on The Hill know when to come in when the sausage is fresh—on Monday mornings and Thursday afternoons."

"John Carney's Supreme" is another sure-selling sandwich. Carney, the KMOX radio personality, "came in asking for a sandwich that combined red wine and garlic sausage, tomato sauce, pepper cheese, onion, and mustard," says Coll. "John asked for the sandwich so often that we named it for him."

Fassi's building dates to 1927 when Joe Fassi Sr.'s parents, Paul and Rose, moved in upstairs and began a period of family occupation that lasted through 1976 when Joe's grandmother, Rose, died. Joe Fassi, by the way, never worked much at the family business. For most of his life, Joe labored at the neighboring brickyard. After retirement, Joe worked behind Fassi's bar.

"Every Sunday, the whole family came to the family quarters for dinner," says Rosemarie Coll, Joe's sister and Tom Jr.'s mother. "Usually we had Italian rice and some form of chicken. There was always a salad because we had a vegetable garden out back. Also out in back was a chicken house. World War II rationing meant that we could sell only one chicken to a household. Neighborhood ladies came in to pick out a chicken; we would then take the chicken to the basement and strangle it. It was the same with rabbits. There is still a rabbit house in back.

"During the war, men from the neighborhood helped us cook fish, sausage, or corned beef in the basement. Men from the local packing house would 'drop off' packages of hot dogs at the tavern so our customers could have a free lunch so long as they paid for their beer."

For years, Rosemarie continues, "We never had an 'employee' here, just family. On Friday night, the staff would work until nine and everybody went upstairs to eat. When you worked here as family, your pay was a salami sandwich. If you stuck around and helped mix the sausage by hand, your pay was dinner. Our first real employee was when we opened as a deli in 1992."

Joe Fassi Sausage & Sandwich Factory
2323 Sublette Avenue, St. Louis

 (314) 481-2626

 10 A.M. to 5 P.M. Monday through Saturday
11 A.M. to 4 P.M. Sunday

 Wheelchair accessible

No smoking

Fatted Calf

Clayton, Missouri

THE FATTED CALF in Clayton is the oldest Fatted Calf restaurant in America; it is also the only Fatted Calf. Its primary product, the calf burger, is as edible now as it was in 1966 when the Fatted Calf stores first opened.

Two St. Louis food icons, Vincent and Anthony Bommarito, opened the first Fatted Calf at Tenth and Locust in downtown St. Louis and featured the one-third-pound, fresh-ground choice beef charbroiled calf burger and sibling cheddarburgers and bleuburgers.

"We used to do a thousand customers a day at our first location," recalls Vincent Bommarito, who owns Tony's, downtown's foremost restaurant. "You would see people line up around the room and outside the door. Everybody ate a hamburger in those days and lots of people ate one every day. We had an egg bun that was so popular that the football Cardinals would call in orders for one hundred-twenty-five calf burgers on those soft buns for players and staff. That experience we had at Fatted Calf was lovely; it was great, innovative fun." (By the way, the same calf burger formula is applied to the burger at the Vincent Bommarito-owned Anthony's Bar. The calf burger also influenced the six-ounce Dooleyburger at the now-closed Dooley's Ltd., a perennial downtown St. Louis fixture. Alex Dooley managed the first Fatted Calf.)

The Fatted Calf became a modest five-location local chain that included a cafeteria-style store at 12 South Bemiston in Clayton that opened in 1969. Eventually the Bommaritos sold their stores to American Snacks Corporation in Boston, which expanded the chain to twenty branches coast-to-coast including one in Chicago's Sears Tower. By 1985, American Snacks, in financial distress, had closed all the stores except the one in Clayton. "That Clayton outlet hung in there, but the manager got sick and American Snacks wanted to get rid of it, too," said Kathy Sellenreich, who managed the Clayton store from 1972 to 1976 while attending Fontbonne College. In 1987, when Sellenreich was district manager of another restaurant chain, The Lettuce Leaf, she decided the opportunity to own her own restaurant was too promising to avoid so she bought the Clayton Fatted Calf.

"This restaurant is like an old English pub," Sellenreich would say. "The Bommaritos went to England to research how to decorate it."

Many of the restaurant's mostly round tables are of custom-made solid oak. The original pewter mugs hanging by the front entrance are battened down to forestall theft, a problem in earlier days. And this is St. Louis's only restaurant with decorative trash bins along the walls.

Each hallmark burger is cooked to order, from extra raw to extra well done. "We recommend the medium burger, our best seller," Sellenreich advised. "Our mushroom and cheese toppings are popular. We have one man who gets two bottom buns for his calf burgers so he can order double portions of mushrooms and cheese. He needs the extra bun to absorb all the rich juices from the toppings.

"People love our onion rings, which we don't cook until you order them. They don't just sit around. And steak fries sell big here. We buy only the best-prepared steak fries on the market. Our salads are fresh every day—we never use bad lettuce. We make all our own dressings except the French. Our Parmesan vinaigrette is the best seller. We also make our own coleslaw daily because coleslaw only holds for 24 hours."

One strong departure from the Fatted Calf norm was Sellenreich's introduction of a charbroiled swordsteak sandwich. "When I bought Fatted Calf, all they had were burgers and fried fish," Sellenreich recounts. "I know that I had to add lighter, healthier foods." She said the swordfish, as well as the charbroiled tuna steak, grill well. On the other hand, customers like the deep-fried deluxe fish sandwich because "it is price-oriented. People are afraid of swordfish sometimes because it sounds exotic."

In early 2008 Sellenreich surprised the food community when she announced her intention to sell her proprety and return to teaching. At first there was speculation that the Bommaritos might purchase Fatted Calf. Later Sellenreich said that she had sold the place to Jason and Kathleen Portman, local restaurant managers with spotless credentials. ""We're keeping the Fatted Calf much like we found it and that means sticking with much of the food offerings," said Kathleen Portman.

"We are known locally as a neighborhood restaurant," Sellenreich would explain, "but we draw from all over. We're known as a place in the neighborhood where kids can get their first jobs. Kids can work here and then get home at 8:30 or 9 to do homework. We're closed Sundays and holidays. Parents know their kids are in a safe environment here."

So strong is the sentimental attachment to Fatted Calf that two Clayton High School classes—1970 and 1972—held their reunion mixers at the restaurant. And employee longevity is extraordinary. Busboy Tom Schmid, for example, has been a staff member since 1987. "People come back from out of town and say they can't believe that Fatted Calf is still here and that most of our the employees are the same," Sellenreich said.

An architectural note: next door at 14 S. Bemiston is International Diamond, Incorporated, a building with a black marble face. According to St. Louis architect William Bowersox, a Fatted Calf fan for decades, the building was designed by noted American architect Cesar Pelli, who went on to do the U.S. embassy in Tokyo and the World Financial Center in New York.

Fatted Calf

12 S. Bemiston, Clayton, Missouri

 (314) 726-1141

 11 A.M. to 8 P.M. Monday through Saturday

 Wheelchair accessible

 No smoking

48

Fischer's Restaurant
Belleville, Illinois

THE BELLEVILLE, ILLINOIS chamber of commerce touts the city's 98-block Main Street as the longest Main Street in America.

One of the oldest businesses on Main Street is Fischer's Restaurant, which started in 1935 as an ice cream store, added plate lunches and sandwiches in 1937, then moved west on Main Street in 1941 as the Dutch Girl Drive-In. After World War II, the restaurant became Fischer's.

Owner Ken Fischer has been a Main Street fixture since 1935 when he helped his dad, Ardel, scoop ice cream at the original shop. "I'm here every day," says Ken, who thinks nothing of making sandwiches or frying chicken when his kitchen crew is overly burdened. "I can cook anything on the menu," Ken once told a reporter. Every Friday morning for nearly forty years Ken has stirred up three to five gallons of clam chowder, a mix that's usually gone by day's end. He doesn't make the acclaimed Fischer's cheeseburger soup, always a sure sell-out when it's on the menu, but he's proud of the recipe. "Does your cheeseburger soup incorporate the bun?" I asked. "It tastes just like a real cheeseburger," Ken replied with a grin, "but I can't tell you what we do with the bun."

The bulk of Fischer's sandwich, salad, soup, chili, and lunch specials are throwbacks to 1941 when Ken's dad developed the hamburger, fried chicken, and shrimp baskets for the drive-in. Their "descendants" and their "offspring" are on today's menu that includes enduring sandwiches such as the beef patty Fischerburgers, the ham-and-cheese Monte Cristos, and the Reubens, endowed with bottom round corned beef, sauerkraut, and Swiss cheese.

And don't forget the art deco-era rarebit sandwich. Fischer's defines it as "broiled turkey topped with a rarebit sauce, bacon, and tomato." Beyond the sandwich form, the rarebit can be ordered in a casserole dish, too. "It's very good with French fries," adds Annette Fischer, Ken's daughter and a restaurant manager.

Fischer's has long been grateful for its fan base. "My grandpa started our annual customer appreciation week forty years ago," says Annette. "We always have it from Monday through Thursday evening during the first full week in January. Anywhere from twelve hundred to fifteen hundred of our customers come in for our eight-ounce filet mignon that we sell for $9. They also get an Italian salad and a Kaiser roll."

"We are also known for our funeral lunch business, which can be brisk," says Corea Buck, general manager. "For instance, on one Sunday we looked at our calendar and saw little ahead. But by Monday we had seven funerals lined up. We usually suggest to the families that they order our salad and sandwich buffet that features roast beef and fried chicken. We always put our funeral people in one of our nine party rooms."

Fischer's, for its size (perhaps the busiest restaurant in St. Clair County) and breadth (it serves breakfast, lunch, and dinner seven days a week, caters widely, and fills its party rooms with regularity), has but one signature dish: turtle ice cream pie. "We make the butter pecan ice cream ourselves and add our own fudge sauce, caramel mix, and the pecans," says Ken. Fischer's runs through ten turtle pies a week, eight slices per pie.

During the lunch hour, Ken sits at Table 41 near the kitchen where he can answer any summons for help or see who's entering the dining room who needs a greeting or a hug. "One thing I don't do with many of my elderly customers," says Ken, "is ask them how they are. We don't ask because we don't have time to listen!"

The round Table 45 in the main dining room is the celebrity or official guest table. "Ronald Reagan was here for a speech and sat at Table 45," recalls Ken. "Our waitress was so thrilled to serve him that she spilled gravy on his suit jacket. We never saw her again. Milton Berle once ate dinner and had a cigar at Table 45. Phil Donahue, Rory Calhoun, Whitey Herzog, and Tommy Lasorda and all the Illinois governors since the 1940s have sat there."

Fischer's, a warm and restful place vaguely reminiscent of the old Schneithorst's restaurant in west St. Louis County, is garnished in deep burgundies, greens, and purples. White tablecloths cover its tables; rolling casters support its barrel chairs. "We have pushed some elderly ladies on those chairs from the main dining room to their card-playing rooms," says Ken. "They're like wheelchairs."

Fischer's Restaurant
2100 W. Main Street, Belleville, Illinois

 (618) 233-1131

 7 A.M. to 11 P.M. daily

 Wheelchair accessible

 No smoking

49

Frank & Helen's Pizzeria

University City, Missouri

I F YOU WANT to save yourself a trip into St. Louis to visit everyone's favorite ice cream shop, you can drive straight to Frank & Helen's, a 1950s-style pizza and broasted chicken joint in University City, and order a dish of Crown Candy ice cream, including black walnut and Oreo. The deal is that F&H owner Scott De Polito's father has a sister who married into the Karandjeff family that owns Crown Candy. On Fridays, the dad, James De Polito, who bakes the lasagna and makes the marinara sauce, is dispatched to Crown Candy to pick up the weekly order of eight gallons.

Scott De Polito says that—besides kinfolk—his place and Crown Candy share another menu item: no-bean chili. "We're one of the few places in town that has chili with no beans but heavy amounts of ground beef that makes up for the absence of beans."

One claim that Crown Candy can't make but that Frank & Helen's can is that F&H is lodged in a structure that was built in the late 1950s as Siwak's Automatic Car Wash. "Dirty cars would come around back and drive from north to south in the wash lane that now houses our kitchen and half the dining room," says De Polito.

In 1965, Frank Seitz and his sister, Helen, moved their Frank's Pizzeria from Olive and Midland where they had started up in 1956 to the vacant car wash. They transformed the building into what is now a University City dining destination.

There are no car wash relics left at Frank & Helen's, but reminders of the 1950s are everywhere: golden oldies play on the radio; comfortable light-blue booths line the east and west sides of the dining room, which is filled with out-of-stock white Formica-top tables. Café curtains hang in the windows. A unique vestibule contains a well-worn black leather sofa, candy machines, and a large banner for the University City Lions Club that meets at the restaurant twice monthly.

"This is a fifties place, not a sixties place," emphasizes De Polito, who bought the business in 1997 after serving ten years as a University City policeman. "A lot of people who come in here still know what things looked like in the 1950s. To them, there is an attachment in their minds to those years. We like to pack people in here so they're closer to their neighbors. That's part of our intimacy. Everyone seems to enjoy the same kind of experience in here, if you know what I mean."

A long wall of mirrors spans the west side of the dining room—twelve four-foot glass panels that require constant cleaning. "We clean the mirrors every day," says De Polito. "We do touchups in between because kids can really smear the glass." Because it's an arduous task, De Polito and his employees rotate the cleaning assignments.

(A popular local poet who frequented Frank & Helen's mentioned the mirrors in a poem. The late Constance Urdang, who ran the writer's program at Washington University, wrote: "America rediscovers itself … in the mirrors behind the booths where time has been arrested and everything Remains what we recall, as Frank—or Helen—dreamed it. Here we are all fed, we can all love one another.")

People come to Frank & Helen's for pizza and chicken. At lunch, Broasted chicken is popular; so is the eight-inch pizza with one allowable ingredient that usually turns out to be pepperoni, and the lunch-only eight-ravioli platter. The "Geniune Broasted Chicken" is prepared in a pressurized deep-fry cooker with special flouring, seasoning, and marinade supplied by the Broaster Company, Beloit, Wisconsin. "You have to be a licensed commercial food service operator in order to sell Broasted," explains De Polito. Frank & Helen's is currently the only restaurant on the Missouri side of the Mississippi that offers Broasted. For your information, Broaster's website reveals that Mr. L. A. M. Phelan, who invented the Broaster pressure fryer, also invented the first automatic toilet. Frank & Helen's restrooms have the manual kind.

Chicken, Broasted and non-Broasted, nearly overruns the lunch menu. Chicken tender salad is the most ordered salad; the chicken Parmesan sandwich plate sells well; the chicken club sandwich is the sandwich leader. "Some people come in just to order a drumstick," says De Polito. "When they do, they also get a slice of French bread. Others come in and order a pizza and then request a single thigh with it. Or somebody comes in with a young kid so they order the kid a drumstick."

For years, Kremer's Tavern, which closed in 2005, was Frank & Helen's next-door neighbor. Kremer's served a popular open-face meatloaf platter and memorable daily specials. Their bartender-waitress once recited the daily specials to me until she reached Thursday. "Pot roast is on the Thursday special," she said, "unless our chef forgot to turn on the crockpot."

Kremer's owner, Grace Rasor, dressed in her best finery, invited her smartly attired friends in for lunch at her special table for two on most weekdays. Each September, Rasor sponsored a customer appreciation day when Dick Lurk, "one of our great customers," as she used to say, "came in to roast a pig."

"Gosh," reflects De Polito. "I hope that when we decided to start up lunch a while ago we didn't put Kremer's out of business." He didn't; it turns out that it was Kremer's time to close shop.

Frank & Helen's Pizzeria
8111 Olive Blvd, University City

☎ (314) 997-0066

🕐 11 A.M. to 10 P.M. Tuesday through Friday
    4 P.M. to 10 P.M. Friday, 4 P.M. to 9 P.M. Saturday

♿ Wheelchair accessible

🚬 Smoking permitted

50

Fresh Gatherings Café
St. Louis

INSTITUTIONAL LOANS OR personal savings typically finance new restaurant start-ups.

On the St. Louis University (SLU) medical campus on South Grand Blvd., however, Fresh Gatherings Café was financed by a hard-to-obtain "curiosity" grant, seed money intended to develop a student-run cafeteria.

Initially the anomalous eatery in the Edward and Margaret Doisy School of Allied Health Professions was given a concept name, Billiken Boulangerie (bakery), but that handle didn't exactly express its originators' intention to involve students and to buy locally and organic. So in November 2004 Fresh Gatherings, which did, set sail with a short cafeteria line, table seating for one hundred-fifty, and "culinary aspect" students from the dietetics and nutrition program fully engaged in the fledgling operation.

Mark E. Miller, chef of the year in 2000 of the prestigious St. Louis Chef de Cuisine organization and the former executive chef of Westborough Country Club in Webster Groves, was one of the original grant-seekers, along with Eddie Neil, who ran Café Provencal restaurant and who was on the premises during the café's debut year. Miller has remained on board as manager, executive chef, and head of the twenty-five-student culinary program.

Miller is part of what he calls "the only university dietetics and nutrition department in the United States with a strong culinary aspect," which in everyday parlance means "restaurant." "Usually dietetics programs are science-based and provide little knowledge of food," Miller explains.

At the lunch hour, medical and nursing students as well as students and staffers from the main SLU campus, one mile north, fill Miller's dining room. "People come here for quality meals that are wholesome and taste good," Miller says. The dining room is open to the public.

Miller himself helps make Fresh Gatherings' hearty soups. "We go through eight to ten gallons of soup in an hour-and-a-half," he reports. The wild mushroom and smoked Gouda cheese soups are highly sought-after, as are the chicken barley and broccoli cheddar soups. Miller gets his shiitake mushrooms from an Ozarks mushroom farm. Free-range chickens for his soups come from Benne's Best Meat, described as "a 127-acre farm in the city" in St. Charles County. Operated by family members since 1801, the Benne farm raises "natural" pork, beef, and poultry "without the use of sub-therapeutic antibiotics or artificial growth hormones." That's the kind of vendor Miller admires.

"In cooler months, black bean soup is popular," adds Miller. "We get our black beans from a local bean farmer. Today, we went through all of our clam chowder, half the bean, and already we're out of broccoli cheddar," he said on a typical day in the cafeteria.

"Our salad bar is not just another salad bar; ours has new and exciting things throughout each season," Miller says. "We get different varieties of beets, lettuces, greens, or radishes that you may find at some farmers' markets but not at any grocery store or supermarket. Our salad offerings represent peak freshness and they haven't traveled 2,000 miles to get here."

Although Miller is not heavily into meats, he is proud of his beef taco salad. "Our beef is farm-raised at Benne's Best Meat—and just for our taco salad!" he exclaims.

Miller often sells out his chicken and tuna salad wraps and entrées such as spaghetti and meatballs and lasagna. Whenever he prepares an entrée that incorporates the beautiful purple asparagus or striking sweet potatoes he buys from Arlene Kruse's farm in Columbia, Illinois, there's usually nothing left in the pan. Students in the program's baking class make all the breads, muffins, rolls, and pastries sold at Fresh Gatherings.

Whenever he can in his food creations, Miller uses multiple herbs. "We have an herb garden right outside the dining room window for quick snip; our main vegetable garden is a block or so away at Rutger and Compton," he says. In the summer, students decorate the dining room tables with flowering dill, basil, or Italian flat-leaf parsley, all conveniently quick-snipped.

Green plastics, sugar cane-reed dishware, and cornstarch and wooden utensils used in the cafeteria and in food preparation are environmentally safe and decompose naturally, says a brochure that the cafe circulates. "Our cups and utensils will not stay in the ground for one hundred years but only for nine months or so before they degrade," amplifies Miller. "We are not only farmer-friendly here, we're earth-friendly."

Fresh Gatherings has spread into the community. It recently completed a U.S. Department of Agriculture grant to teach youngsters in inner-city St. Louis schools how to plant vegetable gardens and enjoy fresh produce. A partnership with schools in Maplewood and Richmond Heights to teach nutrition and develop vegetable gardens is underway.

Miller coolly expounds on an occupational sideline: ice-carving. "In 1996, I was on the international team that placed fourth in the ice carving world championship held in Japan," he says. A few years earlier, his team took first place at the national ice carving championship in Chicago. He has taught ice-carving classes at Forest Park Community College and demonstrates carving at hospitals, schools, and day care centers around town. He's serious about his sideline. "I am a member of the Japan Ice Sculptors Association and the National Ice Carving Association here in the states," he says.

Fresh Gatherings Café
3437 Caroline, St. Louis

 (314) 977-8523

 7:30 A.M. to 6 P.M. Monday through Friday

 Wheelchair accessible

 No smoking

51

Geno's 140 Club

Bethalto, Illinois

AT GENO'S, A pond-raised crappie sandwich comes lightly breaded atop two pieces of rye bread with a big onion slice and a tiny cup of tartar sauce. It is delicious. "What pond was this crappie raised on?" I asked the waitress. "A nice clear one, I hope," she replied. Later, noting that my wife had quickly reduced a meltingly tender boneless barbecue beef sandwich, the waitress returned. "You didn't ask us 'How's everything' like they do in most restaurants," I said. "I didn't have to," she said. "I already knew by looking at youse two." Feisty, friendly banter between servers and the served happens daily here.

Geno's savors its customers. When Dennis Cooper, co-owner with his wife, Sandi, is around, he stations himself at the front door to thank customers as they leave. "It's common courtesy," he says. "I've been saying thank-you since day one. I usually add: 'Come back and see us.' It also says that on our printed receipts."

Geno's sells more than its share of rib-eye sandwiches, half-pound hamburgers, and breaded or grilled pork tenderloin sandwiches. A house specialty is the stromboli, pizza dough wrapped around cheese, pepperoni, or some other meat. "We bought a $20,000 oven to make stromboli," said

Dennis. "When it leaves the oven, it looks like rolled-up pizza. They come in large and small sizes. We even have a six-inch personal stromboli for kids. All kids who visit Geno's receive suckers. Some parents tell us they can't drive past here without their kids saying 'Stop and get us some suckers.' A waitress will sometimes take a bouquet of suckers to a table with kids. Those suckers have been good for our business."

Cooper, past president of the Illinois Licensed Beverage Association and board member of the national licensed beverage group, is not only friendly; he is loyal. Sandi says that around the time she and Dennis married in 1963, Dennis and his buddies from the Bethalto High School class of 1961 would hang out at Geno's, sometimes from 10 A.M. to 4 P.M., when its then-owner, Lenore Floriana, would tell them "It's food time and you all have to leave." "His classmates still come in," says Sandi. "Everybody says that Dennis bought the place because Lenore threw them out so many times." The classmates prefer to sit in the bar section at "The Drinking Table."

After founder Geno Floriana died in 1964, Lenore re-married and is now Lenore Hayley, in her late eighties and still a presence at Geno's. In the recent past, she would arrive at Geno's at 6:30 A.M. to wipe down the bar, serve morning beer to the hearty, chat with salesmen, and reminisce. When she left around noon, she took home a load of blue bar towels to wash and return the next day.

In 1937, Lenore and Geno lived upstairs at their grocery store, a place they later converted to a tavern called the 140 Club, which gradually was transformed into a full-fledged restaurant. "We sold Geno's a couple of times, but we always purchased it again. I kept the place up myself until the Coopers bought it in 1983," says Lenore.

In the 1930s, Geno's mother, Delphina Floriana, called "Big Momma," did much of the cooking. "She would take us down the basement and feed us her homemade tortellini and ravioli at a big table," remembers Lenore, who adds that recipes and sauces for Geno's popular spaghetti, ravioli, lasagna, and chicken and dumplings originated with Big Momma.

In more wide-open days, Lenore recalls, "Three SIU-Edwardsville students took off all their clothes in their car and streaked through our dining area; Rich Winslow rode his horse through the place, and a fellow rode his motorcycle into the barroom then left when we told him his dad, who was justice of the peace, was eating in the middle dining room. One day a man came in with a large box. I opened it and a large turkey flew out. We caught it and Big Momma made us a great turkey dinner."

Geno's suffered a major fire in 1983, re-opening in 1984 under the Coopers' ownership. "Our back bar was completely ruined, but Lenore had photographs of what everything looked like before," says Dennis. "People came in and asked how we managed to save the back bar; we had to tell them it was a new and brilliant reproduction." Original features remain, such as the brown terrazzo floor in the barroom and Booth 6 between the barroom and the main dining room. This lone booth is love-nesty. One couple, Jim and Ruth Balmer, met in Booth 6 and eventually married, reports Dennis. "Every year on their anniversary they return to Booth 6; we supply flowers and candles."

As we have noted, the Coopers have a penchant for hiring staffers who can be pretty frank and forthright. "Once we had a rule that if the food didn't look right to the waitress, she didn't have to serve it," says Dennis. "So one day our waitress told the cook 'I'm not carrying this plate of spaghetti out to the customer.' When the cook balked, she picked up the spaghetti and threw it in his face." That rule was soon modified.

Geno's 140 Club
120 W. Bethalto Drive, Bethalto, Illinois

☎ (618) 377-9394

🕐 11 A.M. to 10 P.M. Monday through Thursday
11 A.M. to 11 P.M. Friday and Saturday
11:30 A.M. to 10 P.M. Sunday

♿ Wheelchair accessible

🚭 No smoking

52

Gioia's Deli

St. Louis

IN THE 1940s Emil Garavaglia, a student at St. Ambrose School, wore a white shirt and tie to work on Saturdays at Gioia's Grocery at Macklind and Daggett on The Hill, St. Louis's renowned Italian neighborhood.

"All the males at Gioia's, and that includes the butcher, wore white shirts and ties on Saturday because that was the day the old ladies came in to pay their bills," recalls Garavaglia. "During the Depression and into World War II the women would charge their groceries all week and then Poppa would bring his paycheck home on Friday and the old lady would be in Saturday to settle her bill—and to get enough groceries, including a chicken live or dressed out, for their big meal on Sunday, when we were closed."

Garavaglia remembers being directed to Gioia's chicken coop out back, something he might do twenty or more times on Saturday. "I'd go to the coop, pick out a chicken, wring its neck, and bring it in to Aunt Teresa (Gioia) who would have one of her grown sons cut the head off. Then she dipped the chicken in boiling water, plucked the feathers, gutted it, and dressed it out. Then we'd sell it to a customer. This same thing happened at small groceries all over The Hill in those days."

Then as now at Gioia's the most popular food item was the hot salami.

In the early days of Gioia's Grocery, neighbors came in for hot salami, offered only on Wednesdays and Saturdays. "Most people would buy a loaf of bread, order their salami, and take it home," Garavaglia said.

Gioia's was founded by Charles "Challie" Gioia who came to America from Marcellano, Italy before World War I. He and his wife, Teresa, purchased the former Pellegrini's Grocery, like so many other structures on The Hill reportedly built with materials salvaged from the 1904 St. Louis World's Fair. One irreplaceable possession that Challie brought from Italy was the recipe for hot salami.

"The Gioias were a beautiful family," says Eleanor Berra Marfisi, author of *The Hill: Its History-Its Recipes* and a close neighbor of Gioia's Deli. "During the Depression any family on The Hill with financial difficulty could come to Gioia's where Challie would give them food and keep their names in a little book. Whenever they could pay him back, they did. It was sheer trust on the part of Gioia's."

"I remember Challie's son, Steve, who took over his dad's store with his brother, Johnny, saying to customers: 'You came in for your penicillin, I see.'" recalled Garavaglia. That was the hot salami sandwich that Gioia's began selling customers in the 1960s and 1970s. Steve would tell everybody that hot salami was like penicillin—it could cure everything." "It will put hair on your chest," Johnny would add.

Gioia's Grocery has been Gioia's Deli since 1980 when Cathy Conley responded to a small "For Sale" sign in Gioia's window. "I am proud to say that I am only the second owner of Gioia's since 1918," says Conley.

The new owner's first task was to remove grocery shelves and aisles, re-start the corner place as a sandwich shop-deli, and continue Gioia's hot salami tradition.

Everybody seems happy with the deli arrangement, even Challie's youngest daughter, Mary Gioia Felix, who visits Gioia's most Saturdays to treat any available niece, nephew, or granddaughter to a round of hot salami.

"Eighty percent of our lunch customers—we only serve lunch—order hot salami," reports Conley. "We make it every day instead of only twice a week. Challie and his sons would be astounded to hear that Gioia's goes through 700 pounds of salami a week. We serve fresh-sliced hot salami as an Italian sub on long French bread although some customers buy whole rolls of salami that they take home to cook themselves. We make between three hundred and five hundred sandwiches a day for walk-ins and on some days we cater two hundred to three hundred box lunches for delivery. Most customers want their hot salami all by itself in a sub, but others like a combination of hot salami and hot roast beef and still others prefer the Italian trio sub, a mix of Genova and mortadello sausages with the salami."

First-timers should not get the impression that Gioia's is all salami. "Our hot roast beef sandwich is amazing," Conley claims. "We bake our own roast beef—it's not pre-cooked like you get at so many other places." Conley offers homemade lasagna ("a must try" the menu says) as well as hand-rolled meatballs and chicken and tuna salads.

"A lot of our sandwiches got started because customers requested them," Conley says. "I made up the 'Trio' myself when I was pregnant. Most of our sandwich ingredients come from here on The Hill: salsiccia from De Gregorio's Market, bread from Fazio's Bakery, and mortadello and Genova sausages from Volpi's. Our salad dressing is called Roma—it is from the Imo family and they are headquartered here on The Hill."

Customers order at a high counter, sit at clear plastic tables, and pay as they leave. At the cash register, Dad's Old Fashioned oatmeal cookies and fudge brownies are displayed prominently. For many customers, those sweets are dessert.

When Challie and Teresa and their family owned the store they lived in the red brick building behind the deli on Daggett. Before that, says daughter Mary, the family lived squeezed into the back room of the grocery. "When I grew up on The Hill," Mary said, "there were grocery stores on every corner and people would buy fresh lunch meat every day. Every day it was the same routine, for years and years." When Gioia's Grocery closed upon the death of Challie's last surviving son, it was said to be the last remaining corner grocery on The Hill.

While visiting St. Louis, Yogi Berra, the Hall of Fame baseball player who was raised on The Hill along with his pal, Joe Garagiola, would stop by Gioia's to chat. "Yogi and Joe both send customers to us now," says Conley. "But Yogi doesn't come here in person anymore because he was always bombarded for autographs. So now he sends his wife to say hello."

Gioia's Deli
1934 Macklind Avenue, St. Louis

☎ (314) 776-9410

🕐 9 A.M. to 4 P.M. Monday through Friday
9am to 3 P.M. Saturday

♿ Wheelchair accessible

🚭 No smoking

53

Charlie Gitto's Downtown

St. Louis

ON MOST DAYS, Charlie Gitto sits on a corner stool at the bar in his Sixth Street restaurant, a habit since he opened in 1974. A wall sign by the stool is emphatic: "Reserved for the Boss," it reads. "Do Not Sit Here."

"I watch who walks in and who walks out," Gitto says. "I say 'Hello' and 'Goodbye' to almost everybody. Today, unfortunately, we had forty or fifty people who came in and turned around because we were too busy at lunch.

"I started bussing dishes at thirteen at the old Ruggeri's restaurant on The Hill," says Gitto. "Later on, I got maitre'd experience at Rich and Charlie's, Stan Musial and Biggie's, and Angelo's, which I later bought. I recently got elected to the Missouri Restaurant Hall of Fame, which was a great honor. A lot of guys come in here and smoke their cigars and see me sitting on the phone and think that owning a place like this is a breeze. They are really wrong. But you do have to be a little nuts."

Not only is Charlie Gitto's a well-regarded Italian restaurant, it is also a museum of fairly contemporary art. Photos and memorabilia that lean heavily toward baseball line the walls. "I have nine dozen autographed baseballs on our walls and fourteen dozen more at home. My son, George, who passed away in 1999, was an outdoorsman. All the deer heads on our walls are those that George killed with his bow and arrow. He was a great fisherman; the grouper over the bar area was something that he caught.

"Tommy Lasorda of the Los Angeles Dodgers came in here all the time," says his friend, Gitto. "Keith Hernandez is a buddy. Dusty Baker was in. Ken Boyer was a very close friend" (Gitto's guest-celebrity table is round and located next to the hostess-cashier stand. A wall plaque designates the site.)

"We're not *all* about baseball," Gitto assures us. "Bill O'Reilly from Fox TV came in recently. George Foreman, the boxer, popped in one day. His picture is on our wall. Bill Moyers of PBS gave me a picture. The commandant of West Point was here. And when the American Theatre was still open, Dennis Day and Don Ameche were in here talking with me until three or four in the morning. Tony Bennett once talked with me until three in the morning, too."

If someone well known crosses Gitto's threshold and doesn't happen to be carrying a personal photograph, Gitto will walk out to his black Cadillac Escalade parked in front and fetch his camera. "People want to be up on my wall," he says. "Let me say that you don't have to be a celebrity but you've got to be somebody I like. If I get pissed off at you, I will have you taken down."

Karen Gitto-Vangel, Charlie's daughter and restaurant general manager, began bussing for her dad the day he opened. She remembers that "Ernie Borgnine, the actor, was here and so was Vincent Price, who made all those horror movies. I was scared to death waiting on Mr. Price because I remembered all his movies so vividly."

Almost any celebrity you can name is commemorated on Charlie Gitto's walls. St. Louis Channel 5 meteorologist Cindy Preszler hangs alongside George Bush 1. Bill Clinton hangs below Joe DiMaggio. Mike Huckabee has wall space and so does John Ashcroft, who visited while U.S. attorney general. "Ashcroft came in here with three guys in black looking one way and three guys in black looking another way," recalls Jim Vangel, assistant general manager. "Once Ashcroft was inside, the Secret Service men made us lock our front door. Senator John Kerry was here and the same thing happened."

"First-timers here like to order their meals then get up and wander the restaurant studying the walls," observes waitress Katie Lilley.

Jim Vangel says that one of his jobs is to maintain separate index cards for all the photos, baseballs, bottles, and assorted mementoes and to organize dusting efforts on slow days. "We'd spray the stuff but we can't because we're a restaurant," he explains.

"Mick Jagger of the Rolling Stones once ate here alone," says Jim. "He was very low key, having arrived in a chaufferdriven Ford LTD with tinted windows. He was in town to give a concert the next day. And that's when we got a call from Mick. 'I left my special tour jacket at your place last night and I'm sending someone over to get it,' Mick said. Well, one of our waitresses had taken the jacket home with her thinking Jagger would never return for it. But when his phone call came you've never seen anyone scramble so fast to return home for that jacket. She brought it back shortly before Jagger's driver arrived."

Gitto's menu offers the usual Italian foods. "One best seller is the Charlie Gitto house salad, which many customers order for their main meals," says Jim. "It has iceberg and Romaine lettuce and we call it the 'Pasta House Salad.' Every Italian restaurant in St. Louis since 1970 serves the same salad with a different twist. Our meatball and the Italian sausage sandwiches go over big. Our daily specials like meatloaf and chicken or eggplant parmigiana, which were created by my mother-in-law, Annie, always do well. Annie also perfected our famous tiramisu for dessert.

"Toasted ravioli is huge here, especially during conventions and when there are ball games at Busch Stadium. You do know, don't you, that toasted ravioli was discovered at Angelo's Restaurant On The Hill in St. Louis in the 1960s and that Angelo's became Charlie Gitto's On The Hill when Charlie bought it in 1981?"

Charlie Gitto's has become a direct supplier of after-game feasts for St. Louis Cardinal baseball players. Gitto's sends the club big pans of toasted ravioli, tortellini, spaghetti, penne, lasagna, chicken Marsala, meatballs, house salad, and garlic cheese bread. The ball club tends to order the same Gitto's comestibles, game after game, win or lose. "Sometimes we drive the food over and other times we push our large cart down the street," says Jim.

Charlie Gitto's Downtown
207 N. 6th Street, St. Louis

 (314) 436-2828

 11 A.M. to 10 P.M. Monday through Thursday
11 A.M. to 11 P.M. Friday and Saturday
Closed Sunday except for special sports and other events

 Wheelchair accessible

 Smoking permitted

54

Giuseppe's Ristorante
St. Louis

THERE AREN'T TOO many reincarnated restaurants in the St. Louis area, but Giuseppe's is one of the best of them.

Giuseppe's is the latter-day extension of Rose's restaurant, situated from 1927 to 1973 at Tenth and Franklin near downtown St. Louis and eventually razed for what is now the St. Louis Convention Center.

When Roses's faced its demise, chef Giuseppe Pugliese (known as Joe) transferred Rose's fixtures and equipment to South Grand Avenue and Meramec, moving into space long inhabited by the Chex Grill, a venerable institution in the Dutchtown neighborhood. Ditto for the restaurant's upstairs neighbor, the Alwa Apartments, a thriving office building for doctors, dentists, and midwives as far back as the 1920s and 30s but seedier now.

Time flies! Giuseppe has retired, but still comes in for take-out weekly, and two brothers-in-law, Mark Manfrede (who is northern Italian) and Eric Stockmann (who isn't Italian) operate the business, painstakingly carrying on the tradition of the original Rose's. "All our recipes—one hundred percent of them—are from Rose's," says Manfrede. "And, by the way, people who were old customers of Rose's let us know they were old Roses's customers. They have high expectations of us!"

Jasper Bonaventre, who bought Rosario's Restaurant in 1933 and shortened the name to Rose's, would likely be astonished at the restaurant's current marketing tactics, though he would be delighted that his breaded veal cutlet hoagie bun sandwich with homemade bread crumbs remains the lunch-time favorite. "Not a lot of places sell veal anymore since it is so expensive. But we continue to do it here," says Manfrede.

Fresh Italian bread and an olive oil dipping mixture are brought to all customers awaiting their main meal. "We get our bread from two bakeries, Vitale's and Marconi," says Manfrede. "We once only got bread from Marconi's but their Breadmaster machine broke down and Vitale's bailed us out of trouble. So now we get three dozen loaves from Marconi and one dozen from Vitale's."

Until recently, Giuseppe's issued a glossy newsletter that has been temporarily discontinued. Its contents were unusual to say the least. Manfrede, the editor, wrote about Dave Radliff's Sinclair station across the street. "For your next gasoline purchase, you might want to stop by our neighbor, Dave Radliff's Sinclair station," he advised. Manfrede tells me that he fills up twice weekly at the station. "You can get an oil change there and while you wait you can come in here for lunch," Manfrede says. "Dave is a good customer here. Most often, his employees get a to-go order for lunch and it's usually pasta."

A fast-growing part of Giuseppe's business—something that would have confounded its founders—is a weekday lunch catering venture. "We prepare between thirty and one hundred lunches every day for employees of doctor's offices and clinics," said co-owner Eric Stockmann. "We take the meals to a pharmaceutical salesperson for distribution to doctors, nurses, and staff members. This is a completely separate business and a great marketing tool for us because all these people get exposed to Giuseppe's." Besides the catering, Giuseppe's opens its dining room evenings for large private events.

Another headliner on the lunch menu is Giuseppe's homemade meatball sandwich. "We use fresh ground veal, not ground beef. Several of us sit around a table and make three hundred-fifty meatballs at a time," says Manfrede. "When the meatballs are ready, we pan-fry them instead of baking them as most restaurants do."

As for noonday pasta, spaghetti and meatballs leads the way followed by cavatelli with mushrooms, and shrimp and clams made with a butter and garlic, instead of a cream sauce. Manfrede's favorite kitchen concoction is a tomato-based cacciatore sauce loaded with onions, celery, carrots, and spices. "These are not the ingredients you'd think would be in an Italian tomato sauce," said Manfrede. "A real tomato sauce is only tomatoes and water."

Giuseppe's offers daily specials, including Friday's baked whitefish. More than sixty percent of Friday lunch customers order the whitefish. "People phone us and have us save three or four orders of whitefish so we won't run out of it," says Manfrede, who adds: "It's the only day that people call ahead at noon time. And, yes, we do run out of whitefish." Manfrede also covets his Wednesday special, boiled beef and a potato mixed with rosemarina pasta. "We use a big hunk of beef and boil it all morning long," he says.

Giuseppe's has a tradition of keeping its lights somewhat low in its four dining areas—the barroom, two middle rooms, and the back bar which is actually a large dining room seating forty that was the original Chex Grill. The dark mahogany wall panels in the dining rooms were salvaged from the old Rose's. The brass and amber lighting globes came either from Europe or from Charlie Gitto's downtown restaurant, says Manfrede. White linen tablecloths have always been a Giuseppe's practice.

"On the day we closed on this property, a van crashed though the windows on the Grand Avenue side and took them all out," recalls Manfrede. "We decided that windows weren't the best thing to put back up so we built walls and put in murals on the inside where the windows had been. If you look closely at the mural in the second room, you'll notice Giuseppe and his wife, Antoinette, posed on a balcony scene painted by our muralist, Allison Larkins. We had another crash: a car came through our front door and crashed into our bar when we had just opened. That wasn't a catastrophe; we served food that very night. But when we remodeled the area, we installed roses in and near the new front door as a tribute to our past. And we installed concrete posts in front of the restaurant so that no one else can run their vehicles into Giuseppe's."

Giuseppe's Ristorante
4141 South Grand Boulevard, St. Louis

 (314) 832-3779

 11 A.M. to 2 P.M. Monday through Friday

 Wheelchair accessible

 Some smoking permitted

55

Grassi's West Italian Deli

Frontenac, Missouri

Grassi's West is an Italian deli and restaurant where nine out of ten lunch customers order the giant Italian salad at the wet steam table line done up in green, red, and white, colors of the Italian flag. "We put fourteen heads of iceberg lettuce in a big plastic salad bowl then we custom-mix each salad in a silver bowl with croutons, green olives, cheese, and the house dressing," explains co-owner Glen Pariani. "Our Italian salad dressing consists of soybean oil, vinegar, and spices; we make six gallons of it every day and there is no sugar in it, so that's good news for diabetics. As you can imagine, there are some bizarre requests for salad toppings. Some say 'put meat sauce on it,' others want sausages, meatballs, or anchovies on top. Some women want broccoli sauce, which consists of broccoli, mushrooms, onions, and a cream base. I've seen about everything."

Pariani says his cafeteria line is like a school lunch line where you don't serve yourself. As they push their trays down the line, many customers settle for the whopping salad as a meal in itself, but others opt for toasted ravioli or the hot roast beef sandwich on French bread or the made-from-scratch meatball sandwich (there is a special ingredient in the meatballs that

Pariani says he can't discuss). "We can put meatballs in a bowl by themselves, on a French bread roll, or couple them with pasta," advises Pariani. Grassi's offers veggie dishes such as a veggie pizza; a best-selling linguini dish topped with a tomato-based marinara sauce with red wine, mushrooms, red, yellow, and green peppers, broccoli, zucchini, and yellow squash; and an eggplant parmesan.

Located on German Boulevard in Frontenac slightly west of Forshaw's of St. Louis, the outdoor furniture store, Grassi's can be hard to find for first-timers. "But, dare I to compare our place to Ted Drewes or Carl's Drive-In and state that we're a destination restaurant for many people," says Pariani, "particularly those who've been out of town for a while and who will come to us straight from the airport for our Italian salad or our roast beef or meatball sandwiches? We're that popular." Pariani says he tries to keep his food offerings and Grassi's interior decor unchanged. "A guy leaves town for a year and comes back and he wants the same as before he left."

Grassi's walls contain photographs of customers such as sportscaster Joe Buck and his late dad, Jack. "Joe is great," says Pariani. "He goes out everywhere to eat. His dad came in here, too, as did Hale Irwin before he moved. Former baseball Cardinals Al Hraboski, Bob Forsch, Andy Bettis, and Jim Edmonds are regulars. "Edmonds is laid back, just as he is in center field," comments Pariani. "He's usually dressed in shorts and a California-style button down shirt and sandals. When he is done eating, he'll walk around and talk to people. He's very friendly. Mark McGwire would do that too, when he came here."

Grassi's has countless regular customers. "We expect loyalty from our regulars," says Pariani, "and we expect them to advertise for us. But you have to make them want to advertise (word-of-mouth). I have to admit that when it comes to advertising, I've tried coupons and mailings and the only thing that works is keeping customers happy. As for coupons, it's usually your own regulars who end up bringing them in, so coupons don't really work."

Among the regulars have been local sports teams. "We have the whole Mary Institute-Country Day football team coming in here for dinner before their home games," says Pariani. "In 1996, they won the state championship and gave me a team jersey. I also get the St. Louis University high school football team once a year; they eat everything in sight." Grassi's has long been a meeting spot for soccer lovers. Shirts from top European teams hang on the walls in Grassi's back room.

Grassi's started around 1970 in a storefront on South Kingshighway near Uncle Bill's Pancake House and was called Grassi's Ravioli, and later Grassi's Deli. In 1976, the Kingshighway store closed and Grassi's moved west to Frontenac. With a degree in petroleum engineering, Pariani worked on the Tomahawk cruise missile project at McDonnell-Douglas, then took positions in engineering management and sales before buying Grassi's West in 1993.

Grassi's West Italian Deli
10450 German Boulevard, Frontenac, Missouri

 (314) 994-1111

 10 A.M. to 9 P.M. Monday
10 A.M. to 10 P.M. Tuesday through Saturday

 Wheelchair accessible

 No smoking

56

Hilltop Inn

St. Louis

HILLTOP INN HAS occupied an exalted spot in the Boulevard Heights section of south St. Louis since Steve Ghiodini opened the place as a saloon in 1937—it had started in the early thirties as Goeckel's Grocery—and Joe Garavaglia and his wife Julia assumed control in 1939, introducing limited food service.

"As a little girl I always called this place a saloon," says Rosalie Garavaglia LaGates, Joe and Julia's daughter, "but older customers told me to say 'tavern' because 'tavern' sounds better."

During Hilltop's growing days, hamburgers and ham sandwiches were the main food focus. "Back then we fried our hamburgers in a black iron skillet on the basement stove," recalls Emil Garavaglia, Joe's youngest brother who is now in his eighties. "The problem was that the fry cook was also the bartender so when someone wanted a burger he'd leave the bar and rush to the basement to fry up a burger."

"Our cheeseburger is about the same as in 1939," says Rosalie LaGates, main food preparer and co-proprietor. "We always use a creamy white brick cheese which is rare for cheeseburgers." (Rosalie's husband, Al LaGates, a former homicide detective, added a note about cheeseburgers. "Did you know that long ago Famous-Barr served cheeseburgers in their downtown department store restaurant but that the cheeseburgers were really from Garavelli's Restaurant on DeBaliviere in the Central West End? Every weekday for years, Garavelli's delivered the cheeseburgers by taxi to Famous-Barr.")

Early on, Hilltop installed a modest steam table with a wood foundation. Lunch customers would expect to see roast beef, ready-to-eat bone-in ham, and meatloaf on display most every day. Nothing much has changed: food is prepared in "the old army kitchen downstairs," as Rosalie describes it; a successor steam table survives as does the roast beef and ham; the pasta with red sauce; Julia Garavaglia's house salad with a special vinegar, oil and garlic dressing; and all the meats, soups, and specials added over the years. "The only change is that I quit putting cloves in the ham," says Rosalie. The short steam table-cafeteria line is open weekdays from 10 A.M. to 2 P.M.

Rosalie's daily specials most often include meatloaf (Mondays), spaghetti and meatballs (Tuesdays), roast pork (Thursdays), and cod tails dredged in light flour, then pan-fried in butter and olive oil and seasoned with garlic, and meatloaf again (Fridays). "Actually I cook on a whim," confesses Rosalie. "I don't always have the same special every day because maybe that morning I get another idea, maybe something I see or hear about on television. We are cooking many more vegetables now, including Brussels sprouts. When people taste some of my Brussels sprouts they say 'My heavens, I haven't eaten these in years.' I'm finding that I have some customers who are coming back just for my Brussels sprouts. Of course I never know when I'll be preparing them since I do cook on a whim."

In the mid-twentieth century, Boulevard Heights was not as dense with subdivision housing as it is now. Truck farmers were located just across Morganford Road. "Those farmers sold cases of tomatoes to the Hilltop and Julia made a tomato salad every day all summer," said Emil Garavaglia. "The truck farmers bought half-pint containers of whiskey from us, put them in their back pockets, and walked across the street to work their fields. Once a year, at least, a load of manure was delivered to the truck farms and unloaded and stacked right across from the Hilltop. We had to keep our front door closed because of the odor since we had no air conditioning.

"In the late 1940s," Emil continued, "it was common for beer drummers to stop at the Hilltop around lunchtime to buy the house a drink and promote their beer brand. One day, Joe Garavaglia stood at the window and noticed a beer drummer slow his truck, then speed away. Joe thought the drummer fled because he saw so many cars parked near the Hilltop—the cars were owned by construction workers building bungalows where the truck farms had been. So Joe devised a plan: the next time the drummer came inside the Hilltop around noon he would blow an air horn to signal the workers across the street to rush over to the Hilltop for a free beer from the drummer. Well, it happened. Joe blew the air horn, the workers all came over, and Joe forced that poor drummer to buy not one but two beers for everyone in the house."

When you walk into the Hilltop Inn today you're back in the 1950s. Glass bricks are prominent; the bar is 1950-ish; the wall art includes a personalized Andy Capp cartoon, the barebottom lady poster that customers like to pose next to, and scores of family and customer photographs. Customers will linger over the photos and some will say to Rosalie or Al: "Why don't you have a picture of me on the wall?" "I tell them:

'Do something that makes me want to take a picture of you,'" says Al.

Where's the hill at the Hilltop? "Back sixty years ago, you could stand down at Gravois, about a mile away, and look west up the hill and you could actually see our tavern up there." says Emil Garavaglia. Today, with all the new housing and street changes such a sighting would be impossible.

Hilltop Inn

6902 Morganford Road, St. Louis

☎ (314) 481-9191

🕓 11:30 A.M. to 2 P.M. Monday through Friday
Bar: 11 A.M. to 1 A.M. Monday through Friday
4 P.M. to 1 A.M. Saturday (burgers, ham sandwiches during bar hours)

♿ Wheelchair accessible

🚬 Smoking permitted

57

Hodak's

St. Louis

"SOMEWHERE BACK IN the early days, Hodak's started to sell chicken, then somewhere they brought history in," muses Ralph Hegel, owner since 1989 when he bought the place from the Hodak family, which started business in 1946 at a tavern on Fourteenth Street near downtown St. Louis. The "history" Hegel's business forbears brought in was record sales for fried chicken in this area. "It's hard to change history," states Hegel. "We're so known for our fried chicken."

With the Hegel's purchase, they inherited Tony and Helen Hodak's fried chicken recipe, one that requires all extra fat and bones trimmed and each piece breaded by hand. "A lot of restaurants just cook all of that up," Hegel adds. "Most customers, when eating chicken, start with the wings and many of them will leave the breast and take it home with them," observes veteran waiter and bartender Rick Kuehn. "The only way to eat fried chicken is with your hands, though I see Europeans come in here and use a knife and fork." (A fried chicken order at lunch or dinner usually consists of half a breast, a wing, a leg, a thigh, great coleslaw and fries.)

Kuehn clearly remembers customers with bizarre chicken-eating routines. "One of our chicken customers starts with a leg first, then he wraps it in a napkin and puts it under a table leg to level the table where he always sits. Another guy chews and sucks the marrow from chicken bones. And one fellow orders three chicken dinners in a bag to go and one dinner for here. When they're delivered to him, he slips the three to-go dinners from the bag one by one so nobody sees him, puts them on the plate and eats them all here." (Take-outs constitute thirty percent of Hodak's business. If you're inclined, you can take home two hundred pieces of crispy fried chicken for $202.)

At Hodak's, fifty percent of lunch orders are for fried chicken (at night, seventy percent). But don't forget chicken and dumplings, the premier special at the restaurant. Chicken and dumplings are available only at lunch and only on the second and last Tuesday of the month. "We don't have them at dinner," explains Kuehn, "because by then they're sold out." What makes Hodak chicken and dumplings so special is that the dumplings are rolled out and dropped into a pot of chicken broth to rise. Then the dumplings are layered over half the plate and half a chicken is set on top. Homemade flour-based chicken gravy is ladled over the whole mix.

Each month, the restaurant publishes a detailed list of weekday lunch specials. On it most months are items such as breaded pork chops, stuffed peppers, taco salads, Polish sausage and kraut, beef stroganoff, fillet of cod, pork roast and dressing, and so on. Plus fried chicken and the extra-special chicken and dumplings.

Donna Bozovich, a Hodak's fixture for nearly forty years, is the chief chicken breader and fryer and helps with the chicken and dumplings. "She makes homemade chicken soup just for us employees (nearly eighty of us) and uses leftover chicken to make us chicken salads," says Kuehn of the talented cook known as "Grandma".

"We do about fourteen thousand to fifteen thousand pounds of chicken a week," reports Hegel. "We're probably number one in sales for a single non-chain restaurant; chances are we're tops in Missouri and maybe the whole country." Hegel adds that "In the old days, when it ran out of chicken Hodak's simply closed for the day. We're better prepared now."

Hodak's has three dining sections: the bar side, the middle room, and the top side, which customers seem to prefer, especially on Fridays when customers line up to the front door. "The top side has an ambience about it," says Hegel. "It used to be a part of the old Heimburger Trucking Company that outgrew the place and moved to Fenton."

Naturally, Hodak's is extremely popular, especially on weekend nights when stretch limousines often stop out front and let off large bachelor or bachelorette parties. Lines waiting to get inside at both the front and side doors can string out to more than one hundred hungry folks. "People call us and ask how long the lines are," says Hegel. "Human beings really don't like to stand in line, so I kill them with chicken kindness—that means chicken jokes—while they're standing there," says Kuehn. "People expect to be pushed around when they line up here," Kuehn says. "Gently," he adds.

One Friday and Saturday night a southside tradition starts at Hodak's. "People come here for a fried chicken dinner, then they leave and drive over to the Ted Drewes custard stand on Chippewa for dessert," says Kuehn. "In St. Louis, fried chicken and sundaes seem to go hand in hand."

Hegel is one of several St. Louis restaurant proprietors who greet customers at the door. "Welcome home," he'll say, as if customers re-appear after a lengthy absence, which they probably don't do at all.

Hodak's

2199 Gravois Avenue, St. Louis

☎ (314) 776-7292

🕐 10 A.M. to 10 P.M. Sunday through Thursday
10 A.M. to 11 P.M. Friday, Saturday

♿ Wheelchair accessible

🚬 Smoking permitted

58

Horseshoe Sports Bar

Collinsville, Illinois

"When people return to Collinsville, Horseshoe's is the place they want to go," says Lois Metzer of Collinsville. Floyd Sperino says the spot has long been a hangout. "After bowling, someone will say 'Let's go to the Horseshoe' and away we go."

Now known as the Horseshoe Sports Bar, its life started in 1946 as the Horseshoe Restaurant. "The first owner was Mr. Beck—I don't know his first name," says Cookie Sedlmeier, who co-owned Horseshoe with her husband, Chuck, until mid-2007 when it was purchased by Kim Kirchoff, the restaurant's manager for twenty years. "Supposedly Mr. Beck bought this lot, got a truck, went to East St. Louis and filled up the truck with concrete blocks and started building this place," said Cookie. "His original front door is now in the middle of our restaurant. Mr. Beck's back bar and mirrors are still there. His horseshoe-shaped bar made of glass blocks still exists. Beck had the place for three years then sold it to John Saggio. I understand that when Saggio owned it, they pumped out fried chicken as fast as they could cook it."

In 1963, Cookie's dad, Roy Jenkins, bought the Horseshoe and kept it until his death in 1977. "When Roy died, my mother-in-law didn't want to sell the business to me," said

Chuck, "so she sold it to three women from Bruno's Bakery. They owned it for six years; we finally bought it in 1983."

Fried chicken is no longer the trademark food item at Horseshoe; it has given way to Crazy Chicken Wings. "You fry them and dip them in our special sauce, drain them, and serve them," Cookie would explain. "On a Super Bowl Sunday we'll sell hundreds to take to house parties. We've had hot wings for more than twenty years. We had them and so did Culpepper's (the St. Louis chain) and no one else did. We got our hot sauce recipe twenty years ago; it includes Tabasco, cayenne pepper, and butter and we play with it and refine it as we go. You take a quart of this sauce and use it for three days."

Horseshoe is also a steak house. An eight-ounce sirloin steak sandwich is very popular on Thursdays. "We have the eight-ounce steak special on Wednesday nights and we keep enough of the steak to sell for Thursday lunch and make a sandwich with it," Chuck said. "We have a lot of traditional char-broiled burgers on the menu including the Helluva Hamburger and the Helluva Cheeseburger. The Helluva is like a hamburger that you drag through the garden, with vegetables and so on. It's like a California burger. I traveled for thirty years and would always bring back ideas for burgers. One popular item we have is the Tina Burger with cheese, bacon, and French fries. Cookie's dad named it for a waitress.

"Besides our luncheon pizza, we have our club sandwich, which is the best club going," Chuck claimed. "It's big and has lots of stuff. I've eaten clubs with Cookie everywhere, but I can't fine one club that's close to ours. We've got turkey, ham, lettuce, and cheese and it's just big and fat. We put more in ours than most restaurants do."

The restaurant's Caesar salad has no anchovies, but has a great dressing, said Chuck. "We make our own dressing with celery, a dash of mustard, Accent, lemon juice, Parmesan cheese, onion, and some garlic. It sells well." What doesn't sell well anymore is the golden horseshoe sandwich, still celebrated occasionally in central Illinois. "In the horseshoe, you have a hamburger and French fries and melted cheese and make it like an open-face sandwich. People who come in today don't know what it is." The horseshoe in the restaurant's name refers to nearby horseracing venues like Fairmount Park and the late Cahokia Downs and not the sandwich.

Thanks to Chuck, a fanatic collector, the Horseshoe is a quasi-sports museum. "When I started this place, I put in five TVs and started to collect sports memorabilia," stated Chuck. "I've gone to all the Super Bowls and have brought back souvenir footballs from all of them—most are displayed over the back bar and in cases around it. I have all my Super Bowl ticket stubs, game programs, and posters on display." When the Sedlmeiers sold the place to Kirchoff and his wife, Tanya, most of the memorabilia came with the sale including the baseball pennants, baseballs, jerseys, and early bobblehead dolls. That's good news!

Horseshoe Sports Bar
410 St. Louis Road, Collinsville, Illinois

 (618) 345-9372

 11 A.M. to midnight Monday through Friday
11 A.M. to 1 A.M. Saturday, Noon to 1 A.M. Sunday

 Wheelchair accessible

 No smoking

59

Illinois Riverdock Restaurant
Hardin, Illinois

FOR A CAFE that hugs the river in the remotest peninsula in Illinois, you would think that the Illinois Riverdock Restaurant would feature catfish, buffalo, or walleye on its menu. But, no, beef brisket, barbecued ribs, smoked pork chops, and smoked chicken are the items that sway luncheon guests.

"Nobody has beef brisket like mine," says Mel Heffington, proprietor, cook, chef, and smoker. "It's the way I apply seasoning, they say. I also probably cook it longer. It's so tender it's unreal—it just falls apart. A man came here from Texas after participating in numerous cook-offs and he said of my brisket, 'Oh, my God, I've never tasted anything like your brisket before.'" Heffington often walks around the restaurant with samples of his brisket and pork chops.

In 1993, Heffington decided to convert his 25-year-old Mel's Refrigeration shop into a restaurant because he liked to cook so much and was tired of the repair business. "We were two weeks from opening when the great 1993 flood put five feet of water into this place," says Heffington. Riverdock finally debuted in January 1994.

Out behind sits Heffington's well-used 600-pound smoker. Although his lunch menu lists smoked Texas chicken breast, smoked catfish and turkey, and a smokehouse half-pound burger, Heffington smokes just about anything in the food chain. "People bring me salmon and I season it and smoke it. I do deer meat and duck and goose breasts; I charge a dollar a pound to smoke them. When some people go off on hunting trips they will bring me parts of animals such as black bears, mountain lions, and caribou. I smoke them but don't serve them for lunch.

"If I can get any spoonbill catfish—it comes fresh out of the Mississippi River at Hamburg, Illinois—I will make it a noon special," says Heffington. "I would compare the spoonbill to a walleye, but it's thicker and it's boneless." Heffington also smokes river sturgeon that is fished in January and February below the Winfield, Missouri dam. "Sturgeon is very rich and flavorful," Heffington claims. According to the *Penguin Companion to Food* sturgeon meat most resembles veal.

"We make about ninety percent of everything we sell," says Heffington. "For example, we make our own barbecue sauce, salad dressings, maple butter, and our own pork tenderloin. In summer months, we do one hundred homemade pies a week and I make some of them myself—coconut cream is the most popular. On weekends, we offer my grandma's fried bread. She taught me how to cook."

Boaters can tie up at Heffington's 250-foot dock where the water is usually nine- to eleven-and-a-half-feet deep and amble over to the restaurant. "Every year we have boaters from Florida and other states who travel up the East Coast then come down through the Great Lakes to the Illinois River and stop here. Boaters talk about us on their radios. They'll have lunch or dinner, stay overnight, and come in for breakfast." Occasionally, a helicopter lands beside Riverdock and unloads its passengers for lunch.

Inside Riverdock are walls with photographs of Calhoun County residents serving in the Middle East. In one corner Heffington sells Watkins products (he is a registered dealer) as well as hats, mugs, coolers, and T-shirts "to cover bikini-wearing tourists who come by boat."

On Fridays, Heffington offers no fish specials as most riverside restaurants along the Illinois and Mississippi Rivers are prone to do. "We offer fried chicken buffet-style with mashed potatoes and gravy," Heffington says.

Illinois Riverdock Restaurant
S. Park, Hardin, Illinois

☎ (618) 576-2362

🕐 7:30 A.M. to 10 P.M. Friday and Saturday

♿ Wheelchair accessible

🚭 No smoking

60

John's Town Hall

St. Louis

"MR. RUBRIGHT, THIS is Patty McMenamy from Town Hall. We have chicken-and-dumpling soup today. Bye." In a flash, I arrived at John's Town Hall on the ground floor of the Dorchester Apartments ready to slurp.

At least a dozen chicken-and-dumpling soup phone alerts are phoned to customers whenever owner and soup-maker John Ruprecht stirs a batch from his grandmother's recipe (once every two weeks or so). Other regulars are alerted by McMenamy regarding the Tuesday meatloaf and the Thursday roast beef brisket and French bread specials. "I also call when we have liver and onions and the turkey pastrami sandwich," she adds.

Ruprecht brought stability to the space that houses Town Hall. "Before I came here after being the manager for twelve years at the original Town Hall (at 6736 Clayton Road, now an Applebee's), there were five restaurants here in less than ten years," he says. "The first one, which opened in 1964—the same year the Dorchester opened—was the VIP, co-owned by legendary St. Louis Cardinal shortstop, Marty Marion, who was a competent carpenter. He built or installed much of the woodwork you see here today, including the paneled doors from the old Women's Exchange in the main dining room."

From the original Town Hall, Ruprecht brought some signature items: breaded fried mushrooms; Reuben sandwiches infused with Thousand Island dressing, and braunschweiger on rye sandwiches with raw onions. "We serve braunschweiger (smoked liver sausage made with milk and eggs) mostly to people over forty; young people don't like it because it has liver in it," says Ruprecht. "Some men say their wives tell them 'braunschweiger is not good for you' so the men come here and order it anyway."

From another Clayton Road landmark restaurant, Medart's, Ruprecht appropriated its famed hamburger. Town Hall's menu states that it is the "Home of the Medart Burger" and declares that "This piece of St. Louis history stands head and shoulders above all other burgers...piled high with lettuce, pickle, onion, and dripping with The Original MEDART Sauce." The mayonnaise-based sauce is so secret that Ruprecht has it copyright-protected. Like other restaurant owners, Ruprecht reiterates that he'd have to be slain before divulging the ingredients in the Medart sauce. The Medart burger comes wrapped in a tiny napkin that resembles a diaper.

The cheeseburger club, Ruprecht's version of the traditional triple-decker sandwich, is a hit with people of all ages. "In my version," he explains, "I take the turkey away and put in a whole cheeseburger in its place along with the lettuce, bacon, and tomato."

When Ruprecht debuted his own Town Hall in 1971, he started with three cooks, three waitresses, a bus girl, bartender, and hostess. "We were packed, but losing money from too much overhead for the space," he says. Since then, he's pared his overhead to one waitress-bartender (Patty McMenamy), one lunch cook, and an evening chef.

Golfers in nearby Forest Park occasionally steer their carts across Skinker Blvd for a quick drink in the Town Hall bar, long a gathering place for bon vivants and friends of Ruprecht's. "People say our bar is like Cheers," he says.

Town Hall has been a good tenant of the twenty-two-story Dorchester, where Cardinal outfielder Lou Brock resided for years and more recently, Cardinals Edgar Renteria and Fernando Viña. Each year, Ruprecht throws a Christmas party for Dorchester residents and staff; it sponsors gourmet nights and cocktail hours at other times.

Armin Schwarz owned the original Town Hall on Clayton Road. He was known to greet customers with a handshake and a felicitous "Hello, Schultz!" "That just means that if Mr. Schwarz didn't exactly know your name, he'd greet you with 'Hello, Schultz,'" says Ruprecht. "I say the same thing myself at times."

John's Town Hall
665 S. Skinker Blvd., St. Louis

☎   (314) 725-3555

🕐   Lunch: 11:30 A.M. to 3 P.M. Monday through Friday
Dinner: 5:30 P.M. to 9 P.M. Monday through Friday
Dinner: 6 P.M. to 9 P.M. Saturday

♿   Wheelchair accessible

🚬   Some smoking permitted

61

Johnson's Corner

Alton, Illinois

IN HER BOOK, *American Sandwich*, Becky Mercuri says that the birthplace of the breaded pork tenderloin sandwich was the still-existing Nick's Kitchen in Huntington, Indiana in 1908. "New initiates are sometimes alarmed by the sight of the tenderloin, which hangs from the bun by at least an inch, and often much more, all the way around, creating a two-fisted dining experience," writes Mercuri, who lists the top sandwich from each state. In her view, "The Midwestern Pork Tenderloin Sandwich" represents Indiana.

One claim that Johnson's Corner doesn't make is that it is the home of the area's first pork tenderloin sandwich, an honor it concedes to the long-gone Comet Drive-In near the Mississippi River bridge in downtown Alton. It does claim, however, that its Bloody Mary cocktail, available at lunch, is the best in America.

This north Alton neighborhood restaurant thrives on its pork tenderloin sandwiches, which, despite twenty-two other sandwiches, including pollock, golden horseshoe, and the "Vegas dog with chili," always heads the customer want list. Years ago, says Bob Johnson, proprietor since 1979, the Comet Drive-In offered pork cutlet sandwiches, "but we have the improved version. We buy fifteen whole pork loins a week and grill half of them and bread the other half. The public likes the breaded the best."

"We bread with all-purpose breading, then we soak the pork in milk, cover it with cracker meal and freeze it. When a customer places an order, we deep-fry it," says kitchen manager Deb Farris. A Johnson's Corner tenderloin measures eight inches across and six inches long, says Johnson, who uses a metal measuring tape to be sure. Take-outs are plentiful. A pair of one-time Altonians who now live in Texas told Johnson that they can't get pork tenderloin sandwiches where they live. So Johnson packed a dozen breaded tenderloins in a box and sent the couple back to Texas in a state of euphoria. Similar transactions occur regularly.

First-timers who ask about the house specialty are told of the pork tenderloin; the homemade onion rings (made with Johnson's special batter in which each onion is double-dipped singly, the final product resembling a typical bakery-bought doughnut); homemade soups; pond-raised catfish strips; and the Johnson's Special salad where ham and beef intermingle with lettuce, tomatoes, onions, cheese, pepper, artichokes, olives, and croutons. I always order a large house salad that is saturated with the sweet vinegar-and-oil-based house dressing carefully mixed by Deb Farris. Interestingly, a Johnson's Corner policy is clearly stated in the menu under salads. "Cheese and crackers are served with salads only! Without a salad, cheese and crackers will cost $1 per person."

Friday's daily special is pond-raised crappie, a fixture at many Metro East restaurants. "My supplier won't tell me where the crappie pond is," says Johnson. "All he'll say is that the pond is four hours north of Alton. We've had it on the menu for at least fifteen years."

One phenomenon of the lunch business at a casual neighborhood place like Johnson's Corner is that "Many people who eat lunch here come back that evening for take-outs," says Jim Johnson, general manager. "They see our menu and like what they see and so they return that evening."

Johnson's bar is a factor at lunch. Besides the Finlandia vodka, horseradish-optional Bloody Mary, a drink special is available each week. On one visit, the "Between the Sheets" martini was highlighted. "It's made with rum, brandy, Cointreau, and lemon juice," says Jim Johnson. But is it a martini, typically a mix of gin or vodka and vermouth? "So long as it's alcohol, it's a martini," says Jim smiling.

Johnson's Corner opened in 1945 as Watson's, a combination bar and grocery that offered hefty ham-and-cheese sandwiches and chili. "They piled ham and cheese on bread and put it under a broiler if you wanted it hot," recalls Jim Stromske, a customer since the first days. "Every Saturday some of the locals would drop into Watson's around 7 P.M. to pick up the Sunday paper and stay until Watson's closed. Around 10 P.M., Mr. Watson would start sweeping the place. He would bring his broom to your bar stool and say 'Get up, sir, and I'll sweep here. And don't forget that we close at eleven.'" Hint, hint.

Johnson's Corner
2000 State Street, Alton, Illinois

 (618) 465-5640

 11 A.M. to 10 P.M. Monday through Thursday
11 A.M. to 11 P.M. Friday through Saturday
Noon to 8 P.M. Sunday

 Wheelchair accessible

 No smoking

62

JV's Downtown Bar and Grill
Waterloo, Illinois

HERE'S WHAT ITS menu says about JV's Downtown Bar and Grill in Waterloo, Illinois:

- It was the former headquarters of Schorr Family Brewery, built in 1880 and operated until Prohibition. Under the restaurant are three fermenting levels with arched stone ceilings below street level; the bottom story is totally under water.
- Slow-smoked BBQ specials are available daily, one of which is the Pulled Pork Sandwich—"slow cooked, for the fall off the bone taste."
- Barbecued pork cutlet is not an entrée but a JV's sandwich. "A tender cut of pork, smothered in JV's barbecue sauce and on bread," says the menu.
- The Mackie Burger, named for a customer who sang 'Mack the Knife' ad infinitum, is a "succulent burger cooked to order and topped with melted provolone cheese, bacon, grilled onions and mushrooms." You can also opt for a mini or super Mackie. The Super, the menu states, is "able to tackle large appetites in a single sitting."
- On Friday, you can get a codfish sandwich; fish cut-ups; "bite-size chunks of Iceland cod, lightly breaded and

deep fried; breaded filet of cod or one-pound filet or cut-ups." And there is a caveat: "As hard as we try, we are not a fast food restaurant: all meals are cooked to order."

"We are not a destination restaurant; we are an everyday restaurant," amiable owners Jeff and Denise Vogt note on the menu.

On Friday, JV's hands customers a separate fish menu in addition to the regular menu. A fish plate, cut-up plate, walleye plate, and seafood platter are on the menu. Jeff explains that all the "fish plates" are actually sandwiches. "Plate means that the order comes with fries or slaw," he says. By contrast, the seafood platter does get served on a plate. For additional explanation of why plates are actually sandwiches on Friday, please contact one of the owners. Fish orders, by the way, constitute seventy percent of JV's Friday business.

JV's chili is different because it's seasoned with paprika instead of chili powder. "We have a man who works for us who made a mistake that turned to our advantage," says Jeff. "The man made up a batch of our chili for a Chamber of Commerce cook-off. It tasted different. I said to him: 'Where's the spice?' Well, we discovered that he had accidentally put in paprika instead of chili powder. That was fortunate for us since we won first prize in the cook-off. Now we always use paprika in our chili."

Soup, plus the famous chili, is a JV's staple. "My bean soup has smoked ham and great northern beans," Jeff notes. "Here of late we've been making chicken fajita soup and beef barley is something we do often. We had a waitress who couldn't spell well who put up our menu board. Once she put 'beef barely' on the board. She couldn't spell ravioli, either."

The Mackie Burger is a sentimental favorite among locals. It was named for Gary Bradley, a newspaper reporter who was enamored with the song, 'Mack the Knife.' "One day at the 21st Amendment Bar here in town Gary gets up on the bar and sings 'Mack the Knife'," says Jeff. "The tavern owner says to me that Gary should not be standing on his bar so we all came down here to our place where he got up on our bar and sang 'Mack the Knife;' again. The name stuck so we called Gary 'Mackie' after that and that's why we named our one-pound burger with bacon, grilled mushrooms, and onions on grilled rye bread after him. Every time he had a few drinks he would climb up on the bar and sing 'Mack the Knife.' He left Waterloo to work in St. Louis but was always worried that the Mackie Burger would be taken off our menu. Sadly, he has died but his burger is still on the menu—it's his memorial. His daughters live in Belleville and come in here for their Mackie Burgers."

In an "everyday" restaurant such as JV's, customers are extended family. "One of our best customers died," said Jeff. "She came in every night with her husband and had a martini while he had a Manhattan. Before her funeral the pastor came in to get her empty martini glass and put it on the altar so he could make a toast. When the funeral procession was on its way to the cemetery, our bartender went outside and toasted her with another martini glass as it went by. I was a pallbearer."

JV's bar, wreathed in red and maroon, is popular with the matrimonially inclined. "We have wedding parties who make it a tradition—sometimes two or three of them on a Saturday—to come by after the ceremony to have their picture taken sitting on top of our bar," said Denise.

JV's three dining areas are the barroom or front room; the "waitress room" with three tables next to the kitchen; and the EL, shorthand for executive lounge, once the living room for former owners of the restaurant. The Rotary, Lions, and Optimists meet in the EL.

Waterloo fascinated Helen Rippelberger Richter, who wrote a book about it in 1988. In *A Cameo Collection of Historic Waterloo*, she claims that the Bellefontaine area of town where JV's is located was "the first permanent American settlement in the Northwest Territory in about 1778." She said the town got its name from English settlers who were so delighted by Napoleon's defeat at Waterloo in Belgium that they gave the name Waterloo to their new town. Others have differing versions on how Waterloo got its name.

The Schorr family, Germans from Bavaria, took over the brewery in 1871. They put up a third story and erected an icehouse that stored ice from Schorr Lake that they built (it is now known as City Park Lake). Author Richter states that the Schorr family sat down for five meals each day. "Birds nesting in the brewery building were killed, cleaned, stuffed, and served along with dinner," Richter discovered in her research.

Jeff and Denise live upstairs at their restaurant. They constantly get asked questions about the old Schorr Brewery. "People ask: 'Can we go see the three levels?'" says Jeff. "I always say: 'not now.'"

JV's Downtown Bar and Grill
117 N. Main Street, Waterloo, Illinois

 (618) 939-7127

 11 A.M. to 2 P.M. Monday
11 A.M. to 8:30 P.M. Tuesday through Thursday
11 A.M. to 9 P.M. Friday, Saturday

 Wheelchair accessible

 No smoking

~~~
───── 63 ─────
~~~

Kilroy's Homestyle Restaurant
Portage des Sioux, Missouri

KILROY'S IS NAMED for the World War II-era "Kilroy Was Here" cartoon doodle character who was always seen as peering over a wall. The restaurant sits amid floodplain cornfields on the road to the Grafton Ferry over the Mississippi River and right beside St. Charles County Airport, better known as Smartt Field. Speaking of walls, the Ozark Airline Employees Commemorative Wall is Kilroy's immediate neighbor.

Much about Kilroy's evokes World War II: the Betty Grable and Cary Grant omelets, wartime plane models on tables, and shelves and color photos of fighter planes on the dining room walls. Outside Kilroy's window, diners can view old runways that served Allied pilots training here early in the war as well as the museum down the road that shelters a North American B-25J Mitchell bomber, Stearman bi-wing, and C-47 cargo plane. More often than not, the C-47 is parked by Kilroy's window as if ready to take off.

"Kilroy's is sort of a Cheers lunch place," says owner Lori Cotton, who once named an omelet with grits in it after herself but dropped it from the menu because so many customers insisted the grits should be on the side. Homemade soups and the Wimpy and Wimpy, Jr. hamburgers, succulent and substantial, are popular at lunch but omelets and the breakfast burrito form the major share of noontime business. Most likely customers are St. Charles County policemen, boaters, hunters, fishermen, sightseers, bicyclists, motorcyclists on poker runs, and patrons of the ferry operation a mile-and-a-half away.

Prior to World War II, the farm field behind Kilroy's became a U.S. Navy air training site. Eight macadamized all-weather runways and a peripheral circular taxiway made the field special for American, British, and Scottish airmen, says Mary Yates Villeret, president of the Portage Des Sioux Historical Society in *The History of Portage des Sioux Township, Missouri—The Land Between the Rivers*. "They would spiral the planes in and out all day, practicing takeoffs and landings," wrote Villeret. After an early trainee was killed at Pearl Harbor on December 7, 1941, the field was named for him: Ensign Joseph Gilespie Smartt.

Smartt Field had H-shaped barracks, a chow hall, chapel, PX, officers club, and other trappings. It was mostly dismantled by 1948, giving way to several airfield-related successors. In 1984, the Confederate Air Force moved its Missouri wing to the field, maintaining two hangars for the vintage aircraft this national group has pledged to restore and preserve. (During a one-week run of the musical *South Pacific* at the St. Louis Municipal Opera in the city's Forest Park, CAF members wheeled out the B-25J and flew it nightly over the outdoor theater.) The museum complex is open to the public several days a week. In 2003, the organization changed its name to be more politically correct—Commemorative Air Force. Its volunteers lunch at Kilroy's.

In 1984, historian Villeret opened Mary's A-Frame Restaurant near the hangars. She put "Mary's Flying Hamburger

Specials" on her menu, including the V-J Day mushroom cheddar hamburger, Kamikaze chili dog, B-25 Mitchell chef salad, Invasion Force pizza, and Atomic Bomb chili. In 1993, Mississippi River floodwaters all but washed out the A-frame, forcing Villeret to move to the elevated building that now houses Kilroy's. In 1997, Villeret closed down her "relatively world famous" dining spot (as her menu put it) and later Lori Cotton, a former efficiency expert at the old McDonnell-Douglas Aircraft Company, opened Kilroy's.

Cotton, daughter of an Air Force veteran, has been taking flying lessons at Smartt Field and is anxious to pilot a plane of her own. If she wants instant air travel, however, she can hitch rides with customers. "Many people come to Kilroy's and want people to fly with them," Cotton says. "And if you fly over us, you'll find this is one of the prettiest places in America, especially with the Mississippi River bluffs. Over fifty percent of our customers fly out of here. We're at mid-point between Milwaukee and Oklahoma, a place where pilots stop by, get gas, and come in for lunch. We're a truck stop for small planes."

In recent years, about one thousand retired Ozark Airline employees have formed an alumni association that meets annually by the Commemorative Air Force hangars. Started in 1950, Ozark was sold to Trans-World Airlines in 1986. The alums have funded a plaza on Kilroy's south side that features a commemorative wall with hundreds of employee names on tablets.

Don Ostmann, a former Ozark pilot who chairs the plaza project, cites the cordial relationship between Ozark alums and Kilroy's. "We will soon install an Ozark memorabilia display case in the dining room," he says. "And when we meet every year for our reunion, half of us eat lunch at Kilroy's."

Since the Ozark project has been erected at Kilroy's, the restaurant menu has a new breakfast/lunch item that seems off-the-wall: "Bird Strike." It's a dish that contains chicken fried steak, American fries, and two scrambled eggs smothered in gravy. You'll have to ask Lori Cotton for an explanation.

Kilroy's Homestyle Restaurant
6390 Grafton Ferry Road, Portage Des Sioux, Missouri

 (636) 250-3303

 9 A.M. to 10 P.M. Friday
8 A.M. to 4 P.M. Friday and Saturday

 Wheelchair accessible

Smoking permitted

64

La Bonne Bouchée

Creve Coeur, Missouri

For twenty years—1982 to 2002—Olivier Leguez labored as a pastry chef in the decidedly French restaurant, La Bonne Bouchée. In 2002, he had a chance to buy the restaurant from founder-owner Alphonse Dirrenger. "I didn't want this place to die, so I said 'I'm going to try it,'" said Leguez. Five years later, his pastry and restaurant sales had doubled.

La Bonne Bouchée has three things in its favor, says Leguez, who presides over the operation in a nicely starched black or white double-breasted tunic with his name embroidered in red over the shirt pocket. "Before anything else, we are a pastry shop. Then, we are a restaurant, and, third, we're not too expensive and we're family oriented."

Although a full breakfast is served, Leguez focuses on lunch where eighty-five percent of customers are women. "Ours is a French restaurant run by a Frenchman. We're one of the only restaurants around that can make that statement," says Leguez.

Nearly fifty percent of his lunch patrons come in just for his French onion soup, Leguez claims. "For this soup we buy and wash the veal bones and make the stock, then we peel and slice fresh yellow onions. We cook the soup for a long time. Its success is all in the timing. The longer you steam it, the better the flavor. When it's ready to serve, it's somewhere in between a soup and a thick white sauce like a veloute."

Another twenty-five percent of lunch sales is captured by Leguez's chicken salad, either on a plate or in a sandwich. "For the salad, we bake a fresh chicken that is surrounded by carrots, onions, celery, and some garni. Baking the chicken with vegetables around it gives the chicken so much more flavor. We use the chicken meat for the salad and we frankly waste the vegetables. We lose a ton of carrots but we gain all that flavor in the chicken!"

Quiche Lorraine, a savory pie, heads La Bonne Bouchée's "specialties" list. "We make our quiche from scratch," says Leguez. "We break our own eggs and you don't find that hardly anywhere; we don't use frozen eggs like so many other restaurants. We add Swiss Gruyere cheese and pieces of fresh bacon that we slice ourselves. Many of the ladies order Quiche Lorraine and a salad."

Most "specialties" have been around since the restaurant debuted in 1981. One of them is Le Vol Au Vent, which combines diced chicken, fresh mushrooms, and Bechamel sauce and is served on a shell. "Some people come here just for this," observes Leguez.

Along with seven siblings, Leguez was raised on a farm in the Loire Valley of central France. "My dad was in the field and my mom took care of the cows. Every night we'd eat omelets and potatoes because my mom had little time to cook. So, when I was ten years old, I started to make dinner for the family and did much more than meat and potatoes. For birthdays, I started to bake cakes. When I was fourteen, the only thing I knew was cooking. At eighteen, I went to cooking school—Ecole Hoteliere de Tours—and then I worked in restaurants in Paris and Versailles before coming here in 1981 because I had the urge to travel to America."

Eventually landing in St. Louis, Leguez went to work for a short-lived Clayton restaurant, Chez Louie, until the owner of La Bonne Bouchée asked if Leguez could help out on week-ends as a back-up pastry chef. Leguez's skill in making his family's favorite chocolate mousse cake plus his knack for mass-producing tarts, éclairs, Napoleons, cheesecakes, cream puffs, strawberry, and Black Forest, mocha, and carrot cakes—pastries he now makes daily in addition to his huge wedding cake busi-ness—so impressed Alphonse Derringer that he was invited to be the restaurant's head pastry chef. He accepted immediately.

Before entering the restaurant part of La Bonne Bouchée, customers must pass the bakery display cases. "How many bakery customers do you convert into restaurant customers?" Leguez was asked. "All of them! When you buy pastries up front you just know that the food in the back rooms must be good, too."

La Bonne Bouchée

12344 Olive Boulevard, Creve Coeur, Missouri

 (314) 576-6606

 Breakfast: 7 A.M. to 10:45 A.M. Monday through Saturday
Brunch: 8 A.M. to 1 P.M. Sunday
Lunch: 11 A.M. to 3 P.M. Monday through Saturday
Dinner: 5 P.M. to 9 P.M. Tuesday through Saturday

 Wheelchair accessible

No smoking

65

Lubeley's Bakery and Deli

Marlborough, Missouri

FOR YEARS, CUSTOMERS have returned to Lubeley's Bakery on Watson Road for their famous gooey butter, deep crumb, and fancy wedding cakes, and customized dog biscuits. As for me, I head to Lubeley's for a chicken salad sandwich at lunch.

When I carry my chicken salad sandwich from the counter to the wedding cake consultation room that serves as the dining area, I sit down amidst displays of non-edible "wedding cake models" that Lubeley's has rigged up to lure brides-to-be in planning mode.

According to the Lubeleys, their establishment—which started in 1937 at Neosho and South Kingshighway in St. Louis—is classified as a traditional, full-baker bakery. In St. Louis and beyond, these places are becoming rarities. "We have six to eight full-time skilled bakers as opposed to some of the new breed of fast, casual bakeries where people in kitchens push buttons on electric ovens and turn out baked goods all day," says deli manager Carol Lubeley. "When we were kids in St. Louis, there used to be a bakery on nearly every corner, but not anymore. There are just a few of us old-fashioned bakers left."

Lubeley's is a family affair, Carol's husband, Robert, is general manager and owner. Sisters-in-law Helen Lubeley

Murry and Sue Lubeley-Suardi are bakery manager and head cake decorator respectively. Ninety-six-year old Helen Lubeley, matriarch of the family, is on hand most weekdays as a volunteer to help Carol prepare the chicken salad, stock shelves, and greet customers. "We pick Helen up each morning at her assisted living complex and bring her here," says Carol.

Carol makes ten pounds of chicken salad daily, a mix that includes real Hellman's mayonnaise and a secret concoction of ground garlic and red bell pepper.

"Other bakeries already in the deli business told us that when we started (in 1981) we had to have a 'signature sandwich,'" says Carol. So "Lubeley's Special," a quartet of roast beef, salami, turkey, and ham with Swiss and American cheese, lettuce, and tomato on a six-inch poor boy bun lathered with a homemade yellow mustard and salad dressing has become the mainstay sandwich—in addition to the chicken salad sandwich, of course.

Penetrating the marketplace even further, Lubeley's has its own signature bread, buttermilk rye; signature Danish, the "Paradice;" and signature cake, the "Dobash," a six-layer butter cake filled with chocolate pudding and topped with a butter cream icing with sprinkled chocolate. All signature products, as well as the gooey butter cake and its siblings, are available for lunch.

Surprisingly, Bob's Dog Treats have become part of Lubeley's product bundle. "My husband, Bob, makes about twenty dozen dog biscuits a day from wheat flour, bacon bits, and chicken broth," says Carol. "The dog biscuits sell especially well around Christmas time since they're big and soft and the dogs love them. Some neighbors with dogs often walk over here, tie up their dogs, and we give them a free biscuit. If you drive here with your dog in the car, we'll come out and give your dog a biscuit. We even have a dog biscuit cookie cutter in the kitchen."

Since you'll be taking lunch in what doubles as the wedding consultation room, particularly on Saturdays when prospective brides come in to view the model cakes, flip through wedding cake books, and take bites of real ones, you should know that Lubeley's is known for custom cakes as well. "Bob made a birthday cake for Bob Hope when he was in town," says Carol. "The cake was shaped like a golf course and came with a sand dune and traps. For various Missouri governors, we've made cakes that look like the state capitol in Jefferson City. When Charles Hoessel was director of the St. Louis Zoo, we baked him a six-foot-long python cake. It took three of us to carry it into the Zoo that day."

Lubeley's Bakery and Deli
7815 Watson Road, Marlborough, Missouri

 (314) 961-7160

 7 A.M. to 7 P.M. Tuesday through Saturday
8 A.M. to 1 P.M. Sunday

Not wheelchair accessible

 No smoking

66

Luna Café
Mitchell, Illinois

SINCE THE DAY in 1927 it turned on its neon sign and opened its door, the Luna Café, then situated on the original U.S. Highway 66 in Mitchell, Illinois, has had a robust business life. In 1929, the nearby $2-million Kingshighway Chain of Rocks Bridge across the Mississippi River accepted its first tolls. It was a stroke of good luck that the Luna, a quintessential Depression-era roadhouse, just happened to be the last spot in Illinois that a trucker or motorist could find food and drink before crossing into Missouri. Nice gambling and ladies of the evening could also be found at the Luna in those days.

In Luna's first decade, "Most ordinary people couldn't afford to come here—you had to know somebody to get in," former co-owner Alan Young once told me. "It was rumored that Al Capone came down here from Chicago and stayed upstairs where the prostitutes were. The gambling was conducted in our basement."

Irma Rafalala was the original Luna owner. "With its tall false front, the Luna looked old when Rafalala built it," writes Quinta Scott in *Along Route 66*. Scott marveled at the still-existing neon sign that reads: "Luna Café. Steaks. Chicken. Sea Food. Fine Dining. Package Goods." The sign's main visual feature is a full cocktail glass topped with a cherry. "When the cherry, which has been dark for years, was lit up, it meant that the girls were available upstairs," Young explained. Aficionados of old Highway 66 are working to get the sign fully restored and operative.

Current owner Larry Wofford, who bought out Young in 2007, has placed all sorts of dogs, ducks, roosters, owls, and a string of little lunas (quarter moons) around the barroom and dining area along with street and road signs, Capone-era memorabilia, and an Alcatraz poster. An impressive mahoghany luna is displayed near the back bar that allegedly came from a long-closed house of ill repute in Granite City. A prominent wreath of hot-glued condoms and Life Savers that hung on the back bar was stolen some time ago.

Luna offers a typical menu of lunchtime specials: hot roast beef sandwich, half-pound hamburger, homemade meatloaf, chicken breast with sauce, homemade chili, homemade dressings for salads, and crappie. Free chicken wings are handed out on Mondays and Fridays, provided customers buy enough alcohol.

A ten-inch taco stuffed with a half-pound of ground beef and piled high with cheese seems to be Luna's signature offering. "I had a shiny bald-headed scuba diver in here and I bet him he couldn't eat three tacos. He ate all of them but said that if he ate the fourth he'd make a fool of himself," recalled Young. "That big-ass taco you get here is a kick," a regular sitting at the bar said to me. The customer ordered a taco to show me how enormous it was then he had it boxed for take-out. "I'll have it for dinner," he said.

When they were business partners, Young and Wofford sat at the bar during the lunch hour conspicuously nursing bottles of Stag Beer. "When our customers see Larry and me drinking our Stag Beer, they're likely to do the same thing," said Young. "We sell more Stag Beer than anyone else around, maybe twenty-five cases a week."

The partners pumped new life into the Luna with special events, Young told me. "When we first bought this place, our Fourth of Julys were notoriously bad. So we perked them up with a whole-hog luau and horseshoe tournament. The first year we took in $89; the next year, more than $2,000, and so on. When we see a dead business day coming, we try to perk it up. We do many fundraisers here. If a regular is sick or goes to the hospital, we have a big fundraiser for them like a spaghetti dinner, barbeque, or raffle. All the proceeds go to the person who needs it, such as a dead person's family."

Much as they do at the Ariston Café in Litchfield, Illinois, foreign followers of historic Route 66 stop in at the Luna. In rental cars, motorcycles and even on bicycles, visitors from abroad show up regularly to see what a 1920s roadhouse looks like. "We get more publicity about the Luna in Europe than we do around here," Young would assert.

Luna Café
201 E. Chain of Rocks Road, Mitchell, Illinois

 (618) 931-3152

 8 A.M. to 3 A.M. Saturday

 Wheelchair accessible

 Smoking permitted

67

Mangia Italiano

St. Louis

MANGIA ITALIANO, MEANING "Eat Italian," has been a fixture in the Tower Grove Heights-South Grand Boulevard ethnic food district since it debuted in December 1982. Its founder was Dr. Richard Parmley, an avowed gourmand and dentist who specialized in cleft palate problems of handicapped children.

Parmley, whose ancestry was British, was obsessed with Italian food and cooking. "I do not choose to eat American," he proclaimed. "I do not choose to eat pre-packaged, mass produced and quick frozen." He became intrigued with fresh, as opposed to store-bought dried, pasta and installed four pasta-making machines in the front window of his deli and Italian gourmet food shop.

"We at Mangia Italiano," he told a newspaper reporter, "recognize that every supermarket in St. Louis offers packages of dried pasta in every shape conceivable but we are confident that once people taste fresh pasta…and discover it only takes two minutes to prepare…as compared to ten to fifteen minutes for dried pasta, once people discover the excitement of watching their pasta being created just for them, they're going to realize they've been missing a lot." For a while, Parmley wrote "The Pasta Doctor," a weekly column for the old *St. Louis*

Globe-Democrat in which he told how to prepare concoctions like black rabbit of eastern Sicily or "golf ball-sized" zucchini pieces for a pasta dish.

Although he kept busy at both Cardinal Glennon Hospital for Children and his Ballwin dental practice, Parmley, a huge, towering man, especially when wearing a billowing chef's hat and a white uniform braided with the red and green colors of the Italian flag, enjoyed appearing in his storefront window with his pasta machines to turn out batches of linguini, tortellini, and ravioli.

David Burmeister, a manager at the former Balaban's Restaurant, bought Mangia Italiano in 2001, a decade after Parmley's premature death. Burmeister and his partners kept the old pasta machines but added five more and moved them to a separate "factory" on Cherokee Street. The team has doubled the seating, put in a tall contemporary bar, refurbished the interior, added a new non-smoking room, introduced a tantalizing luncheon buffet with trademark pizza not on the regular menu, and generally retained Parmley's ideas about Italian food.

"We make 1,000 pounds of fresh pasta a week," said Burmeister. "We use it here in the restaurant, sell it for take-out, and make it on contract for twenty-five or thirty other restaurants." On summer Saturdays, the restaurant runs a retail pasta stand at the Tower Grove Park farmer's market and one or two other farmers' markets.

On weekdays from 11:30 to 2:30, Mangia's buffet line displays a savory pasta salad with a spicy mayonnaise sauce in addition to noodles that change daily, green salads, soups, fresh vegetables, toasted ravioli, cheese and tomato pizza, meatballs, bread pudding by the slice, and chocolate cake.

Although Parmley offered sandwiches in the early days, he didn't name them for Roman warriors as the new group has done. You can order a Marcus (roast beef, cheddar, jalapenos, cream cheese, red peppers, and olives), an Antonius (marinated portabella, carmelized onions, pesto, and mozzarella), a Caligua (housemade meatballs with tomato sauce and mozzarella), and the sandwich best-seller, the Nero (pan-seared tilapia with romaine, tomato, and chipotle aioli). At least eight pasta items are on the lunch menu, including the popular Spaghetti Mangia, baked in a cream sauce that is a Parmley legacy. "All the pasta was made fresh this morning and so were our sauces," Burmeister reminds us.

Along most of Mangia Italiano's south wall is an earthtone mural begun in 1995 by St. Louis artist Wayne St. Wayne. "It starts with the dinosaurs but also has images of Alfred E. Newman, Mikhail Gorbachev, President Reagan, the Frankenstein monster, and even the old Grand Avenue streetcar," observes Burmeister. "We call it Mangia Evolutiano because Wayne comes in here about once a week to work on it and we don't know what he'll add or change. The mural has some grotesque images that some customers don't want to look at. Other customers can spend their entire lunch or dinner studying it."

Mangia Italiano
3145 S. Grand Blvd., St. Louis

 (314) 664-8585

 11:30 A.M. to 9 P.M. Monday through Thursday
11:30 A.M. to 10:30 P.M. Friday, Saturday

 Wheelchair accessible

 Smoking permitted

68

Mimi's Subway Bar and Grill

Ferguson, Missouri

WHEN IT OPENED as The Subway Bar during World War II, the building that contains Mimi's was a designated bomb shelter, says Mimi Fowler, restaurant owner since 1994. Mimi's is the only St. Louis area restaurant where customers must walk down twenty concrete steps to enter. "Local families still tend to come down here to get away from the threat of scary weather," she says. "Our older folks know that this is the best place to be in a tornado." The building has 16-inch walls.

"We have no waitresses here, only a serving system," Fowler explains. "Customers come to the window to read the posted menu, order, and pay the bill. When a meal is ready, I serve it but I don't waitress. For beverages, customers walk over to the bar and order anything they want. I go later to pick up the dirty plates and cups since we have no busboys." Fowler says the only complaint she hears is that she feeds customers too much food. "We have a saying here," she says: 'We'd rather see you walk away full than hungry.'"

A rarity for local restaurants is Mimi's all-you-can-eat soup or chili that chef Kim Bargart stirs up daily. "It's our trademark right alongside our half-pound angus ground beef hamburgers, our Signature Burgers, Thousand Island Burgers, and Bacon Cheeseburgers plus our Cajun Chicken Barbecue sandwiches. We also have homemade pizza and famous salads like our Large Fried Chicken Salad and our Large Lemon Pepper Chicken Salad." Bargart's soups—such as stuffed green pepper, Wisconsin blue cheese, cream of broccoli, or chicken-and-dumplings—are so popular that the kettle often runs dry before lunch hour concludes. The all-you-can-eat soup or chili special can be wickedly tempting to gorging customers. "One fellow ordered the equivalent of four 32-ounce salad bowls of my stuffed green pepper soup," recalls Bargart. "That about drained the pot that day."

Before Mimi bought the place, Bud Barger, who described himself as the oldest bartender in the St. Louis area, was Subway's longtime barkeeper. "In his early days, kids would skip school and come here to play pool," says Fowler. "There were still truant officers back then. When the real squeaky door opened on top of the stairs, Bud knew it was the truant officer. So he hid the kids in the back closet until the officer left. When Bud died after bartending for sixty-seven years, we planted a tree in his memory at January Wabash Park in Ferguson."

Lunch hour at Mimi's attracts its share of regulars. "Fifty percent of them drink at least one beer at lunch; on Fridays they buy pitchers of beer because the weekend's coming," observes Fowler. "Friday is the day the Raccoon Lodge meets here for lunch. They're nine or ten guys who work down the street at the Emerson plant. When they first started eating here they always wore raccoon hats, which they still wear to our annual Christmas party. They love our bacon cheeseburgers."

Customers can lunch at Mimi's 100-year-old bar with a brass footrail and solid cherry strip along the bar edge. Some old-timers believe that the back bar may have been produced by Anheuser-Busch in the early 1900s, but AB archivists insist their company never made back bars. In a nearby corner, a 1930s-era phone booth stands tall. "The phone company wanted to remove it, but I stopped them," says Fowler. On a wall in the dartboard and pool table room is a wooden Anheuser Busch eagle. Fowler has heard that the eagle once was mounted outside the brewery's headquarters on Pestalozzi Street.

Fowler says that she and her co-workers have nicknames for most of her regular customers. "We must have a hundred guys named Bob, so we have special handles for each of them like Handy Bob or Old Bob. We have lots of Jims like Keno Jim and Dammit Jim because he loves to swear. We have two construction workers we call 'The Extra Meat Boys' because they are always begging us to toss some extra meat on their open-face roast beef sandwiches. There is Subway Dave who comes in mornings to clean the bar, sweep, mop, police the parking lot, and make sure the cooler is filled with beer. At lunch, he usually sits at the bar near the tapper. He gets special draft beer pricing because of who he is."

Mimi's Subway Bar and Grill
46 N. Florissant, Ferguson, Missouri

 (314) 524-6009

 11 A.M. to 10 P.M. Monday through Saturday
11 A.M. to 6 P.M. Sunday

 Limited wheelchair accessibility

 Smoking permitted

69

Mother-in-Law House
St. Charles, Missouri

WHEN DONNA HAFER purchased the Mother-In-Law House she was enrolled in a Lindenwood University "awareness class" taught by a psychic. "I once told the psychic that I thought someone had left the windows open in the fine arts building because it was drafty in our classroom. The teacher studied me closely, then said: 'Donna, I'll see you after class.'"

Afterwards, the psychic told Donna that a ghost had been sitting next to her during class. "That was an enlightening experience," Donna says, leading her to question the unusual vibes that she had sensed in her newly acquired restaurant. Hafer soon phoned the psychic and said: "We may have a ghost. Can you come over and tell me what may be going on here?"

After her visit, the psychic told Hafer that "the mother-in-law who spends her day looking out the window in your front dining room is lonely. So, every night before you leave you must tell her that you love her, then everything will be all right."

Years later, the upshot of the psychic's advice is that Hafer, her son Robert, or a trusted staff member, bids the mother-in-law ghost a warm "good night" before locking up.

"I've been here twenty-five years and I want to stay another twenty-five," Hafer says.

Hafer explains that the mother-in-law sits at Table Number 1, "the first on the right as you enter the dining room. Some customers tell me that they feel that the mother-in-law is there. I have never seen her but when I need help, I think that she goes out and finds help for me. She may find a friend who will come in and pour coffee or water when we're short-handed or send us in a new employee when we need one. I'm truly thankful for her presence."

Who was the mother-in-law? Local historians believe it may have been Christina Becker, whose son-in-law Captain Francis X. Kremer (alternately spelled Kramer or Krammer) erected a red brick "double" or duplex home—a structure originally divided down the middle by a thick brick wall—for himself and his wife on one side and his mother-in-law, Christina, on the other. "Kremer (around 1860) handed his mother-in-law the keys to her new quarters and told her she could remain there as long as she lived," Edna McElhiney Olson wrote in the *St. Charles Journal* in 1960. Apparently, she has.

Little is known about Captain Kremer, a local mill operator who moved to St. Charles in 1853. "We don't know if in his earlier years he was a captain on the river or a captain in a war," says Hafer.

When you order the restaurant's popular lunchtime half-pound "Salt Lick Trail" burger—"It's ninety percent lean ground beef and only ten percent fat with hand-packed best- quality bacon and the best-quality Cheddar cheese," Hafer explains—you'll probably be seated in reasonable proximity to the mother-in-law ghost. She sits at a table for four by the window.

Hafer purchased the restaurant in 1982 from Carl House, a former chef at the Brown Derby restaurant in Beverly Hills, California. House had operated the Mother-In-Law House since 1969 and had redone the interior in heavy Victorian. The bar area supposedly replicates the pilot house from the Golden Eagle, a Missouri River packet boat. When Hafer bought the place she considered renaming it "Tara" because, as she often says, "I have some Scarlett O'Hara in me." Hafer's mother talked her out of it.

Hafer brought along many of her favorite recipes from The Copper Platter restaurant, a business she started in 1979 and continued to run simultaneously with her new restaurant until 1996. For a while, Hafer recalls, "I would supervise lunch at the Platter then rush down Main Street to help cook dinner at the Mother-in-Law House." That got burdensome.

Hafer's mother contributed a celery seed dressing that she mixes into her fried chicken salad as well as the Russian dressing that tops the signature Mother-in-Law salad—spinach, lettuce, water chestnuts, eggs, bean sprouts, and bacon. "We package and sell the celery seed dressing," Hafer adds.

Every weekday there is a special entrée plus a special soup that belongs to a twenty-four-soup lunchtime rotation. "Today it is corn chowder," said Hafer. "My son Robert, who is our general manager and a cook, too, invented our salmon chowder, and I like both his vegetable and prime rib soups," she says. "I can make anyone well with my prime rib soup," says Robert. "We boil the bones to get all the marrow out and we use lots of vegetables in the process. Then we pick off the prime rib from the bone and get the fat out."

As for desserts, "Mother-In-Law's reputation for having the best pies and the flakiest crust in town is growing," the menu claims. Although the only official dessert entrée on the lunch menu is coconut cream pie, customers are urged to "ask about other desserts of the day." Those other desserts might include Robert's cheesecake or Hafer's brownies, peppermint ice cream, fudge sauce, or ice cream pie.

Hafer calls her basement banquet and special events room "The Cider Cellar." The space is unusual—walls made from Missouri River stone, floor joists fashioned from white oak tree trunks to which Hafer has attached apple tree branches from her family farm in Gillespie, Illinois. Rustic picket fence swatches and old millwork from the area add to the décor. A sign by the basement bar reads: "I Love Pigs." That message explains all the pig memorabilia and artifacts that populate the basement, an area that could just as well be called "The Pig Room." It's worth a look after dessert.

Mother-in-Law House
500 S. Main Street, St. Charles, Missouri

☎ (636) 946-9444

🕐 Lunch: 11 A.M. to 2:30 P.M. Monday through Saturday
Dinner: 5:30 P.M. to 9:30 P.M. Tuesday through Saturday

♿ Wheelchair accessible

🚭 No smoking

70

Nadine's Gin Joint

St. Louis

IT'S BEEN UPHILL all the way since Nadine Soaib cut the ribbon at the eponymous Nadine's Gin Joint in 2000.

"I bombed with just about my first creation here," she recalls with a wince. "I had come up with a dish that featured three or four White Castle hamburgers covered with home-made sausage gravy and I was excited about it because nobody in town offered anything like it. But I was shocked when no one ordered it—no one—and I wondered seriously about my future in this business." Years later she now says: "I'm here through God's grace and no one put me here to fail."

Nadine's inhabits a solid red-brick building from 1850 that accommodated neighborhood saloons for decades, more recently McIntire's, then Tim and Judy's, a kind of "politician's" bar with assorted characters and regulars where one could gamble and enjoy a merchant's lunch.

"When we moved in, we were cleaning out under the bar and discovered an urn with cremated remains," says Nadine. "The remains turned out to be those of Ray Bennett, who was a popular bartender at Tim and Judy's. When he died, we understand, many of the bar customers pooled their money and had Ray cremated. Tim and Judy probably forgot about Ray when they sold the place. Once we found out whose remains they were, we gave them back to Tim and Judy. I don't know what they finally did with Ray."

In her first few months as an owner of an ancient building, Nadine found some unexpected eeriness. On several occasions, she entered the building to find candles burning but no melted wax and no reasonable explanation why. On their first return visit, Tim and Judy were eating lunch at a table under a firmly attached wall cabinet when the brass top of an old candy dish mysteriously dislodged from a shelf and crashed at their feet. "They haven't been back since," said Nadine.

Now that Nadine's spectral run-ins have waned, she prefers to talk food and ambience. "Our salmon Caesar salad is very popular," she says. "The salad is so sprawling that we have to smash down the six-ounce salmon because it tends to tip off the plate." Her chicken salad, loaded with dill, is a major lure at lunch and so is the blackened salmon salad, the beef tenderloin salad, and appetizers that can be full meals like flash-fried spinach and toasted ravioli.

Beyond salmon, Nadine now offers oysters on the half shell, monkfish, grouper, and, on weekends, "all the fried fish (pollock mainly) you can eat." "I'm turning this place into a seafood restaurant, it seems," she says.

One side dish is on Nadine's permanent menu, the "Neighborhood Famous Beet Salad." "When we bought this place, we found a single can of beets in the kitchen," says Nadine. "I asked my girlfriend, Brenda: 'What do I do with this?' She said do this: 'add Italian dressing, seasoning, celery seed, and some red onions and mix them with the beets.' I did and customers can't get enough of it."

Nadine's has added a spacious patio lined with oleander plants, tubs of canna lilies, and other masses of flora—plus a long patio bar and a collection of "unwanted" artificial Christmas trees used year-round for "insulation." A huge tent over the patio allows food service all year.

In February, Nadine's pool table room is converted into a workstation for Soulard Mardi Gras volunteers who make costumes; work with paint, glue guns, and glitter; and plan Nadine's Mardi Gras parade float. "Our floor is literally covered with glitter but I tell the volunteers to leave it there. It lets everyone know we're part of the team."

Nadine's Gin Joint
1931 S. 12th Street, St. Louis

 (314) 436-3045

 11 A.M. to 1:30 A.M. Monday through Saturday

 Wheelchair accessible

 Smoking permitted

71

Old Town Donuts
Florissant, Missouri

A VETERAN DUNKER at Old Town Donuts in Florissant says that what he likes best about donuts is that "They have no bones." He speaks for all of us.

At Old Town, there are no bones and only yeast in the very popular glazed donuts (twenty-five percent of sales) and the nearly equally applauded oblong chocolate- and vanilla-filled long johns. Since Old Town is the only twenty-four-hour donut shop around, with three eight-hour baker shifts, "We know we have to have fresh donuts at least three times a day," says Keith Took, owner. "The best time to buy fresh donuts here is between five and six A.M., between ten and noon, and from four to five in the afternoon."

Take-out donuts, muffins, and bagels bring in the bulk of Old Town's revenue. Coffee, a revenue sideline, brings the shop to life.

Old Town is located in a small strip center near the historic part of Florissant. Large glass windows provide a sweeping view of busy tables, full display cases, and a long coffee counter. "Donut shops with large windows tend to bring in more impulse customers," a veteran donut maker once told me. At Old Town, those large windows beckon scores of regular patrons.

Some donut operators get rankled when customers linger too long over donuts, some even invoking "20-minute chair" rules to discourage protracted stays. Not Took. "We love coffee drinkers sitting at our tables because their cars fill our lot and when the lot is full, more and more people come in to take out donuts. I don't care if our coffee people stay here three or four hours. Besides, many of them buy donuts to take home."

Took says his coffee regulars—mostly retired men—come in shifts. "There's the 6 A.M. table, the 7:30 table, the one o'clock Coffee Club and so on. A lot of the men are World War II veterans including a B-29 pilot who was a squadron commander. For most who come early in the morning, coffee and donuts constitute breakfast."

Most weekdays around 7:30 A.M. two men in pickup trucks, each with one dog, park side by side in front of Old Town's big window. Before leaving their trucks, the men nudge their dogs—a Pomeranian named Lady and a bulldog named Gus—to their windows so they can bark to each other while their masters sip coffee for the next two hours. After an hour, one of the men will take donut holes (always supplied gratis by Took) to the dogs. "They want to keep those dogs talking," said Took.

Ed Riley, a former Florissant councilman, says he was present at the ribbon-cutting to open Old Town by members of the Took family thirty years ago. A regular, Riley belongs to the 8 A.M. group. "Keith (Took) usually has samples out on the counter for us then brings us a pot of coffee. We'll usually get a big donut and share it. Sometimes we get a chocolate long john and cut it four ways."

After the daily workout at a fitness center, Don Tanner, a retired dean at Florissant Community College, and Greg Campbell, owner of Crest Bowl, retreat to Old Town to figure out Mindbenders word games and puzzles from the daily *St. Louis Post-Dispatch*. "After we tax our brains and take some coffee," said Tanner, "we're off to work." Tanner chairs the board at Lutheran School of Theology.

Clarence Raup ran a nursery that sold rich black Florissant topsoil, once coveted by gardeners and now pretty much vanished. "I just came from the dump truck show in St. Charles," he told his pals. "Years ago, there were nothing but truck farms out here in the Florissant Valley. I guess the glaciers put the topsoil here. Sometimes it would run ten feet deep. Now that the Valley is so built up there's no more ground in North County to take topsoil off of."

Took boasts of two veteran employees, 9 P.M. to 5 A.M. cashier Mary Anselmo, with Old Town since its inception, and Vera Marlowe, donut box folder for twenty-eight years. Marlowe, ninety-one, folds anywhere from two hundred to four hundred half- and full-dozen boxes each day. For a head start, she partially folds two hundred boxes at home then, with her daughter's help, brings them to Old Town around 10 P.M. to complete. As she folds, her daughter stacks the boxes.

"I always sit at the front table," says Marlowe, who uses a walker. "If anyone is sitting there when I come in, they always graciously get up and let me sit down. Once in a while, young people who come in late for coffee come over to help me fold, especially the kids from the Christian college over on Dunn Road." Marlowe worked for the old Velvet Freeze ice cream company for twenty years before joining Old Town. What happened at Velvet Freeze? "They folded," she said.

The always-cheerful Mary Anselmo has acquired an insider's knowledge of the donut business. "You can tell which one of our bakers baked a batch just by looking at the donuts," she observes. "Each baker is different. Their donuts have different sizes, different colors, and different consistencies."

Anselmo is pleased that Old Town has banned smoking. "Our donuts were absorbing too much cigarette smoke so we had everyone quit."

Old Town Donuts
510 N. New Florissant Road, Florissant, Missouri

☎ (314) 831-0907

🕐 Open 24 hours

♿ Wheelchair accessible

🚭 No smoking

72

Papa Fabarre's

In downtown St. Louis

THE WAIT AND support staff at Papa Fabarre's second-floor hideaway restaurant in Macy's downtown department store in St. Louis is a tightly-knit, playful bunch. Most of them have been together for years.

"One morning, just before our 11 o'clock opening, we were all attempting to skip," recalls Joyce Skaggs, longtime manager. "It is really hard to skip after not doing it since childhood. Nevertheless, we were skipping through the dining area and having lots of fun. When our first customers congregated in the entrance area, they saw what we were doing and five or six of them joined us. We all went skipping together and we covered every inch of our space but the kitchen. The best skipper was a St. Louis circuit court judge. We all stopped to watch her—we were in awe of her talent. And we were roaring with laughter.

"You should see our team when a customer is celebrating a birthday," continues Skaggs. "Our staff ceases whatever they're doing and walks over to the birthday table and opens up. We call ourselves 'The Worst Singing Group Downtown.' Come on down on or near your own birthday and we will prove it."

Most of the servers at this thirty-three-year-old lunch-only restaurant, with its turn-of-the-twentieth-century motif, have logged at least a decade of service. Barbara Howard is one of them. "When I arrived in 1977, all the waitresses had to wear long, pink 'Little House on the Prairie' dresses with white bonnets. Back then we were really busy and stayed open to eight or nine at night." Papa's regularly scheduled disco nights with live bands and professional dancers then tapered off to just a piano player before the era ended in the mid-1980s.

"For lunch in those early days," says Howard, "the restaurant was much different from today. We had a Biloxi salad in a big shell with real crabmeat, shrimp, eggs, carrots, tomatoes, and green pepper. People swarmed this place to get that salad. Our lunches were like dinners. We had shrimp Rockefeller, shrimp Thermidor, whole catfish, huge crab legs."

When Famous-Barr was acquired by Macy's in 2005, the staff at Papa Fabarre's (Fabarre's is an imaginative play on the words "Famous-Barr") transitioned easily. There were no personnel changes, the Midwest dining club continued (club members get their cards punched after each meal, with the eleventh meal free) and the menu was hardly touched except for the French fries. "We were used to the thin fries that we'd been eating here for years, especially with our burgers," said architect Fred Powers, a devout regular. "When Macy's introduced curly fries we expressed our displeasure. There was enough commotion over this that Macy's did a public opinion poll so customers could vote for the old fries or the new curly ones. So we stuffed the ballot box in favor of the old straight-cut fries. I signed one ballot 'Bubba' and Bill Bowersox, my business partner, signed another one 'Al Gore.'" Our side won and Macy's graciously changed back to the old fries."

French onion soup has reached landmark status at Papa's. Austin Johnson, Papa's venerable chef, stirs up nearly fifty gallons of it weekly. Howard, the waitress, states that nearly half of Papa's customers order the soup. Powers recalls arriving for lunch late one day and ordering the soup for himself and a client from San Francisco. "I told my guest that our soup compared to the best he might find in San Francisco," said Powers. "'We can't make the soup for you because we are out of French bread,' the waitress told me. "I said to the waitress that the Famous-Barr baked goods counter on the first floor sold French bread and that perhaps someone could go down and get a loaf. She said she couldn't do that, but that I could if I wished. I took the escalator down to the first floor, bought the bread, and they made the soup for us. My client agreed that the soup was very good."

Powers and Bowersox are such stalwart regulars that someone on Papa's staff will call to remind them of certain daily lunch specials, especially the Sloppy Joes on Mondays. "If we can't make it on Monday, they will keep our Sloppy Joes in the refrigerator for us," says Bowersox. "Once, they kept our Sloppy Joes until Thursday. They still tasted good." "By then, they tasted more like chili," adds Skaggs, the candid manager.

Powers, who cooks for a hobby, is so sentimental about his years of eating at Papa's that he says: "I'd like to cook the staff lunch sometime. I'd cook back in Papa's kitchen and I'd even clean up afterward. I think I'd make them a pasta dish, maybe tortellini with bacon and a cream sauce."

Beyond the daily specials—Sloppy Joes, meatloaf, taco salad, fried chicken, and cod—Monday through Friday respectively—the John White burger is a daily standout. "John White was the chef at Famous-Barr's old Northwoods store," says

Skaggs. "He created the John White, which is a grilled burger with mild cheddar sauce and breaded fried onions. You don't see burgers like this anymore. When conventions come to town they come in and order French onion soup and the John White burger."

Papa Fabarre's opened in 1976 as a tin-ceiling, tile-floor replica of a days-gone-by restaurant. "This place was the creation of our Famous-Barr 'visual man' Dan Clark," recalled the late Helen Weiss, who served forty-seven years as Famous-Barr's director of special events.

"Papa's was forged in the 1970s when restaurants were starting to appear on Laclede's Landing," said Bowersox. "Many of them had the same theme and most of them are gone. If this place ever closed, it would be a crime."

Papa Fabarre's
601 Olive St., Second floor

 (314) 425-3634

 11 A.M. to 3 P.M. Monday through Friday

 Wheelchair accessible

 No smoking

73

Pietro's

St. Louis

PIETRO'S, A DESTINATION restaurant in south St. Louis—much in the manner of Hodak's restaurant, the fried chicken emporium farther south—is a place where customers cherish decades of colorful memories.

One continuous customer cluster is the Retired Southwest Doctors' Group that has met regularly for lunch at Pietro's since 1960, Pietro's debut year, when the Southwest medical building was a neighbor on Watson Road. In earlier years, the doctors met Saturdays for lunch at Pietro's. Alphonse, a veteran, unflappable waiter was usually assigned to the doctors' table. "What do you want today?" Alphonse would ask, disregarding any need for printed menus. "It wasn't worth our while to request a menu since we all knew that Alphonse would bring us what he wanted us to have, which was usually a medium strip steak," recalled Dr. William Fogarty, Sr., a retired Southwest internist. "Alphonse was a major piece of work."

In the half-century that the Southwest doctors have patronized Pietro's, they've been woven into the institutional fabric. "When we're sitting around the table, we're often besieged by former patients who stop by to pat us on the back or update us on personal health issues," said Fogarty. If the men are in Pietro's during a medical emergency, they're called upon. While the group lunched one day, a man apparently dropped dead at the bar. A Southwest clinic physician examined the man. "They had to lower me so I could feel his pulse, which wasn't there," the doctor recalled.

As to the slickly printed menu, its contents have remained fairly steady. "Chicken Pietro (boneless breast in white wine and mushroom sauce) is our number one seller," says John Iovaldi, co-owner of the restaurant with his wife, Marianne. "Next comes our homemade baked lasagna and then all of our daily specials like sauerbraten with potato pancakes for all the southside Germans, frog legs on occasion, tilapia and filet of sole on Friday." The veal Parmigiana sandwich (chopped cutlet with meat sauce and cheese on French bread) has been a lunch leader along with "Pietro's Famous Fish Sandwich," which the menu describes as "Freshly breaded, served with our homemade tartar or cocktail sauce." The menu doesn't say what kind of fish it is or why it is famous. "It's filet of sole," Iovaldi says.

Pasta Ballal, linguini with shrimp and sweet peppers—a menu fixture—is named for Dr. Herbert Ballal, a retired Southwest internist. "He's another piece of work," says Fogarty.

In its first decade, Pietro's sold its house salad dressing that had been developed by cook Emmy Lou Young. "In those days we sold the dressing in old bourbon bottles, some of which Emmy Lou helped empty," says Iovaldi. "Dad (John Iovaldi, Sr. restaurant co-founder) always insisted that Emmy Lou make and bottle the dressing before she started drinking." One Southwest doctor recalls requests from his sister: "Bring me six fifths of the dressing the next time you're at Pietro's," were her instructions.

John Iovaldi, Sr. and Marco Pietro Griffero, Sr. took over Charley Mittino's Supper Club in 1960 and in the years of their partnership added three dining rooms. John Iovaldi, Jr., who assumed the reins in 1995, has added three more. The elder Iovaldi, who dropped dead during his son's graduating ceremony from St. Louis University High School, was often blunt with customers. "He'd sit at the front door and not get up and always asked 'How many are you?' whether it was one customer or ten," remembers optometrist Tom Bell, still a steady noonday regular. Bob Boaz, a retired St. Louis police officer, recalls that Iovaldi, Sr. was nonplussed when someone complained about a steak being tough. "That's the way some of the steaks come," the restaurateur would casually reply.

"People still remember my dad's gin rummy games down in our basement potato bin," says Iovaldi. "Those fellows had a continuing gin rummy game during the 1960s and 1970s. Sometimes they'd start at two or three in the afternoon and go to midnight. There would be police and fire captains and other notables from the community. On Sundays, when we were closed, the guys would go over to someone's house to continue their game."

Although Pietro's attracts customers of all ages, Boaz likes to joke that the restaurant specializes in old people and funerals. "Sometimes if you walk in here and you're seventy years old, you may be the youngest person in the place," he cracks, drawing laughter from his lunch pal, Bell. As for funerals, there's no joking around. "People put it in their wills that they want their funeral lunch at Pietro's," says Marianne Iovaldi, who handles special events. "In fact, a lady just booked a funeral lunch for Saturday," she said. "We have many happy occasions here, too," she added.

Boaz said Pietro's gets crowded at times, even during lunch. "Sometimes in the middle of our lunch, someone will come up to us and say 'You have to move because we're putting some tables together to accommodate a big party.' They know that we regulars will be back tomorrow, so we move without any begrudging."

Boaz continues: "People can be standing in line waiting to get in for lunch and Iovaldi gets a phone call and someone says 'I have fifty people. Can we come over now and be served?' And the answer is always: 'Come on over.' I don't know how the kitchen does it, but it does."

Boaz and Bell shift conversation to Pietro's bar, which wouldn't be the same without Joe Delworth who sits on the corner stool nearly every day, lunching on a sandwich and sipping a scotch and water. "Joe has been coming in at least twenty years and, in fact, has "trained" many of our bartenders," says Iovaldi. "When people come in looking for the rathskeller where we have meetings, he points them down the stairs." Delworth knows who comes and goes. "The FBI meets here, the Port Authority meets here, the Labor Council meets here, and they all go downstairs. The other day we had two funerals and two baby showers. It was confusing but I got everyone pointed in the right direction." Once a month, Delworth gets off his stool and goes downstairs to lunch with his own group of retired insurance claims managers. They call themselves the Silver Foxes.

Boaz and Bell stretch their memories way back to the days of Brusatti's Bar, the small neighborhood operation that preceded Mittino's Supper Club and Pietro's. "That Gabe Brusatti was quite a piece of work," said Boaz. "Remember when he had that big red Cadillac convertible and would cruise around at ten miles an hour looking at girls?"

Pietro's
3901 Watson Road, St. Louis

 (314) 645-9263

 11 A.M. to 9 P.M. Monday and Tuesday
11 A.M. to 10 P.M. Wednesday through Saturday

 Wheelchair accessible

Smoking in bar only

74

Ricardo's Italian Café

St. Louis

Mark Adams, co-owner with wife, Michelle, of the Lafayette Square Italian restaurant that occupies a string of old storefronts, ghosts of former eateries known as Salvatore's, Café Zoe, and Empire Café, is a self-taught, do-it-yourself restaurateur. The Adams family acquired the drab shells of the buildings in 1989 intent on injecting new color into the neighborhood. This they did by creating an "indoor patio" they call the "Portofino Room," next to the main dining room.

"One day after buying our storefronts we went to a play at Vianney High School in Kirkwood where their theater students had done some great set designs," says Mark. "Why can't we get one of these students to do a mural for us, maybe even design a set for us?' Mark asked Michelle. "It wasn't long before teacher Al Book brought his whole stagecraft class down here to do set design and murals of the Ligurian Sea in northern Italy with people, boats, and other things to remind you of Italy. My sons and I put up shutters and splattered them with grey paint to make them look old. We did research on flowers of northern Italy such as bougainvillea and daisies and we had them painted in the murals. The murals depict Portofino, an elegant village on the Ligurian Sea." (Portofino is an international gathering spot for movie stars, royalty, and business giants.)

"After we finished the 'Portofino Room,' we traveled to Portofino to see if we got the mural right," says Mark. "It turns out we did! The mural has great personal meaning for us since most of our family is pictured in the Portofino village scene: Our kids, Mom and Dad, the in-laws, our dogs. We had boats drawn in and we named the boats after good friends."

For me, the baked lasagna, a recipe from Mark's grand-mother, is a major attraction at lunch. Mark, who oversees the kitchen, uses ground beef for his lasagna, loading the dish with fennel seed and topping it with provolone, St. Louis's ubiqui-tous cheese. "When we first opened in 1989 we made two pans of lasagna to last a week," Mark says. "Now we do ten times that and make it every day."

Beef spedini—a permanent lunch special—is a kitchen favorite. "We are one of very few restaurants that make beef spedini like it's made in Italy," Mark declares. "It's not rolled or stuffed; it's shis-ka-bob on a stick. It constitutes twenty-five percent of our lunch revenue. We have chicken spedini, too." Both spedinis were on the menu of Salvatore's, where Mark cooked before purchasing the place and renaming it Ricardo's in honor of his dad, Richard Adams. The menu's entire pasta list, headed by linguine pesto and cavatelli broccoli, remains intact from the Salvatore's period.

Mark took a cooking class near Portofino and learned to bake bread, something he had not done before. "Now I make all my own bread, five kinds of it," he says. Ricardo's offers a full brace of sandwiches, wraps, and hot grilled sandwiches known as paninis. "The big panini for us is the smoked turkey club," Mark says.

Mark runs a daring message on his menu. It reads: "If there is a dish from a previous menu you wish to have, just ask your server and we will be happy to prepare it for you." Mark says he hasn't been blindsided by any strange requests, but he adds that if he is too swamped in the kitchen he'll send his server to the table to apologize. "I like to say that you can have anything you can pay for unless there is a time constraint," Mark adds.

Few restaurants honor their favorite customers as thoughtfully as Ricardo's. Near the restrooms, the Adamses have created a customer wall of fame with photos and plaques. The wall honors nine customers for whom menu items have been named. Examples: "Chicken Murfellini" honors Father Mike Murphy of Webster Groves. "Although Father Mike is obviously Irish, we told him that any dish named for him has to sound Italian," explains Mark. "We named 'Penne Michelangelo' in honor of Father Michael Joyce who went to Italy a lot and told us we had to make that dish for him. 'Shrimp Oldani' is named for Father John Oldani who now lives in Texas but was posted in St. Louis and came here every Saturday night for fried shrimp. The 'Strip Ricardo' (strip steak) is named for my father. 'Chicken Marie' (a charbroiled breast topped with white sauce) is named for Michelle's grandmother, Marie Riley, who was German and hated garlic. It's our only dish without garlic. By the way, if your name is on Ricardo's wall of fame you get a plaque to display at home."

Ricardo's hominess strikes you immediately. Entrance is through the barroom where there's an eighty-year-old Kimball upright piano, a gift of a friend who allowed the Adams children to practice on it. Photos of the Adams family and friends are atop the piano. A wall filled with photos of employee's children is across the room. "Our bus girl from sixteen years ago just brought us pictures of her kids, which we will hang," says Michelle.

Real plants, as contrasted with the plants drawn into the "Portofino Room" murals, sit in window boxes in the entrance room. Mark salvaged one plant from his grandmother and others from funerals of in-laws. "I tell my servers: 'When you water the plants, don't over-water or you'll kill them. They're about all I have left of my family!'"

The main reason Ricardo's serves no breakfast and offers lunch from 11 to 2 only is Mark's swim schedule. He is the head diving coach and assistant swimming coach for Vianney High School and Parkway Central High School in west St. Louis County. "I am at Parkway weekday mornings at six and at Vianney at three in the afternoon," he says. That makes for an unusually busy day.

Ricardo's Italian Café
1931 Park Avenue, St. Louis

☎ (314) 421-4833

🕐 Lunch: 11 A.M. to 2 P.M. Tuesday through Friday
Dinner: 5:30 P.M. to 9 P.M. Tuesday through Thursday
5:30 P.M. to 10 P.M. Friday through Saturday

♿ Wheelchair accessible

🚬 Smoking permitted

75

St. Louis Tearoom

St. Louis

UNLESS I HAVE overlooked something, I'd say that the St. Louis Tearoom is the only place in town that dishes up lines of poetry right in the middle of the lunch hour. Co-owner Judy Rusch delivers the poetry, mostly lines by the late *Detroit Free Press* resident poet, Edgar A Guest. Judy walks to the center of the Garden Room, pauses while diners set aside their quiches and salads, opens a dog-eared Edgar Guest and reads away. "Edgar's poetry (from the 1920s to 1950s) has topics that are easier for people to connect to; his language is easier to understand," says Judy, notwithstanding two lines supposedly written by the iconoclastic writer Dorothy Parker:

"I'd rather flunk my Wasserman test
Than read a poem by Eddie Guest."

Judy's fallback poet for lunchtime audiences is Eugene Field, although, she says, "his wording is often pretty flowery." When Judy finishes her poetry, she takes a minute or two to point out who's who among the photos displayed in the room. "My mom and dad are up there with me right after World War II. I was three," Judy explains. "A lot of pictures are people we can't identify although a lady spotted her brother's wedding photo. He came in to see it and brought his grandchildren."

For Rebecca Daake, who manages the tearoom and is one of Judy's daughters, their business—which began in south St. Louis in January 2007—doesn't fully conform to the generally accepted belief that tearooms are only for women. "We are different," she states. "We have lots of male customers; we serve real portions; we actually cook in a working kitchen, and we don't serve your typical tearoom sandwiches that are small and dainty and not enough to eat for a man."

"We had men with us today," observes Judy.

All arguments aside about how the St. Louis Tearoom is unique, it's the quiche of the day that customers seek out. Ten quiche recipes rotate frequently but there are the standby quiches—the bacon and Parmesan cheese; the Lorraine (bacon and Swiss cheese); the Mediterranean with feta cheese, and the veggie.

Most St. Louis Tearoom sandwiches have neighborhood-appropriate names. There is the "Utah Street" classic BLT, the "Grand Oak Hill" egg salad sandwich, and the "Roger Place club" on toasted Vienna bread "livened up with basil and mayonnaise."

Everyone starts off their meal with trademark English sweet scones made daily from recipes found by cook Barbara Obermayer (another of Judy's daughters) in the 1936 *Magic Chef Cooking Book*. Customers can opt for appetizers, salads ,and soups or order a main entrée, including quiche, lemon pepper salmon steak, or raspberry baked chicken breast. Side dishes include "fluffy ambrosia," a kind of chilled fruit salad that mixes cherries, pistachios, and marshmallows; an intriguing three-potato salad; and the Claremont coleslaw with cucumber and carrots in an oil-vinegar, instead of mayonnaise, base.

For your beverage, you can order an endless cup of coffee or for $2.50 per person an endless pot of tea. Each table has its own tea menu that describes forty different teas, led by cherry almond, ginger peach, and a lemon-vanilla combination. Many customers order iced tea. "Today we had blackberry vanilla," said Judy.

An impressive dessert list is headed by English trifle, although, as the menu states, "Barb, 'The Cook,' reserves the right to add any delicious decadent dessert...any time she wishes!" "Ours is the traditional, layered trifle dessert," says Judy. "We have had British ladies here tell us that ours is very close to the trifles at home. Our trifle is actually pound cake with brandy on it with layers of raspberry pudding. You can leave the tearoom under the influence of your dessert! Today I carded an 80-year-old man at dessert because he ordered the trifle with brandy."

In the Victorian Room, the back seating area, Judy and her family have transferred many of their antique and 1940s kitsch collection from their previous business in Kimmswick, Grandma's Parlor and Tearoom. (Their first Grandma's opened in 1993 in the Frenchtown neighborhood of St. Charles.) Rebecca's collection of bird statues and birdhouses is there and so is the collection of World War II salt and pepper shakers. A still useable 1930s ice box stands in a corner. "We had it in Kimmswick and it didn't sell when we had our clearance so we brought it here," says Judy.

Back in Kimmswick, Judy and her daughters performed Victorian skits for customers during the lunch hour. "For five years in a row, we performed 'Haunted Tea' and I was the ghost," Judy says. "We're not inclined to repeat it here in St. Louis."

But the showbiz bug still stings. Besides Judy's poetry readings, Barbara will occasionally emerge from the kitchen to recite "Thomas and the Leprechaun" and during the holidays Rebecca will step up to recite "The Christmas Cup of Tea."

St. Louis Tearoom
4001 Utah St (at Roger Place), St. Louis

 (314) 772-2998

 10:30 A.M. to 4 P.M. Tuesday through Saturday

 Handicapped accessible

No smoking

76

Shrine Restaurant at National Shrine of Our Lady of the Snows

Belleville, Illinois

ACCORDING TO A list in the *St. Louis Business Journal*, The National Shrine of Our Lady of the Snows near Belleville, Illinois is the number eleven tourist attraction in the St. Louis metropolitan area. "If you take out the casinos, we're number five," says Chuck Schumacher, general manager of the Shrine Restaurant. "The Shrine is definitely the biggest attraction on the Illinois side of the Mississippi, if you don't count the casinos." (Restaurant placemats proclaim the Shrine as "the largest outdoor Catholic shrine in North America.")

Schumacher has managed the Shrine Restaurant since 1973, witnessing explosive growth within the 200-acre Shrine complex and within his own restaurant, a modest dining room with fifteen employees when he arrived and now a food behemoth with a staff of eighty. In 2002, the restaurant moved into its much larger current quarters and, since then, has served more than half-a-million people, Schumacher estimates. (From November 15 to January 6 during the Shrine's annual Way of Lights celebration the staff stretches to one hundred-twenty.) Schumacher operates ten banquet rooms; an extensive catering service that once handled a reception for then-President Bill Clinton and a large take-out business. "We are one of the only Catholic-operated full-service restaurants in the United States," declares Schumacher, who has served as president of the St. Louis Restaurant Association and is a long-time board member of the four-thousand-member Missouri Restaurant Association.

"Even though we are a restaurant, our environment here is different," states Schumacher. "All Shrine employees go through a mission enrichment program taught by a trained lay person. Christian hospitality is the main focus. The golden rule certainly applies here."

Lunch at the Shrine Restaurant usually entails a trip to the homemade soup and thirty-one-topping salad bar. In a good week nearly three thousand customers make the trip. "Our white chili made with chicken is very popular," observes Schumacher, "as is our carrot dill soup, which was featured in the *St. Louis Post-Dispatch*. People keep choosing our cheeseburger soup and both the Boston and Manhattan clam chowders. We make twenty-eight different soups and rotate five of them every day. Linda Pass has been with us twenty-five years as chief soup maker and day supervisor; she makes eighty percent of our soups herself. We make an incredible one hundred fifty gallons of homemade soup a week here. When people mention the Shrine Restaurant, you hear them talking about our good soups."

On the lunch menu are "Shrine Favorites" that, with the exception of the lightly charbroiled rosemary crusted salmon with teriyaki glaze, are all sandwiches. If you seek Schumacher's advice he will recommend the top-selling chicken salad sandwich that the menu describes as "St. Louis-style with white grapes, celery, and almonds, served on a fresh croissant." (The Shrine's menu is the only one we've seen with St. Louis-style chicken salad, although St. Louis-style ribs and St. Louis-style pizza are pretty common.)

A fried cod cut-up sandwich is another Shrine favorite. Nearby Illinois restaurants are the most likely purveyors of cut-up fish (see JV's in Waterloo, for example). I can't explain why there are so few restaurants in Missouri that offer cut-up fish, but in Metro East Illinois, where some communities are predominantly Catholic and still embrace fish on Fridays, the special fish dishes seem plausible.

"Cut-up cod is big business around here," says Schumacher. "We can't compete with certain churches, VFW halls, or private clubs because we have labor costs. So we try alternatives to cod cut-ups. We use three or four pieces of cut-up cod for sandwiches and serve them with slaw or hush puppies. Cod is easy to fry; the breading is what makes it. We put cayenne pepper—very carefully—in our breading and maybe a little something else. To begin with, we get a big cod loin, cut it into long squares, then cut it again into smaller pieces."

An astute manager and planner, Schumacher holds weekly kitchen meetings that include the chef, three supervisors, kitchen managers, and the food buyer. "Among other things," he says, "we discuss upcoming events, desserts, special buffets—the last one we had was a five-night German buffet—whether we should back off buying strawberries because of price and quality, when to marinate a certain meat dish and for how long, seafood specials during Lent and how to organize a catering job that calls for fifteen hundred silver dollar sandwiches. We had to talk over when to make the sandwiches, how to set up the assembly line, when to slice the meat, and whether we should rent a refrigeration truck."

Shrine Restaurant at National Shrine of Our Lady of the Snows

442 S. De Mazenod Drive, Belleville, Illinois

 (618) 394-6237

11 A.M. to 8 P.M. Monday through Thursday
11 A.M. to 9 P.M. Friday through Saturday
10 A.M. to 8 P.M. Sunday

Handicapped accessible

No smoking

77

Soulard's Restaurant and Bar

St. Louis

IN 1977, SOULARD'S Restaurant opened in a well-worn building from 1929 and coasted along briskly as the dispenser of its famous peppered pork tenderloin until a fire in 1990 that might have gotten fully out of control was saved by a knight in shining armor.

That knight, left at the restaurant by the previous tenant, still stands sentinel, along with a twin knight, on either side of the fireplace off the main dining room. If you're seated close to the fireplace, as were Steven Spielberg and his wife Kate Capshaw one day in the 1990s, you'd be seated at coveted tables K1 and K2, as the servers call them. Customers in the know like to sit by the protective knights.

"Our fire in 1993 started when a dumpster outside our window caught on fire," recalls Tim Badock, co-owner of Soulard's with his brother, Dan. "We had a linen hamper next to the window and the linens caught on fire, which spread to the window casing and somehow knocked over the suit of armor and that set off the burglar alarm. The police and firemen came and saved us from burning to the ground. It was the knight in shining armor that really saved us."

Tim and Dan, fresh out of college, bought out their parents in 1984. "Soulard was quieter back then," said Tim. "There were a few bars and restaurants like Mike and Min's and the Downstreet Café. We had more fun around here in the 1980s. If it snowed a lot, we'd lock up the restaurant and go barhopping."

Soulard's has two serving floors. On the downstairs level is the bar, the main dining room, and the Fireplace Room. The upstairs dining room has a separate lunch menu with plenty of overlaps from the downstairs menu and both locations are open for lunch.

"If you are sitting upstairs on a Tuesday, for example, and we're having a meatloaf special downstairs, our waitress will run downstairs and get it for you and bring it up," states Dan. "There is competition between the downstairs and upstairs," added Tim. "If it's not a busy day, our upstairs waitresses will snatch customers coming in the front door and coax them into walking upstairs. We have wide windows upstairs that look out to the parking lot. The waitresses can spot customers coming in from up there then rush down to meet them by the front door."

Despite its lofty price, the peppered pork tenderloin with garlic mayonnaise or raspberry sauce and served with soup or salad, vegetable or French fries, is lunchtime's best seller both upstairs and down. "It's amazing how well the tenderloin sells, since it's an entrée, not a sandwich, soup, or salad," observes Tim. "We had two ladies in here yesterday and they both ordered it. 'We get it every time we come in,' one of the ladies said. 'We can't get past it on the menu.'"

"I made up that pork tenderloin recipe in the early 1980s," continued Tim. "I was at a wedding and they served pork with garlic mayonnaise and I came back wanting to do something similar. I put mine together with mayonnaise, sour cream, garlic, Dijon mustard, pepper, and Worcestershire sauce. Ever since, it constitutes twenty percent of sales at lunch alone."

Salads are lunch leaders primarily because of Soulard's house dressing, which is bottled and sold by the front door. "We had the house dressing since the day we opened," said Tim. "People from all over America call for it so we ship it to them. We have our own cookbook that is also for sale but the recipe for our house dressing isn't in it. We don't give it out." By the way, added Dan, "We don't put preservatives in our house dressings so we encourage people to keep it in a cool spot."

Like most first-class small restaurants in the area, daily lunch specials are strategic lures to keep regular customers returning and snag new ones. Some restaurants, as noted elsewhere in this book, vary their specials depending quite often on the whim of the cook and others, such as Soulard's, have settled on mostly fixed daily specials, though there can be some variance.

"If we don't have meatloaf with sautéed green beans and mashed potatoes every Tuesday, people get upset," says Dan. "On Wednesday, we always have seafood gumbo with salmon, grouper, scallops, and shrimp. It's spicy but not overwhelming. On Fridays we have hand-breaded cod joined by homemade macaroni and homemade cole slaw. If we don't serve this on Friday, it is not good for us at all. On Mondays and Fridays we mix up our specials but on Mondays we always offer split pea soup, although my favorite soup is available only on Tuesday, the tomato mushroom bisque."

Before the present Soulard's building was put up, the land served as stables for horses at Soulard Market. There's been quite a run of occupants in the building: Blattner's

Bakery in the 1930s, George Tiefenbrunn's restaurant in the early 1940s, Marie's Bar in the late 1950s, Schuster's tavern in the 1960s, and the French Market AuPetit Café preceding Soulard's. The previous owner, as we have noted, fortuitously left the two knights in shining armor as well as some stained glass windows.

Soulard's Restaurant and Bar
1731 S. Seventh Street, St. Louis

☎ (314) 241-7956

🕐 11 A.M. to 9:30 P.M. Monday through Thursday
11 A.M. to 10:30 P.M. Friday
8 A.M. to 10:30 P.M. Saturday

♿ Handicapped accessible

🚬 Smoking permitted

∽ 78 ∽

Steak & Rice Chinese Restaurant
Kirkwood, Missouri

PAUL LIN, CO-OWNER of Steak & Rice, beat out one hundred-twenty-four other Taiwanese cooks auditioning in Taipei in 1978 for the job of head cook at Sunny Garden Chinese restaurant in Manchester, Missouri. Sunny Garden's owner had flown to Taiwan to conduct the tryouts in person. Mr. Lin won the auditions with a tingling rendition of General Tao's Chicken and a perfect plateful of Bean Curd Szechan Style.

An exultant Lin emigrated, acquired a green card, cooked three years in Manchester, then another three years at the old Yen Ching in Chesterfield before purchasing Steak & Rice in 1984. The previous owner had pursued the strategy of offering both steak and Chinese food as a kind of culinary marketing coup; he failed and the place closed. Lin and his wife, Mei, decided to keep the name.

Taiwanese-style food, not very available in the St. Louis area, dominates the menu at Steak & Rice. "Taiwan-style is lighter, not as salty as Mandarin, not as hot or spicy as other Chinese foods, and has more vegetables," explains Mei Lin, the manager. "We brought over a lot of food from Taiwan, including the prize-winning General Tao's Chicken and the Bean Curd Szechuan Style. You should try our Hot Braised Chicken, which is boneless white meat deep-fried and coated with a special secret sauce. Our Kung Pao Chicken is mixed with green peppers, carrots, and onions and comes in a slightly spicy sweet brown sauce. Most of these are among our luncheon specials. Chicken is the most popular food for lunch here because it's low in calories. People always ask for white meat."

One Taiwanese import is the Assorted Seafood with Crispy Noodle. It's a collection of shrimp, scallops, beef, snow peas, broccoli, carrots, and soft noodles pan-fried until crispy. And then there's the Moo Goo Gai Pan, called "Snow Pea Chicken" in Taiwan. "Elderly people like it," observes Mei.

A lunch in itself is an order of Paul Lin's pot stickers. The finely ground pork and cabbage stuffing is lubricated with high-quality chicken bouillon with a casing that makes each of the six stickers into substantial pillow-shaped morsels.

Mei Lin is a methodical hostess. She takes digital photos of most of the dishes on the menu and prints them out so customers can see what they're ordering. If there's no printout of the item you want, it's probably somewhere in Mei's camera. "I'll be glad to bring the camera over to the customer's table and unroll the photos for them," says Mei.

Mei estimates the metro area Taiwanese population at five thousand to six thousand. Of that there are three hundred or four hundred Taiwanese who frequent Steak & Rice, especially on weekend nights. Besides the nostalgic food, the Taiwan expats favor Mei Lin's bamboo toothpicks. "When I go back home, I return with 30 or 40 pounds of toothpicks. They're great because they don't bend," she says.

Speaking of bamboo, the Lins have become friendly with Kirkwood neighbors who grow bamboo in their backyard. "When they harvest the shoots in April and May, we use them in our Chop Suey, Moo Goo Gai Pan, and Chicken with Vegetables," she says. "Only a few American people like bamboo shoots," she adds.

Steak & Rice Chinese Restaurant
951 S. Kirkwood Road, Kirkwood, Missouri

(314) 984-8889

11 A.M. to 9:30 P.M. Monday through Thursday
11 A.M. to 10 P.M. Friday, Noon to 10 P.M. Saturday

Wheelchair accessible

No smoking

Veritas Café

Chesterfield, Missouri

IN ITS MODEST storefront location in Dierberg's Market Place in Chesterfield, Veritas Café has as its next-door neighbor Starbuck's Coffee, a pretty scary proposition for most restaurant owners.

"We love Starbuck's—they're one of the reasons we moved here in 2004," says co-owner David Stitt. "They send us customers for lunch and we have tea pots here for Starbuck's tea. And we don't have to invest in a cappuccino machine or other equipment for exotic coffees. We encourage our customers who want espresso or cappuccino to go next door."

"Besides," adds David's wife, Stephanie, "we give Starbuck's workers two bucks off lunch."

"We also maintain good relations with Cobblestone, the shoe repair shop two doors west," David Stitt continues. "We often see customers come in here for lunch with only one shoe; the other one is being fixed at the shoe shop."

Veritas belongs to a restaurant species all its own.

"Our shop offers not just meals but most everything else for the table," says David. "While Veritas Gateway to Food and Wine (official name of the business) is a specialty shop that offers a fabulous selection of wines from around the world as well as a fine array of some of the very best in today's table-top and kitchenware, the heart of our shop is a full working kitchen," explains Stephanie. "This kitchen allows us to enjoy and share the very best that the culinary world has to offer." Add to this cooking and dinners called "Wine Bars" on Thursday nights and the first Saturday of the month and you have the most unusual culinary set-up around.

People walking past are often confused about the kind of business Veritas is, admits son Brian Stitt, who cooks and manages weekend breakfasts. "People stick their heads in the door and say 'What are you? Are you a franchise? How long have you been here?'"

Regular diners tend to sit at the counter so they can kibitz with chef Jay Stringer and his helpers, Brian and Kevin Reddy. "Veritas customers are curious and convivial," comments Stringer. "They like to watch me and my crew at work. They want to know everything we do and what ingredients we use and why. They are adamant about what they don't want in their order, such as telling me to leave the butter out or keep beans out of their soup. They love to see me set a flame to their chicken Marsala. And they ask for my advice all the time. A lot of them ask what I recommend they should eat for dinner at home that night."

A faithful customer named Jim exemplifies the kind of patron Veritas covets, says Brian. "Jim sits at the counter and leans over. 'What do you have today?' he inquires. We tell him and he says 'Fine.' Then he wanders over to the wine racks and asks David, 'What's good today with what I'm having?' Then he returns to his seat and, since he's someone who doesn't like to eat alone, he says 'Pour a glass of wine for everyone at the counter.'"

Veritas has some unusual signature offerings that keep regulars returning. Mark, a regular, has a preference for protein. So the Veritas crew expanded their house salad with mixed fresh greens, tomatoes, and grilled asparagus to include a topping of undeniable protein; more often than not, tilapia or grilled chicken. "We have renamed the salad 'Mark's Giant Salad,'" said Kevin, who adds that Mark, being totally health conscious, dresses his salad only with freshly squeezed lemon juice.

Fish, even at market prices, is an overriding favorite at Veritas. As the lunch menu states, fish can be served as part of Mark's Giant Salad, a sandwich, or an entrée with a side dish. Tilapia is the house favorite fish, especially in the form of a lunch plate. It is typically accompanied by a side of spinach sautéed in a sauce of brown butter, lemons, and capers.

Veritas sandwiches originate with Stephanie, the sandwich maven. One of her winners is the most fascinating grilled cheese sandwich in town. "We use multiple types of cheese and wonderful white pillow bread from La Bonne Bouchée bakery for this panini," says David. The sandwich employs a mix of feta and pink peppercorn spread (which you can buy at Veritas), cream cheese and manchego, Muenster, and fontina cheese. The bread is buttered on both sides before it meets the grill. Customers have also taken to the Veritas bison bites, mini-sandwiches topped with pimento cheese or pepper jelly as well as the Nicoise salad that uses Ortiz Spanish tuna, all jarred and preserved.

"Our soups," said Kevin, "are a kind of resting place for our fresh vegetables." David is the principal soup maker; beef vegetable is the pack leader followed by whimsical concoctions that use sweet potatoes, squash, parsnips, turnips, carrots, and white potatoes. "As to chowders," says David, "we let customers choose what goes into them such as fish or chicken. This gives our customers another way to be more participatory."

Veritas is a retail outlet for Missouri pecans, which it buys raw, coats with a glaze of honey, syrup, port wine, and melted butter, and roasts. "The pecans are all natural, one of the last species not affected by hormones," explains Kevin. They're stored in a large jar next to the Dad's Old Fashioned Cookies at the cash register.

Veritas Café
1722 Clarkson Road, Chesterfield, Missouri

(314) 481-2626

10 A.M. to 6:30 P.M. Tuesday, Wednesday, Friday
10 A.M. to 11 P.M. Thursday
8 A.M. to 6:30 P.M. Saturday (to 11 P.M. on first Saturday of month)
10 A.M. to 5 P.M. Sunday

Wheelchair accessible

No smoking

Wagon Wheel Café

Frankford, Missouri

FRANKFORD, MISSOURI IS about 85 miles northeast of St. Louis and 12 miles south of Hannibal, right off U. S. Highway 61. It contains three hundred-fifty people.

Frankford was founded in 1817 by Solomon Fisher, once a captain in the War of 1812. Its first postmaster was Reason Vermillion. "Reason received about two letters a month and carried them in his hat in order to deliver them at the first opportunity," writes local historian Pam Williams.

Perhaps Frankford's most celebrated resident, according to Jerri Tyler, who co-owns two of the liveliest businesses in town (the Wagon Wheel Café and the Wagon Wheel Opry House), was Valentine Tapley, who owned sixteen slaves and declared that if Abraham Lincoln were elected president he would forswear shaving forever. "Tapley's hair got so long he had to stuff it in his pockets," Jerri says. "It was 20 feet long when he died."

When the Shortline Railroad, connecting to St. Louis and Hannibal, dismantled in 1933 after sixty-two years, the town rather imploded, habitués of the Wagon Wheel say. By then, Frankford's population had already peaked—at eight hundred in 1895.

Most Wagon Wheelers are attuned to Frankford's past. For insurance agent Mike Houchins, the Wagon Wheel itself is living history. "I used to live here," he says. "The long room in back where the Friday night buffet table is set up was my living room. Before I lived here, it was a small engine repair place, a body shop where the Wagon Wheel kitchen is now, a grocery store, a dance parlor, you name it."

Jerri Tyler and his wife, full-time cook Pam Calvin, have made the Wagon Wheel into a kind of town center, serving breakfast, lunch, and dinner. Lunch is the busiest meal. "The whole town stops in there," observes Mark Miller, a Frankford fan and manager of Fresh Gatherings Restaurant in St. Louis.

At lunch, the ham cheeseburger is a mainstay. "It's a cheeseburger with a slice of ham on it," explains Jerri. "If you want the ham real thick, we can cut it real thick. Our hot ham and cheese sandwich is just warmed-up ham with a piece of melted cheese on toast. That costs you $2.99. We can also give you that sandwich with no cheese for $2.74.

"We offer a 'plain fish' sandwich for $1.75 as opposed to our 'fish sandwich' for $3.29. The 'plain fish,' just to make it clear, comes without the bread. Probably forty to fifty percent of people at lunch go for the Wagon Wheel special, which is quite often jumbo tenderloin, or the chicken fried steak.

"We're a little old town," Jerri continues. "Everybody knows everybody. This is their home. They order what they want. If you come in here and order jelly on a stick, we'll ask whether you want apple or grape. In here you can order whatever your belly feels like." "We have one breakfast regular who doesn't want toast," adds Pam Calvin. "He only wants warm bread."

Wagon Wheel customers are mostly area farmers and others attached to agriculture. Regulars know that the first table by the door is the BS Table, a seating designation used by untold other restaurants. (At Tony's, a popular café in Bridgeton, Missouri that burned down in 2006 and that advertised the largest omelets in Missouri [six to eight eggs], the table closest to the omelet grill was the BS Table. That's where owner Tony Fileccia would sit and shout orders to his burdened omeleteers: "Roll them tight; roll them tight" and that's where he, most unfortunately, died of a heart attack back in 1996.)

"I sit at the BS Table," says Jerri. "Mike Houchins sits there. Tony Schindler is there. We got a boy named Tom Fagan who sits there. And then there are all the others who gather around us, sitting or standing." In most restaurants, the common conversation topics for males are sports, sex, and politics. Not so at the Wagon Wheel. "We talk about farming, horses, horse trailers, trucks, and tractors," says Jerri.

There is a horsey set in Frankford. "This is a little old Western town," says Jerri. "Everybody in the community owns five or six horses. I own twelve head between my son and me. I have broken in horses, driven them, and traded them most of my life. Our décor on the Wagon Wheel's walls is Western boots, horses, and cowboys."

Jerri's Wagon Wheel Opry House is a block or two away. The building was built in 1909 as a functioning opera house, but eventually the opera audience withered and the building either lay vacant or served as a courthouse, church, movie house (where Will Rogers performed in person), or elementary school. If you come to the restaurant for your fish sandwich lunch on the first or third Friday of the month, plan to stick around town (or drive up to Hannibal to visit Huck Finn), take in the Friday night buffet, then, with most of the other customers, walk over to the Opry House to hear

Jerri's country music band in their "Branson show." The band includes characters from the restaurant: waitresses Jerri Jean Calvin and Brittany Tyler on vocals, Mike Houchins on drums, and Jerri himself on flat-top guitar. "All of us in the band can do vocals, if required; only two of the ten of us can read music, and only two aren't horse-related, which isn't bad for this town," says Jerri.

Wagon Wheel Café
216 N. Main Cross Street, Frankford, Missouri

☎ (573) 784-2258

🕐 6 A.M. to 2 P.M. Monday, Tuesday, Thursday, Saturday
6 A.M. to 8 P.M. Wednesday, Friday

♿ Wheelchair accessible

🚬 Smoking permitted

DINERS

81

Broadway Diner

Columbia, Missouri

AT THIS AUTHENTIC diner it is no stretch at all to conclude that one breakfast item dominates all others—the any-style eggs, the griddle cakes, and all the omelets. An item called the Stretch is the ruling entrée at this college-crowd establishment near the University of Missouri main campus.

On Friday and Saturday nights hungry collegians will consume two hundred to three hundred Stretches. There is a certain mystique about the Stretch, customers say.

Owner Ed Johnson describes the construction of one Stretch: "You start with potatoes which you shred, then fry. Then you add two plain or fancy egg omelets. You cover this with a full order of chili and add salt and pepper. On top of this you put your shredded cheese and usually your diced green onions, green pepper, and Tabasco sauce. Many of the kids like to slather ketchup or mustard on top of this pile then pour ranch dressing over the whole mix. There are about 2000 calories in each Stretch."

Some customers obsess over Stretch. One man ate four-and-a-half Stretches at one sitting. "His name is Gus; I don't know if he is still alive," quips Dave Johnson, Ed's son and overnight grill boss. "There are some fraternity guys who compete for bragging rights as to who can eat the most Stretches. Occasionally guys will come in for breakfast and one says, 'I dunno, I can't eat a Stretch today.' Then his buddies say 'Oh you pussy, you can't eat a Stretch? What's the matter with you?' You're nothing if you don't have a Stretch. We have some women students who can outdo the guys; they order 'Super Stretches', which is half again more of everything. You're not a cheap date if you order one of those."

Ed Johnson has told the story of the Stretch over and over again. "There was a local high school girl into athletics nicknamed 'Stretch' who came in regularly. At one point she said to the cook 'Fix me a plateful of hash browns and put some scrambled eggs or a flat omelet on top of them and put a whole bunch of chili on top of that and some cheese. Got some onions? Add those to it.' Next time she comes in and says 'Remember what you fixed me the last time? That was good. I'll have one of those again.' After a while, others would say 'I'll have what Stretch is eating—give me a Stretch.' That's how the Stretch was conceived."

The Stretch story has romantic edges. "A Mizzou alum who lived in Georgia phoned me," says Ed. "He said he was going to have his girl friend over for an intimate meal and he wanted to make her a Stretch. He needed to check on a couple of things in the recipe. Well, he made her the Stretch then proposed and she said 'Yes'".

The Broadway Diner is a legitimate diner. It arrived in Columbia in 1949 on a railroad boxcar from its maker, Valentine Manufacturing Company, Wichita, Kansas. It debuted as the Minute Inn, several blocks away from the present location. "Many restaurants in Missouri are called diners, but they're not—they're built-on-site places and not eligible to be listed by the American Society of Diners, to which I belong," Ed explains.

Ed is serious about the American diner movement. "I had a customer who moved to Seattle," he says. "I said 'Let's get you hooked up with an authentic diner out there.' So I looked up Seattle in my directory and found some places. We've got to get our customers out of the fast food joints and into diners. We need to bring quality to their lives. Diners are for people who like people. You don't get that at a fast food place that prefers active people who are there and gone in no time flat."

With the exception of Tuesday and Sunday, Broadway Diner opens at 11 P.M. and closes at 2 P.M. the next afternoon. That puzzles many, chiefly those who appear around mid-afternoon and find the place closed. Those loopy hours don't faze the regulars, however. On football weekends, when either the Mizzou football or basketball team wins at home, "the rush starts at 11:30 P.M. and ends about 3 A.M.," says Dave. "We can serve about sixty people in our booths and at the counter and our patio can accommodate fifteen more people."

Insomniacs wander into the diner around two or three A.M. "Insomniacs look for a quiet place to sit and read the paper and maybe get tired," observes Dave. "They get pissed off if other people are loud. Some insomniacs will pace the floor from booth to booth or along the counter area to get more comfortable and maybe a little sleepy. They will drink water or juice and maybe order toast, pie, or a grilled cheese sandwich. When they leave, most of them look very tired. That pleases us."

Among the customers there are some idiosyncrasies. "Customers are my bosses," Ed insists. "If they want their eggs burned, you burn them. If they want their toast put down in the toaster three full cycles to get the toast blacker than charcoal, you put it down three times." Ed says one charcoal-ordering customer puts butter and jelly on the charred toast, crumbles it manfully, and stows it into his mouth.

With his first cup of coffee, another customer pours the whole cupful into the saucer and gets up to visit stoolmates until the coffee cools. Then he pours the coffee back into the cup and drinks it. As a regular, he gets as many refills as he wants. Occasionals and strangers have to live with the diner's two-cup policy. "We don't allow over-drinking of coffee," Ed states.

Most diner customers are mannerly. An unsettling exception is collegians who eat from plates that previous customers have not completely finished, especially their American fries. "Well, fries are at least good diner food," says Dave, shaking his head in disbelief.

Customers come to expect that jovial owners such as Ed Johnson will be standing at the door to greet them with a hello and a smile. "They want you here every time they walk in the door," says Ed. "You see them in the Mall or out socially and they might say 'I was in your diner two or three times and you weren't there; what's going on?' Some alumni kids come back from Kansas City or St. Louis and if I'm not at the diner they will call me at home and give me hell. 'Get your ass out of bed and get down here,' they'll say."

Broadway Diner
22 S. Fourth Street, Columbia, Missouri

 (573) 875-1173

 5 A.M. to 2 P.M. Monday, 11 P.M. Monday to 2 P.M. Tuesday 5 A.M to 2 P.M. Wednesday, 11 P.M. to 2 P.M. Wednesday through Sunday

 Wheelchair accessible

 No smoking

82

Chili Mac's American Diner
St. Louis

EARLY IN THE twentieth century, most large Midwestern cities had their share of Coney Island joints or chili parlors. St. Louis had the O.T. Hodge Chili Parlor chain that was founded in 1904 and grew to sixteen outlets, mostly in downtown St. Louis. "It was the only place in St. Louis where you could order scrambled eggs with chili on top and not get disbelieving glances," says John Eirten, who managed six of them from 1975 through 2003.

Over the past few years, all of the Hodge parlors have gone out of business. The best surviving remnant is Chili Mac's American Diner on North Broadway. It was recast in 1985 as a faithful reproduction of the original Hodge facility on Pine Street. Long before the Hodge operation, the space was called Crescent Sandwich Shop, operated by Mrs. Evelyn McKinney, who lived upstairs.

Decades ago, breweries such as Anheuser-Busch would "build out" taverns for enterprising barkeeps. Large wholesale coffee distributors did the same for coffee and sandwich shops. This is what the Star Coffee Company in St. Louis did for Mrs. McKinney. After getting a bank to co-sign a note, Star brought in contractors to install booths, counters, flooring, ceilings, and kitchen and refrigeration equipment. "The only thing that Mrs. McKinney had to do was buy all of her coffee from Star and pay them the mortgage," recalled Joe Charleville, former president of Chauvin Coffee Company of St. Louis, who was a Star salesman in earlier days.

Beneath Chili Mac's long counter is a sheet of quilted steel made in St. Louis by Laciny Brothers, Inc., an industrial custom fabricator. Red linen-patterned Formica covers the counter and tabletops. Pointing to the counter, Eirten says: "You can see where people put their elbows on it, right along the edges where it's faded and worn. You can judge a counter's age by the elbow marks. You wonder who's been there and what the walls have seen."

Eirten is proud of his floor-mounted counter stools, which have stainless steel footrests anchored by solid brass holders. The stools, all a regulation twelve inches lower than the counter top, are part of the "nostalgia seating" line from nearby Vitro Manufacturing Company, which makes fifties-style furniture for restaurants worldwide. "We have eighty percent of the fifties marketing in America," Mike Scott, vice president, once told me. "The guys from Vitro come in here for breakfast or lunch a lot," said Eirten and, while they're on the premises, they closely examine the Vitro-made oxblood-burgundy Naugahyde counter stools, spinning them and debating ways to improve their product—as if Chili Mac's were their main seating laboratory.

Equipment and building history notwithstanding, a main feature of this classic diner is the early morning sister team of Kay and Peggie Massey, who are cooks, cashiers, and waitresses incarnate. This pair, a fixture at Chili Mac's for more than twenty-five years, was once deeply influenced by the old television sitcom, "Alice," which aired from 1976 to 1985 and featured a pretend restaurant, Mel's Diner. The cast included three waitresses—Alice, a sharp-tongued recent widow intent on a singing career; Flo, a loud-mouthed, soft-hearted waitress; and smart-alecky Vera—plus Mel, the sometimes moody manager. At Chili Mac's, "Kay is Flo and I'm Alice," said Peggy, the older sister. "Nobody wants to be Vera. And John [Eirten] sometimes acts identically to Mel. There are times when we know when to leave him alone and when we can mess with him."

Peggy: "We get involved with customers. If someone is broke one day, we let them pay whenever."

Kay: "We're the only restaurant I've ever seen that doesn't write down orders. We don't write anything down. We memorize them and call them over to the grill in shorthand."

Peggy: "There have been times when we let a new waitress write down orders for short periods of time and then we say we better not catch you doing it again."

Kay (to incoming customer): "What you need, dear? You come to see me again?"

(Peggy calls out an order for four people: "Give me a fry two sausage and one up and one over around a scramble two.")

Kay: "People will come in at 5:30 or 6 A.M. to order a bowl of chili to take out. They order sausage and eggs with a plate of chili on top of it. These people may be coming off a midnight shift and it doesn't bother them. We'll put chili on anything they want."

Peggy: "I had a guy who ordered hot cakes, two eggs over easy, and a bowl of chili. He put the eggs between the hotcakes and, instead of maple syrup, he poured chili over the hotcakes. You see a lot of weird stuff when you work with the public."

Peggy: "Did you mention our 'Tamale Ale'? That's a tamale with two eggs any style all covered with chili. We sell it for breakfast."

Kay: "And we have an omelet named 'The Wilbur' for a man who used to wash dishes here. It is not printed on our menu but all our breakfast regulars know our off-menu items. The Wilbur is sausage, onions, and potatoes inside a cheese omelet with milk gravy on top. We also have 'The Plumber' which is the same as The Wilbur but has chili on top instead of gravy. And we have 'The Slinger' which has two cheeseburgers, American fries, one egg, and comes with chili if you want it. We used to have 'The Roadkill' which John Eirten personally made himself but we don't sell it anymore."

Despite chili's role on the menu, tastes have changed. "Twenty years ago we served between thirty-five and forty gallons of chili a day; now we sell between five and seven gallons," observes Eirten. "Once we were a chili parlor serving diner food and now we're a diner that also serves chili."

Chili Mac's appears to be the only area diner offering fresh chocolate candy. "I make candy from November through March," says Eirten, who takes most of his recipes from has grandfather's recipe book, *Rigby's Reliable Candy Teacher*. "We make turtles, heavenly hash, fudge, and long chocolate bars and sell them inexpensively. My candy is comparable to the best you can buy around here and we always sell out."

Chili Mac's American Diner

3523 N. Broadway

 (314) 231-9546

 5:30 A.M. to 2 P.M. Monday through Friday

 Limited wheelchair access

 Smoking permitted

83

Connelly's Goody Goody Diner
St. Louis

HOW DID CONNELLY'S Goody Goody Diner, the destination restaurant in St. Louis's Hamilton Heights neighborhood, get its current name? The place started in 1931 as the A & W Root Beer and Sandwich Shop and had as its next-door neighbor the original Ted Drewes frozen custard stand and drive-in. The A & W was purchased in 1948 by Cecil Thompson who renamed it Goody Goody. For an answer to the name question, we checked some menus.

The 1995 Goody Goody menu stated that Rosemary Clooney's hit song 'Goody Goody' was the inspiration. But the two-page GG history in the 2007 menu says: "Parents would drive to the restaurant while the children expressed their delight...by chanting 'goody goody.' That's how we got our name." So, take your pick—either explanation works for me. (For the record, 'Goody Goody,' written by Matt Malneck and Johnny Mercer, bowed in 1936 and quickly reached number one on the top tune charts.)

Herb and Viola Connelly bought the business in 1954, appointing their son Richard as a carhop since teenage cruising from drive-in to drive-in was much in vogue. The senior Connellys introduced a "Good Morning Breakfast Plate," which headed their menu for decades and continues to lead it now. They erected a neon Goody Goody sign that has flashed 24 hours a day since 1957. "The city of St. Louis tells me that our sign is a landmark," says Richard Connelly, who, with his wife Laura, bought GG in 1968. "The city has promised that if the sign is ever damaged or vandalized, it will be OK to replace it in its entirety. You couldn't get a sign like this approved today; we're grandfathered."

A Goody Goody breakfast menu from the early Connelly days of the 1950s reflects the era. Besides the "Good Morning Breakfast Plate," there was a "Traveler's Breakfast" with ham steak, a "Handy Man's Breakfast" with two pancakes and two eggs any style, a "High Country Breakfast" with corned beef hash, a "Down Home Breakfast" with two homemade biscuits blanketed with sausage gravy, and the "Great Adventure Platter" with grilled "porkets," three eggs, hash browns, and the usual sides.

What brings neighbors, college students, and hordes of regulars to breakfast these days are the "Fried Chicken-Belgian Waffle" platters, nicely appropriated from Roscoe's restaurant in Los Angeles thanks to a coveting customer; the "Polish Hot Link Platter," suggested by a clergyman who told Connelly that a New Orleans restaurant serves it and so should he; salmon croquettes; catfish and eggs; and the "Hobo Breakfast Bowl," a mighty load of sausage bites, scrambled eggs, tomatoes, onions, hash-browns, white gravy, Cheddar cheese, and "your choice of bread." "The kitchen calls this 'The Mess,'" Connelly explains.

Connelly offers pretty much the usual variety of omelets except for "The Wilbur," a chili omelet. "I don't know who Wilbur is; I think it is an offshoot of the Wilbur omelet on the menu at Chili Mac's on North Broadway," Connelly says.

One reason Goody Goody has flourished on Richard Connelly's watch may well be a course he took as a young man at the Dale Carnegie Institute where memory training was stressed. He did so well in memory drills, reeling off the first and last names of thirty-seven classmates during the first go-round, that his teacher invited him back as a "graduate assistant" to train others. His graduating certificate, with honors, hangs in his office.

In the ensuing years, Connelly has profitably tapped the memory that Dale Carnegie made him stretch. "I have memorized the names and faces of about a thousand of my mostly regular customers," he says. For "irregulars" whose names he has not fully learned, he keeps a coffee-stained cheat sheet under his glass desktop. On it are quick notes to himself such as: "Harold Owen—tire man," "Virgil, friend of Cecil," "Cornelius, tall friend of Ron's." "If a regular customer shows up with his wife, I put her on my cheat sheet, too," he says.

"I make it a point to call all my customers—sixty percent of them who eat breakfast here are regulars—by their first names," says Connelly. "I know their favorite waitresses, what they order, and their preferred seating spots. If they can't get a table they want, I diplomatically hold them in the foyer until a table is available." When regulars have to wait, Connelly makes a point of addressing them by their first names at least two or three times.

Connelly and his waitresses seat customers at tables or window booths. Some regulars seat themselves on their favorite among nine stools at the counter. "Customers stay longer at the counter," Connelly observes. "They're here for food and conversation. People who want to read the paper use the booths or tables and stay to themselves."

One of GG's unique art pieces is an oil painting of waitress Tammy-Lynn Ross, murdered at home in 2002 by her disgruntled boyfriend. The painting hangs on a wall on the east side of the restaurant, which Ross ran. "She was so strong-willed, so giving, and so special to her customers that if I live to be ninety I'll never see the likes of a waitress like her again," says Connelly. "A lot of our male customers still won't come in because they're too upset she's not here."

Tammy-Lynn Ross was on hand in March 2000 when presidential candidate Al Gore came in to shake hands. Connelly said he learned about the Gore visit ten minutes before his arrival. One clue was that Natural Bridge Road out front was completely shut down and a low-flying helicopter hovered overhead. "When Mr. Gore came in the door secret service men dressed informally as customers and scattered at several tables stood up and flashed their badges. Nobody could leave until Mr. Gore had shaken everyone's hand."

"Did I tell you," asks Connelly, "that during our first twenty years of operation, eleven of our waitresses married customers? Two of the waitresses were carhops: Marge and someone else with a French name," adding in a very un-Dale Carnegie way: "Right now I can't remember it."

Connelly's Goody Goody Diner
5900 Natural Bridge Road, St. Louis

 (314) 383-3333

 6 A.M. to 2 P.M. Monday through Friday
7 A.M. to 2 P.M. Saturday

 Wheelchair accessible

 No smoking

84

Del Monico Diner
St. Louis

IN 1926 THE ten-story, fully fireproofed Roosevelt Hotel opened on the site of the recently razed restaurant named Cicardi's, which had opened in 1914 and had a huge church-like dome. In 1929 the hotel was auctioned off at the courthouse steps, then sold again. In 1932 the hotel auditor was robbed in his lobby office by thugs wearing "light-colored felt hats and dark overcoats." Later in the 1930s the hotel was reconfigured into first-floor shops, two floors of offices, and seven guest floors.

In the 1940s, the owners mailed permanent guests terse letters raising rents nearly twenty percent and warning them to patronize the hotel dining room, coffee shop, and bar (known as the Wonder Bar.) "No hotel can exist on room rentals alone," the letter stated. "When someone new applies for a permanent room, we ask them if they intend to eat meals at the hotel or at their grandmother's house. Only those who signify willingness to eat at the hotel and patronize the bar are given permanent rooms."

In 1958, more new owners proudly announced that the Roosevelt would become a "drive-in hotel," first of a supposedly new breed. "Cars can drive into the building, stop at the reservation desk, unpack near the elevators, and then exit to a parking lot though an air door," the owners said. Long after the drive-in idea flopped, the hotel was taken over by the city's economic development corporation that eventually created 154 units of federally subsidized apartments but kept the ground floor open for retail.

In the early 1960s, Mrs. Eva L. Bobo was head cook at the Woolworth store at Crestwood Shopping Center in St. Louis County. One day "something hit her and she said 'I can cook for myself somewhere else,'" her son, Oscar Jones, recalled. She obtained a small business loan, took a leave from Woolworth's (just in case her business failed), and opened a restaurant in the old Miami Hotel at Grand and Enright. "Mother was looking at a magazine ad one day and saw the words 'Del Monico' and said 'that's what I want to call my restaurant,'" said her daughter, Dorothy Dunn. Later on, Bobo moved Del Monico to the present location on Delmar—in that part of the old Roosevelt Hotel lobby where cars drove in to register.

Until she died in late 2005, Mrs. Bobo sat in Del Monico's kitchen on Friday mornings to chat and "pick" greens, which means snapping stems from slick mustard and turnip greens. The greens were served mostly on Sunday, the restaurant's busiest day. One exception was the bowl of greens she had prepared for a favorite clergyman six days a week at breakfast. Dorothy Dunn, longtime restaurant manager, supervises the greens picking now along with the weekday special bowls of greens.

Ray Jones, Bobo's nephew, is Del Monico's chef. He claims to cook by feel. "I have to feel things. I don't have to taste anything," he says. "My food, I can feel. I use no recipes or note cards. When Jesse Jackson came here he said of my food that you don't have to go to school to learn this kind of cooking."

Stewed apples and hash browns are popular breakfast items on the Del Monico steam table line. Until he retired, Oscar Jones, Bobo's son who was breakfast manager, made the hash browns, which he fortified with secret proportions of onion, pepper, and salt and which often sold out early in the morning. Occasionally Oscar returns to help his cousin, Ray Jones, peel and prepare the potatoes. "My stewed apples are best sellers," Oscar would say. "I like to cut up red apples, add cinnamon and syrup and a little butter." When he was overly busy, he'd take his stew apples directly from a can. "I add my cinnamon, my butter, and a little water. You can hardly tell the difference from real apples. I make people's day with my stewed apples; that's what people tell me."

Del Monico is a typical soul food restaurant. Besides the stewed apples, greens, and yams, salmon croquettes are a breakfast mainstay along with biscuits that Dunn makes from scratch. Customers dip the biscuits into a mixture of maple syrup and melted butter. "We provide grape jelly exclusively," Oscar said. "People don't want anything else. If we don't have grape jelly, they ask us for it."

"Mohammed Ali with all his bodyguards came here to eat once," recalls Dunn, who remembers, too, that Aretha Franklin's sister visited, as did associates of Sammy Davis, Jr. who took orders of black-eyed peas back to the entertainer who was appearing at the Chase Hotel. "Later, when he was being interviewed by Johnny Carson on television, Sammy Davis said he'd put on some weight after eating black-eyed peas and ham from a certain restaurant in St. Louis," said Dunn, amused at the reference. Most celebrities who eat at Del Monico autograph the backs of their meal tickets; management tacks the tickets to the wall by the cash register for all to read.

(Years ago, Del Monico had a contract to deliver lunch to the football Rams training facility in Earth City and to supply "go plates" for players to eat on flights to away games. Ray Jones would often send aloft buckets of chitlins along with the go plates. Later on, some of the players, such as Isaac Bruce and Orlando Pace, would drop by for more of Bobo's remarkable soul food.)

Del Monico sponsors a Family and Friends Day every Thanksgiving. "This event is like a reunion," Oscar Jones once explained. "This place will be full; even some homeless folks will be here. Sometimes we have a DJ and people can dance in the main dining room."

There is an overarching sanctity about Del Monico. "You feel different when you walk into our restaurant," Oscar said. "This is a kind of church place. See the sign by the southeast corner set off by pocket doors? It says: 'The Lord is my shepherd, I shall not want.' That area is the Ivory Perry Room, named in memory of the civil rights activist Ivory Perry. Next to the main dining room is a large side room with an organ, piano, and pulpit. We call it the Ronald B. Packnett Room in memory of the beloved former pastor of the Central Baptist Church where my mother was a member for almost sixty years. There have been weddings and church services in that room, especially when congregations find themselves temporarily without their own church because of a fire or something. The banquet room is used on Friday and Saturday nights and as an extra room on Sunday, when people come here directly from church. That's the day that the ladies mostly wear all white. You should see them!"

Del Monico Diner
4909 Delmar Boulevard, St. Louis

 (314) 361-0973

 7 A.M. to 6 P.M. Tuesday through Friday
8 A.M. to 6 P.M. Saturday; 11 A.M. to 6 P.M. Sunday

 Wheelchair accessible

 No smoking